'45

Born in 1926, Charles Whiting joined the army as a volunteer in 1943 and served with the 52nd Armoured Reconnaissance Regiment in Belgium, Holland and Germany. After the war he studied at the University of Leeds and later at London, Kiel, Cologne and Saarbrücken. In 1958 he became a university teacher, first in the USA and then in England and in Germany where he was also German correspondent for the *Times Educational Supplement*. He gave up full-time teaching in 1973 to devote himself to writing.

Charles Whiting's first novel *Frat Wagon* was published by Jonathan Cape while he was at university. Since then he has had nearly a hundred books published ranging from fiction, under the pen name of Leo Kessler, to military history, espionage and linguistics. His most recent publications include *Death of a Division*, *The Battle for Hitler's Wall*, *The German Home Front*, *The Siegfried Line* and *'44: In Combat on the Western Front from Normandy to the Ardennes*.

'45

The Final Drive from the Rhine to the Baltic

CHARLES WHITING

GUILD PUBLISHING

LONDON

Frontispiece
**Two US infantrymen dash past a blazing enemy gasoline tank
in the Square at Kronach.**

Copyright © Charles Whiting 1985
All rights reserved
First published in Great Britain in 1985
by Century Publishing Co. Ltd,
Portland House,
12–13 Greek Street, London W1V 5LE

Designed by Tom Deas
Maps by Frances Pitt
Picture Research Simon Holt
This edition published 1985 by
Book Club Associates
By arrangement with Century Communications Ltd.

Photoset by Rowland Phototypesetting Ltd,
Bury St Edmunds, Suffolk
Printed in Great Britain in 1985 by
Butler & Tanner Ltd, Frome, Somerset

CONTENTS

AUTHOR'S NOTE
page 6

JANUARY
page 13

FEBRUARY
page 51

MARCH
page 86

APRIL
page 123

MAY
page 155

ENVOI
page 182

NOTES
page 184

INDEX
page 188

ACKNOWLEDGEMENTS
page 192

AUTHOR'S NOTE

That winter, forty years ago now, I, too, 'went up'.

I was one of the many thousands in khaki and olive-drab, who were at last swept across that grim border by the great tide of events. There were five of us, three youths I had only met twenty-four hours before and the 'Old Man', perhaps thirty years of age, but very ancient to us at eighteen.

Dumped in a muddy freezing farmyard, our kit piled at our feet, while jeeps came and went and the guns rolled sullenly in the distance, we innocents waited for what fate had in store for us in this forbidding country. The Old Man and one of the youths, a sandy-haired Scot from Glasgow, were 'fetched' – and returned only minutes later: the Scot lying sprawled across the bonnet of the jeep, his face covered in blood, and the Old Man lying ashen-faced and silent in the back, clutching his stomach. The war had claimed them already. I and the other two would survive and become by the time it was all over the 'veterans'.

The real veterans of the Normandy landings and the Battle of France were now long dead, prisoners-of-war, vanished into the German cages, or were broken men, physically or mentally, who could not or would not fight again. The fighting regiments had been decimated by the last six months of battle. Nearly half a million men of Eisenhower's armies had been killed, wounded or taken prisoner in North-West Europe. Now the great gaps in their ranks were filled with hastily trained teenagers – 'trained' infantrymen of three months' service.

Montgomery was running out of infantry and had been forced to break up two divisions to provide infantry replacements for the rest. His American opposite number, Bradley, in his turn had made a five percent levee of his rear echelon troops to do the same. Clerks, cooks, cops became instant infantry. Now even blacks in the old segregated US Army would have the 'honour' of fighting – and dying – for their country.

Divisions were now led by officers in their late thirties, battalions by colonels of twenty-five or so, while companies were commanded by twenty-year-olds. Nineteen-year-old infantry lieutenants, they said, had a life expectancy in the line of some six weeks. We who would fight the Battle for Germany were all very young, at least those in the infantry. But the teenagers who crossed into Germany as reinforcements, bumping along the snowbound, muddy tracks, past the rusting wrecks from the previous year's hard battles for this bitterly contested frontier, had long been prepared for what was to come – especially if they were British.

At the beginning of the war, we had been children in short pants as we listened to that tired old man at eleven o'clock one Sunday morning, making his announcement on the radio: 'This country is at war with Germany . . . Now may God now bless you all.' It probably did not make much impression on us; after all, there was still school on the morrow. My mother cried, as she stirred the batter for the Sunday's Yorkshire pudding. But then her father had been killed on the Somme in the 'Old War', as well as four of her uncles.

For a few days after there was activity for most of us children. We spent all our free time running errands for people with money, who were stocking up with tea, sugar, corned beef, flour and the like while there was still time before rationing started. In my case, there were called-up Army reservists virtually locked up in the chapel next door so that they couldn't escape before being allotted to their units. They tossed threepenny bits and sixpences over the wall, and, patriotic urchins that we were, we ran around buying them Woodbines and Park Drives, and keeping the cigarette cards as our reward.

(Right)
British soldiers keep a watchful eye out for the enemy.

6

But in the end they went and the war settled down. Nothing happened. Everything seemed just as normal, save that we went to school carrying our gas-masks and once a week we had a lesson wearing them, our faces slowly growing wet and sticky as the mica facepiece steamed up.

Yet slowly and unconsciously the war began to prepare us for what was to come, as we changed from short pants to long pants – officially at fourteen in those days. There was no scheme or pattern to it, I realise now, but already we were being readied mentally. The young men disappeared. The police were suddenly all middle-aged and carried steel helmets. We had a woman postie. There were women clippies – *and they wore trousers in public!*

An uncle of mine, a volunteer from his seminary, was killed in France. Something called Dunkirk happened. Overnight the trophy cannon from the Boer War, the German tank captured in France in the Great War, even the two old muzzle-loaders from the Crimea disappeared from the squares of the city in which I lived. They were needed for scrap. Railings, pots and pans followed rapidly. My father brought home a World War One vintage American BAR automatic rifle in a golf bag. It hung in the hall, together with my mother's air raid warden's helmet. For now the mother who had cried the previous year was part of the 'war effort' herself. That summer a lone German bomber – a Junkers 88 – cruised lazily over the river bank where I played in the Home Guard trenches with my pals. Round and round in the perfect blue sky, and not one single shell was fired at the enemy plane. How confident and arrogant that pilot was, I thought. Almost immediately, the alarming thought shot through my mind that perhaps we had already lost the war. But I didn't tell anybody.

In 1941 I was a fire-watcher myself – and eventually received a medal for having been one. Armed with steel helmet and stirrup pump, it was my duty to scan my school's roof for fire-bombs. It was great fun. We slept under the billiard table in the masters' common room, and had the following morning off. The school suffered some slight bomb damage and the masters herded us into the cellars, crying encouragingly: 'Remember you are British, boys!' 'Ay, but do yon buggers up there know?' a dour unconvinced Yorkshire voice called back from the gloom.

Now it was a grey time. Defeat after defeat. The woman rushing into the street in her apron, clutching the War Office telegram telling her that her only son had gone down with HMS *Hood*, screaming in uncontrollable hysterics. My uncle, one of the new-fangled commandos, missing in the Med. Just like the father he had never known, he would be posted 'Missing presumed dead'. My grandmother and her sister bombed out yet again in London. In the end the V-2s would kill them both, while I was deep in Germany. We were all being hardened for what was to come.

The war seemed to have gone on for ever. My home town was really bombed for the first time. Thirty planes attacked it for nearly three hours. They dive-bombed the city centre without a single shell being fired back at them – there were no anti-aircraft guns, and the RAF scrambled its fighters too late. Our roof was riddled with tracer, our water boiler burst and the door blew off, while we huddled underneath the table. There was no military target in our town, save the railway station through which went the traffic bound for our new ally, Russia. There were three hundred casualties and eight thousand homes were destroyed or damaged. A drop in the ocean in comparison to what was beginning to happen on the other side of the Channel. But we were being readied.

Meat ration one shilling and one penny's worth per person per week. Oranges for kids under twelve at Christmas. Whalemeat on sale in the wet fish shops. Long queues for offal at the butcher's. We mended our own shoes with bits of rubber and sewed up split seams with string blackened with shoe polish. Starved of sweet things, we bought arrowroot sticks at the local chemist's. Another uncle went missing, this time in Burma. He never came back either.

Now it was 1943. The first of my friends were joining the service, eager seventeen-year-olds, desperate for the 'adventure' of war: Derek R., killed in action in Normandy, aged eighteen; Terence K., died of malaria in

Two American soldiers inspect an unexploded flying bomb in a field in France.

India, aged eighteen; William T., killed in action in Burma, aged eighteen. But I was still only sixteen and alone in the sixth form with a 'conshy', who wore 'goggles' to boot. One day I locked him out on the balcony, went to the local recruiting station, made myself seventeen, and joined the Army. In October 1943, the authorities were not asking too many questions; they needed 'bodies'. My mother cried again.

We knew more or less what to expect. We had been around soldiers for nearly four years now. We expected to be shouted at, drilled, threatened. 'Come on you bunch of pregnant penguins . . . Get them knees up . . . Move it, or yer feet won't touch the deck to the guard-room!' This was what we had been preparing for all along.

We learned the intricate three-hundred-year-old drill of the British Army. '*General salute . . . Officer on parade, dismiss . . . Slow march . . . By the right, quick march . . . At the double now . . .*' We grew accustomed to the constant noise: the stamp of hob-nailed boots on concrete, the crunch of marching feet on gravel, the whack of palms hitting polished rifle-butts, the hoarse, hysterical cries of the instructors. We learned to 'make do and mend', squatting on our made-up bunks gingerly (for each cardboard-padded rigid roll of blankets was lined up meticulously each morning so that they were all in a dead-straight line), plying our needles from the 'soldier's housewife', darning socks or sewing on buttons

while the corporal lectured us on the regimental history. We fell asleep at ABCA lectures on the fate of the world, given by bespectacled earnest sergeants with socialist leanings. We goggled at the nudes the instructor slipped into the slides of aircraft recognition to keep us awake (though most of us knew German and Japanese aircraft backwards anyway). We got goose-pimples listening to the MO's talk about VD, full of 'pulling back foreskins' and 'handling one's John Thomas as if it is a very precious thing'.

By now we could jump off a truck travelling at 15 mph. We could march fifty miles a day, and speed-march twenty miles in four hours, laden with rifle, steel-helmet and thirty pounds of kit. We could live off the land, without food or money or shelter, stealing and begging from the local farmers, eating stolen eggs raw, scooping milk out of the churns they placed at roadsides at dawn. We spent weeks outdoors in snow and rain, constantly wet and miserable, yet superbly fit, in spite of our grumbling.

Slowly, as 1943 gave way to 1944, we became soldiers, filling out on the plain rough food – and milk, *by order*; for those of us under eighteen were commanded to drink milk. We were contemptuous of 'civvies'. We spoke our own tongue, full of 'old sweats', 'stick men', 'lead-slingers' and the like. We learned how to 'come the old soldier' and walk around the barracks purposefully with a bucket, as if we were working. We learned how not to

WE'LL MEET AGAIN
Words & Music by
ROSS PARKER and
HUGHIE CHARLES
FEATURED & BROADCAST BY
JACK PAYNE
AND HIS BAND
6D
Irwin Dash Music Co Ltd
17, BERNERS ST, LONDON, W.1
Put DASH in your Programmes

be around on a Saturday afternoon when fatigues were given out; 'out of barracks or in bed' was the order of the day. We learned that all soldiers were not so eager to die as we young enthusiasts, and that there was a surprisingly large number of 'senior soldiers', as they were called, who had never heard a shot fired in anger since 1939, and an equally large number attempting to 'work their ticket' and get out of the 'Kate Karney' (Army) before the shooting commenced.

Finally, for those of us who were not reluctant 'senior soldiers' or 'working their ticket', the time had come. Like thieves in the night we left our camp, packed in blacked-out trains speeding through the darkness to London, all badges and unit signs removed along with anything else that might have identified us to some lurking German spy. We marched through an empty, bombed, pre-dawn London, laden down with field marching order, with a blanket strapped around our big pack, much as our fathers must have marched in the Old War. We departed from the same station they had gone from, too – Victoria. From here my own grandfather, after whom I'm named, had departed also, never to return.

All was hectic hustle and bustle among the steam. Self-important Railway Transport Officers hurried back and forth with their clipboards; good ladies handed out jamjars filled with bitter, sugarless tea; hard-eyed Red-caps (Military Police) armed with service revolvers stood around in pairs, watching out for anyone who might be tempted to 'go on the trot'.

Here and there was a weeping woman seeing her husband or lover off. But there was no woman to see us off. 'Baa . . . baa,' we bleated like sheep ready for the slaughter, 'why are we waiting?' The sergeant-major saluted when the train finally began to pull out. *He* was staying behind. 'You'll get no promotion this side of the ocean,' we bawled, scared of him no more, 'so cheer up my lads, *fuck 'em all!*'

Another midnight. Now we marched to the waiting ships. More good ladies handing out bars of bitter chocolate wrapped in blue paper and wishing each of us 'Good luck, boys.' Out into the inky Channel in a convoy – to be dumped in Europe at dawn. We were almost there now. Soon it could start.

For a while they kept us in Belgium. An ancient lecher of a sergeant-major, whose skinny chest bore the ribbons of the Old War, took us on a leisurely route march around the Flemish town and showed us the brothels – including the one run by his mistress, who was half his age; but then he was a big man on the black market. We guarded a bunch of deserters from the front, all of them 'senior soldiers'. They escaped in the middle of the night by cutting a hole through the floor of the cavalry barn in which they were housed. We slept a couple of hundred to a room on bunks recently vacated by the Germans and still bearing their eagle stamp. There was no sanitation save 'piss buckets'. The latrines were holes in the earth,

swilled out with hosepipes wielded by sabot-wearing Belgian soldiers – also 'senior soldiers' no doubt. Some American deserters raided the clothing store at pistol point and stole blankets to sell on the black market as coat-material. We collected the scraps of marge left at meal-times, and pressed them into empty cigarette tins to sell. We visited the cafés, thinly disguised brothels with new names (now the Germans had gone) like Café Alaska and Café Washington, full of cigarette smoke, drunken women's laughter and the tinny clash and blare of *bal musette* music. But we were innocent. Besides, our pay was only a guinea a week. To pay the price the whores were asking, we would have had to save up for a couple of months and we were not staying that long anyway.

Then the news came: the Germans had broken through somewhere in Belgium. Panic. The permanent staff – those 'senior soldiers' again – started burning secret papers, whatever they were, in the square. We were all given two bottles of beer from the NAAFI, while the staff began to smash bottles of spirits; it seemed they didn't want us looting the spirit store when the Germans came, in case we ran away or surrendered.

The sergeant-major deserted. Perhaps he went to his mistress. We didn't know. We were completely cut off from the outside world now. It was said that the 'Belgies' had taken down all the Allied flags and pictures of Churchill and Roosevelt that had once decorated every window, and they no longer talked to Allied soldiers. Even the black market was dead. The Germans were coming back again.

Overnight long lists of names appeared on the landings of that great echoing barracks. We could hear typewriters clacking far into the night in the company offices. We were being posted to the front, as quickly as they could get rid of us. All of us were going. One morning we awoke to find a dead man sprawled out in a red star of his own blood in the snow of the courtyard below. Late the previous night he had found his own name on the posting list. Rather than go to the front he had killed himself. Perhaps he had been another 'senior soldier' caught at last.

Whiting C. 175. There it was. My name, too.

That last morning they fed us porridge, soya links (sausages made of soya flour) and cocoa. Each of us was given a 'haversack lunch': two thick doorsteps of jam and bully beef sandwiches to last us to wherever we were going. They loaded us into open trucks. Outside the barracks Belgian kids were snowballing each other. They didn't look up as our convoy started to roll. Neither did their elders, 'liberated' these three months now. Perhaps they had seen it all before. Perhaps they just wanted rid of us so that they could get on with their own lives.

We didn't care. We had other problems. At last we were 'going up' . . .

CW. Winter 83/84.
Wittlich, West Germany.   11

US infantrymen take cover from enemy artillery fire in Luxembourg during the Ardennes Offensive.

JANUARY

"We can still lose this war"

That night the fighter pilots of the German Luftwaffe, some one thousand of them, did not celebrate, as they would have done normally. They even missed the Führer's speech. At five minutes to midnight, Adolf Hitler declared boldly to his hard-pressed people: 'Our nation is resolved to fight the war to victory . . . We are going to destroy everyone who does not take part in the common effort . . . The world must know that this State will never capitulate . . . Germany will rise like a phoenix from its ruined cities and will go down in history as the miracle of the twentieth century!'[1] But the pilots who would fly the great surprise attack did not hear his words, for they were already asleep.

At five o'clock the next morning they were wakened. They were served their 'nigger sweat' (black coffee), 'dog biscuits' (cookies), and, for those who could stomach them, rubbery scrambled eggs made of egg powder. A final briefing – there was a touch of ground fog in places – and then they were airborne: nearly one thousand Focke-Wulf 190s, Messerschmitt 109s and Junkers 88s from ten different wings, spread out in four massive formations, each wing assigned to attack a specific target behind the enemy lines.

From the Rhine to the snow-bound front they were led by old-fashioned 'Auntie Jus', the lumbering three-engined Junkers transports, piloted by veterans (many of the pilots taking part in this mission were inexperienced, straight out of flying school). Down below German flak opened up. In spite of the fact that flak divisions had been warned to expect something unusual this icy morning, the sixteen-year-olds who manned the 88 mm flak cannon could only think this massed formation had to be the usual Anglo-American 'air gangsters' returning from one of their nightly terror raids on the Reich's

Debris litters an Allied runway after the Luftwaffe's surprise attack.

shattered cities. Four of Oberst Buehlingen's Focke-Wulfs from the Second Group went hurtling down in flames, shot down by their own people. But the rest kept on flying, steadily and purposefully, westwards.

Now the old 'Auntie Jus' began to turn back. They were too slow, too vulnerable. Below coloured searchlights flicked on and started to sweep the heavens. Flares hissed into the sky. Here and there, ground troops ignited coloured smoke pots, as arranged. Great red arrows of fire suddenly appeared in the snow, always pointing westwards in the direction of the unsuspecting enemy.

Inexperienced as they were, the eager young pilots flying their first combat mission were glad of any assistance that would guide them to their targets. They flew on. Now the 'old hares', the veterans of five years of aerial combat over three continents, such as Colonel Buehlingen and Lieutenant-Colonel Baer, waggled their wings and indicated that their pilots should follow them down. Soon they were to cross the front and they did not want to alert enemy radar prematurely.

The four great waves dropped dangerously low. Still observing the strictest radio silence, as ordered, they skimmed across the barren, snow-sheeted landscape at tree-top height, flying up the deep frontier valleys wherever possible in order to escape detection at the hands of those Anglo-American radar operators unfortunate enough to be on duty this particular day. Soon they would attack and they knew the surprise would be total. They flew on.

Later the crestfallen Allied pilots would call it the 'hangover attack', for most of them had been on a long binge the night before. They were taken completely by surprise when the icy-blue sky suddenly erupted in fury that morning. The German fighters and fighter-bombers seemed to fill the skies over Holland, Belgium and northern France, shooting up the Allied fields.

Wing-Commander 'Johnnie' Johnson, DSO, DFC, stationed with his Canadians at the Brussels-Evere Field, had been celebrating with the rest. He was watching as Canadian Squadron-Leader Dave Harling, a close friend of his, led twelve Spitfires along the slippery, narrow runway, through a field crowded with aircraft and completely undefended except for a handful of light guns. Harling was to fly the morning weather reconnaissance mission. With his 'Spits' in a tight formation behind him, he was just beginning a slow turn onto the runway.

Suddenly, without warning, it happened. A mixed bunch of some sixty Focke-Wulfs and Messerschmitts came zooming in over the boundary in a loose formation. Their cannon started to pump tracer shells at Harling's squadron. Johnson, who had celebrated the wedding of Harling's pretty nurse sister only hours previously, watched with horror as three of the aircraft immediately behind his friend fell apart. Their pilots

Ground crew stand helplessly by as another aircraft burns.

scrambled out and scuttled for safety, followed by vicious purple spurts of flame as shells struck the tarmac behind their flying feet.

Dave Harling opened his throttle wide and raced down the runway to meet the intruders. All alone, he hurtled into the hard blue sky towards the weaving, curving enemy planes. Johnson clenched his fists as Harling brought up his undercarriage and at the same instant pressed the button of his cannon. A German plane staggered as if it had run into an invisible wall. Next moment it was careering downwards, trailing smoke. But the odds were too great for the lone Canadian.

The enemy planes concentrated their fire on Harling. Great chunks of metal dropped off the lone Spitfire's fuselage. White glycol began to stream from its engine. It was all over within seconds. Harling's plane fell out of the sky. As the few guns fell silent – they had run out of ammunition – Johnson and his pilots could do nothing but watch in helpless rage as Spitfire after Spitfire burst into flames before their eyes.

Further up the field, Flight-Lieutenant Frank Minton, a short, stout officer who owned a dairy back in Canada, was hiding in the Ops caravan as the attack reached its climax. Suddenly the phone rang. Minton eased himself up from his prone position on the floor and lifted the phone.

A staff officer spoke urgently, the fear obvious in his voice: 'Large gaggles of Huns near your airfield! *Get your Spits off!'*

Minton, who did not lack a sense of humour, shouted back: 'You're too late! If I stick this phone outside, you'll hear their bloody cannon!'

The staff officer was indeed too late. Ten minutes later, when the enemy planes finally disappeared over the horizon to the east, they left behind them eleven Spitfires destroyed on the ground and twelve damaged. On the west side of the field many transport aircraft were blazing furiously and Field Marshal Montgomery's own personal Dakota was a total write-off, lying among the shattered planes whose undercarriages had collapsed so that they lay on the ground, looking to a frustrated Johnnie Johnson 'like tired cattle'.[2]

Fifty miles away from the Brussels field, Lieutenant Colonel John Meyer – he was America's ace pilot in Europe, with thirty-five and a half kills to his credit – was drinking a last cup of coffee at Aachen Field and waiting for the ground fog to clear. He was already strapped into his Mustang fighter and in touch with Control.

At five minutes past eight that morning, Marmite Control gave him the order to start. He began to taxi up the runway, followed by the rest of the planes from his 487th Fighter Squadron. Suddenly flak began to explode in black puffballs at the far end of the runway. He hit the button of his R/T. 'Anything coming?' he called.

A Typhoon is stranded in Holland, by the atrocious weather.

'No, not a thing,' the radar station answered.

Meyer gave his plane the throttle in the very same instant that a Focke-Wulf 190 came rocketing towards him. Meyer knew he didn't have a chance. But abruptly the enemy fighter-bomber changed course. It broke to the right, did a wing-over, and started firing at an empty C-47 transport plane parked at the edge of the runway.

Meyer didn't wait for a second invitation. Hardly daring to believe his luck, he roared into the sky. While he was still retracting his undercarriage, he pumped a savage burst into the Focke-Wulf. The enemy plane exploded and hurtled down, hitting the ground in a flurry of snow and earth as it did a pinwheel skid and broke apart.

By now the sky was teeming with German planes. As if he were diving through a shoal of great metallic fish, Meyer zoomed towards his next victim, another Focke-Wulf. But each time he got onto the enemy plane's tail, friendly flak ripped the length of his wings. A whiff of acrid smoke, a belt of icy cold air, and a big hole had abruptly appeared in the front of his cockpit. That did it for Colonel Meyer. The Krauts were bad enough, but he had no intention of being shot down by his own flak. He veered off a little so that the gunners below, trigger-happy as they were, could see that he was friendly. There, with his last belt of ammunition, he knocked the German out of the sky with a burst from about twenty percent deflection. He had just made his thirty-seventh and a half kill.[3]

Two hours later it was all over. The attackers had lost 232 pilots, nearly a quarter of the force that had set out so confidently that dawn, but they had wreaked a terrible vengeance on the Allied 'air gangsters' and their planes. At Brussels-Evere alone, 123 transport aircraft, Flying Fortresses, Typhoons and Spitfires were wiped out. At Eindhoven in Holland, a Canadian Typhoon Wing and a Polish Spitfire Wing were nearly destroyed. In all, twenty-seven Allied air bases were in ruins and over three hundred aircraft were knocked out. As Flight-Lieutenant Pierre Clostermann, the Free French air ace, commented cynically: 'This operation had been brilliantly worked out and superbly executed. Allied public opinion would have been dealt a staggering blow if it had known it. The American censorship and the Press services, in a flat spin, tried to present this attack as a great Allied victory, by publishing peculiar figures. We pilots were still laughing about them three months later . . . In the week following, 122 Wing [Clostermann's unit], in effect, alone kept the aerial offensive going, from dawn to dusk, and in sixteen days lost 18 pilots and 23 aircraft.'[4]

New Year's Day, 1945, had started with a bang!

On that beautiful, bright, if freezingly cold first day of the new year, Private O. B. Voss, who had been severely wounded on D-Day, was returning with a draft from England, chugging along in a boarded-up troop train from Ostend where the draft had landed early that morning for the reinforcement holding unit at Louvain. From thence the Lancashire-born infantryman, who at twenty was already veteran, expected to be sent up the line to his old division, the 3rd. Forty years later he remembers:

There were a couple of hundred of us, mostly green rookies still wet behind the lugs, plus a couple of blokes who had been wounded like me earlier on and two fellows from the Northumberland Fusiliers – both of them old sweats who had refused to go into action, and had been given seven years in the glasshouse. They'd had their sentence cancelled because Monty needed bodies and they'd volunteered to go up again. There were also a few Yanks, mostly black, who had been puking all the way since Folkestone and who were now a delicate shade of light green.

Anyway, we marched from the quay at Ostend right to the troop train, six abreast, blankets strapped around our big packs and singing. You might have thought we were old style Tommies from the Great War going back up the line.

The train started – it was freezing cold and there were no windows (they were covered with boards with just a slit in them to see out) – but not for long. It came to a sudden stop and everybody shouted the Belgie driver must have run out of wood. Anyway, there we were, in the middle of nowhere, nothing but snow-covered fields to left and right, stamping our feet on the floor to try to keep warm. Of course, when you're cold you always want to take a leak. But our NCOs wouldn't have it. 'Piss out of the windows!' they shouted. The Yanks took no notice of them. They got off the train and started wandering down the line to have a piss.

It was freezing cold and the fields on both sides were covered in snow. I can remember to this day how the urine steamed as the Yanks took their leaks. Then suddenly it happened. A Jerry fighter came barrelling down the line, machine guns blazing. The Belgie train driver panicked. Christ, didn't he get that old engine going! We were off in a flash, throwing the lads inside the carriages all over the show. I thought the boiler would blow up, the way that Belgie driver was giving it throttle. And behind we left the Yankee darkies, hands on their cocks, mouths wide open. God knows what happened to them. That Belgie at the controls didn't stop again till we got to Louvain. For all I know they might be still standing there, waiting for us to come back for them! . . .

It was only later that I got to thinking. I worked it out in my head. It was D plus 177, one hundred and seventy-seven sodding days after I had first gone ashore on D-Day – *and the Jerries were still bloody well attacking us!*[5]

They were indeed!

After six months of bitter, hard fighting, ever since the Allies had first fought their way ashore on June 6th, 1944, General Eisenhower's armies were still stalled at the German frontier. Already the Allies had lost three hundred thousand men, dead, wounded, or captured, not to mention a similar figure for non-battle casualties; yet they had only gained a small section of German territory around the city of Aachen. More, on this first day of the New Year, the Germans were attacking, not only in the air, but on the whole length of the Reich's border with France, Luxembourg and Belgium. Even as Private Voss's troop train was shot up by that lone German fighter, four fresh divisions were plunging into French Alsace on a new offensive, aimed at recapturing the key city of Strasbourg, the capture of which would probably bring down General de Gaulle's provisional government in Paris and knock France out of the war for the second time around.

Up in the freezing snow-bound hills along the length of the German frontier, a savage battle was being fought in which no quarter was given or expected. In Belgium 'the Battle of the Bulge', as it was being called, had been raging for sixteen days now, and already the American Army had suffered fifty thousand casualties in men killed, wounded or taken prisoner.

On that first day of January, 1945, twenty-two-year-old Captain Macdonald of the 2nd US Infantry Division, a typical young replacement officer, was leading his company through the thick woods near the Belgian frontier village of Ondenval. Suddenly he and his men were challenged in German. They stopped dead, clutching their weapons in hands that were suddenly damp with sweat, their fatigue forgotten.

'Help me . . .' a voice continued in English. The words were spoken so mournfully that Captain Macdonald felt the hair bristling on the back of his neck.

'Come out with your hands up!' one of the Captain's men cried.

'I cannot come,' the voice answered slowly – 'as if it were torture to utter each word,' Macdonald recalled later – 'I am blind. I cannot see you.'

Macdonald's men finally ventured forward and found the German. He was indeed blind; he had been abandoned there in the forest by his retreating comrades. Standing there miserably, surrounded by the rough unshaven infantrymen, he asked for a cigarette.

'Why you Nazi sonofabitch!' one of Macdonald's men exploded, aiming a savage kick at the captured German's rear. 'Of all the goddam nerve! If it wasn't for you and all your kind, all of us would be smoking now!'

Hurriedly Macdonald stepped in and ordered two men to take the blind German back to company headquarters. He knew the temper of his men, although he had only been with them for a short while: the bitter fighting of the last two weeks had turned them into savage animals. He watched the escort lead the faltering German away and forgot the incident; there were still plenty of Germans ahead who could see only too well.

But the two-man escort returned surprisingly quickly. 'Did you get him back okay?' asked a suddenly suspicious Macdonald.

'Yessir', they answered promptly and turned as if they were in a hurry to get back to their section.

But Macdonald stopped them and repeated his question. One of them stared at the trampled snow at his feet and said: 'To tell you the truth, Cap'n, we didn't get to "A" Company. The sonofabitch tried to make a run for it.' He raised his head and looked the young officer straight in the face. 'Know what I mean?'

'Oh,' Macdonald said slowly, nodding his head, 'I see . . .'[6]

But the men of the 2nd Infantry Division were not the only American soldiers shooting prisoners that first grim day of the New Year. At the other end of the front in the Ardennes, men of the green US 11th Armored Division had just captured sixty Germans at the village of Chenogne.

At the end of the action, the sergeant in charge asked for volunteers. Although even greenhorns had learned not to volunteer for anything in the US Army, this day there were plenty of them. They had all heard of the so-called 'Malmedy Massacre' of the previous December when Nazi troops had *allegedly* machine-gunned captured American prisoners.* They knew, too, that their Army Commander General Patton did not approve of taking prisoners and had *allegedly* ordered none to be taken in his Third Army area.[7]

Soon the miserable Germans in their shabby, overlong greatcoats were lined up against a wall, guarded by the volunteers. The NCO in charge looked around. 'Not here,' he commanded. 'The others hiding in the woods will see. Take 'em over that hill.'

Dutifully the volunteers marched their prisoners away, out of the sight of the other Germans still holding out in the wooded heights beyond the village.

What happened then was short and savage. The muted bursts of machine-gun fire. A few groans and cries for mercy. But this snowy day there was no mercy – for Germans. Prisoner after prisoner crumpled to the ground, dead, shot in cold blood. Suddenly a jeep came racing down the hill, with an officer standing up next to the driver. 'There's been a mistake!' the officer yelled. 'We're supposed to take prisoners, not shoot them!'

But it was too late. The sixty German prisoners were already dead, sprawled out in the snow like bundles of abandoned grey rags.

These men who had survived the bitter battle in the

---

* See '44 for further details.

German dead litter a field near Bastogne during the futile attempt to overturn the American 101st Airborne Division.

Ardennes had become different from the easy-going GIs of the summer, who had been so well supplied and looked after, always confident that the air force or the armour would pull them out of any mess they got themselves into. In the Ardennes there had been little that the air force or armour could do to help them. It had become an infantryman's war, pure and simple, man matched against man. The easy optimism of the summer had disappeared to be replaced by a stubborn bitterness, an anger at the retreats and panics of the first week of the great surprise attack, and at the fact that they had to fight and die under such miserable circumstances. These GIs had tasted defeat and now they wanted revenge. Those who had not been killed or wounded or captured, and who had not 'bugged out' or gone 'over the hill' for good, had become vicious and relentless.

They had learned a lot, too – things that the German *landser* had learned long before in Russia. They had learned how to fight in knee-deep snow in the coldest winter within living memory – and survive. Medics had found out that by tucking frozen morphine syrettes under their armpits, they could defreeze them and plunge their contents into the arms of wounded comrades, giving them the boon of blessed oblivion. Plasma could likewise be kept liquid in these sub-zero temperatures by keeping the flasks under the hoods of the Red Cross jeeps, next to the engine, while they warmed their

C-rations on the little vehicles' red-hot exhausts.

Infantrymen fought frostbite and trench-foot, which were still causing more casualties than the Germans, by massaging their feet and changing their socks at regular intervals. Whenever the long-suffering soldier had a break from the fighting, he made himself a 'tootsie-warmer', cut out from blankets abandoned by dead or wounded comrades and worn around the frozen feet like a muff. They learned, too, these one-time American greenhorns, what their German enemy had learned in that first terrible winter in Russia back in '41: that tight boots killed the circulation and led rapidly to trench-foot. So they copied the old hunter's trick; they found boots a size too large and stuffed old copies of the *Stars and Stripes*, the Army newspaper, between their boots and their black felt 'artics', as they called the overshoes the US Army had issued them with that winter.

Instead of the standard issue overcoat, which was bulky and had long tails that always got soaked and heavy with snow, they wore two woollen GI shirts, which had to be switched every day, with the one next to the body, always wet with sweat, being dried somehow before being put on again. Or they simply cut off the tail of their greatcoats and made a thigh-length jacket of it. (In the British Army, it must be noted, such 'damage' to 'Government property' was a punishable offence: thirty days in the dreaded 'glasshouse' faced the offender.)

The GIs learned to heat food over a wine-bottle filled with stolen gasoline, using a twisted rag as a wick. Or they employed the old English trick of the desert war: a can, half-filled with earth, into which gasoline had been stirred until the mix had a porridge-like consistency; lit by a match, the can would provide a fire for heating or cooking for several hours. And they learned not to eat snow, no matter how thirsty they were, for snow brought diarrhoea, just as alcohol resulted in deadly cooling off after the initial glow had passed. They discovered that metal sweated and then seized up, if the engines of tanks and trucks were not kept running at regular intervals during the night. They discovered that lenses and sights of guns had to be greased with a thin film of vaseline, otherwise they would be useless in combat; unlike the enemy, the US Army had not yet developed a special Arctic grease for winter fighting.

And most of all they learned how to kill, without remorse or pity. For they had finally shed one of the strictest taboos of western society – that killing is wrong. The average GI had absorbed his fear of aggression virtually with his mother's milk. At home and later at school he had been taught to be 'a good boy'. It had been one of the GI's greatest handicaps when he first entered combat. As military historian Brigadier-General H. A. L. Marshal revealed after the war, 'Only about a quarter of the fighting soldiers will fire their weapons against the enemy.'[8]

But the Ardennes changed all that – for the survivors.

On that same first day of January, Pfc Kurt Gabel, a nineteen-year-old German-born paratrooper with the US 17th Airborne Division, was part of a force attacking along the Bastogne-Marche highway in Belgium. With thirty-odd other young paras of the 17th, which was being 'blooded', as the generals liked to call it, in the Ardennes, he was ordered to fix bayonets. They were going to charge the Germans holding them up. '*Geronimo!*' the young soldiers cried lustily, their breath fogging the air, and raced to the attack across the frozen snowfield.

Almost at once some twenty-five Germans rose to their feet in their hiding places, hands aloft. '*Kamerad! . . . Nicht tœten!*' they yelled in a frenzy of fear. Some of the paras were carried away by the blood-lust of battle. They bayoneted the defenceless Germans where they stood. One pushed his blade home so deep that he could not get it out. He struggled frantically for a few moments to release it, foot on his dead enemy's chest, tugging with all his strength. But it didn't work. So he released the bayonet clip and left the blood-stained blade protruding from the dead German's skinny chest.

The paras rushed on. Somewhere to their left a machine gun hissed into action. White tracer zipped across the snow, dragging a fiery light behind it. Four paras went down at once in a flurry of flailing arms and

Snow falls on German prisoners captured by the 82nd US Airborne Division near Hierlot, Belgium.

legs. Abruptly the mad rush came to an end. The rest flopped to the ground, chests heaving, the slugs cutting the air just above their helmeted heads.

Two US medics, both clearly identifiable as such by the red cross painted on their helmets, volunteered to go and fetch the wounded. But the German machine-gunners had seen how the paras had slaughtered their comrades when they attempted to surrender. As the two medics, laden down with their medical haversacks, rose to rush to the wounded, the Germans opened up once more. Both medics fell, severely wounded.

Gabel, rifle clutched in his hand, scurried across to his section commander. The young lieutenant was wringing his hands in utter despair, for the men were bogged down; they could move neither forward nor backward.

'Let's use the prisoners as a shield, sir,' he suggested, gasping for breath.

'But that isn't in accord with the Geneva Convention', the young officer objected.

'*Neither is shooting medics, sir!*' Gabel retorted angrily.[9]

The officer agreed. The paras beat and shoved the surviving German prisoners to their feet, using them as a shield while they rescued their wounded comrades. Then they tackled the machine gun, forcing the terrified Germans ahead of them until they were within striking distance, charging the rest of the way and finishing off the gunners with the bayonet.

By now the light was beginning to fade and the paras knew it would be dangerous to continue their attack in the rapidly growing darkness. The attack was called off.

Standing shivering with the other survivors, Gabel suddenly realised that there were only twenty men still on their feet. Out of the two hundred paras who had gone into the attack that morning, only a score had come through. Everywhere the snow was dotted with the still, dark shapes of young Americans. That January the newly arrived 17th Airborne would be well and truly 'blooded'. When they were finally pulled out of battle they would have suffered some 4,000 casualties out of a total strength of about 12,000 men.

The hard fighting of the frontier was taking its toll. Four hours after the two soldiers had shot the blinded German, Captain Macdonald himself was hit. Somehow or other, he staggered and stumbled back to the Battalion Dressing Station where he was given a pain-killing injection and a glass of neat bourbon which made him feel 'nice and drunk'. In a thin cold rain, he was taken to the divisional clearing station where the surgeon removed the slug from his leg and, as was customary, gave it to him as a souvenir (he still has it).

At the nearest town, the Belgian city of Verviers, he was loaded into a hospital train bound for Paris. Every four hours throughout that long journey across the snowbound countryside, he was given a shot of the new wonder drug, penicillin. The wounded GI next to him in the long carriage, packed with white-painted cots, kept cracking: 'I got those shots once before – but it wasn't on account of frozen feet!'

The military nurse in her helmet and poorly fitting khaki slacks who was attending to them was not amused. She knew what the anonymous GI meant: he had received the standard penicillin treatment for VD.

In that same train Macdonald discovered a boy from his own company, a lanky farm youth from Kentucky, who had been hit in his first battle. The boy refused any assistance from the nurses, in spite of the fact that he had apparently been hit in the back by a fragment from an 88 mm. 'It was four hours before they got me out,' he drawled to Captain Macdonald. 'I almost froze. But that wasn't so bad. Another 88 came in and did this. . .' He shifted his cigarette from one side of his mouth to the other, and then, after some hesitation, lifted the edge of his blanket so that the Captain could see.

Macdonald gulped. The kid's right leg had been severed cleanly above the knee. Half an hour in action and the teenage farmboy was a cripple for life.[10]

It was tragedy after tragedy that first week of January 1945. Staff-Sergeant Giles of the US Engineer Corps, in hospital at Liège for ear trouble, noted in his diary for Sunday, January 7th: 'You can tell we're taking casualties in the battle. Our wing is so full it's overflowing and even the halls are full.'

So it was that Sergeant Giles was detailed to help the overworked Army nurses by keeping an eye on a teenage soldier with a bad leg wound, who had 'taken a turn for the worse'. Now, before the NCO's horrified gaze, he started to die. 'Like a coward,' Giles confessed later, 'I wanted to run away.' But he stayed and held the plasma bottle while the doctor and Lieutenant Gregg, the nursing sister in charge, fought to save the young man. But it was no use; the soldier was too far gone.

'When it was all over,' Giles noted later, 'Lieutenant Gregg turned round and I could see she was crying. I couldn't believe he was gone. Stupid like, I said, "Is that all?"'

The nurse turned on him in fury. 'Goddammit to hell!' she exploded. 'Yes, that's all! . . . *That's all – for one more poor sonofabitch . . .*'[11]

Corporal Alex McKee was seated in a café in the town of Tilburg just behind the British front with a group of Scottish soldiers, none of them more than twenty, who had just come back from the front. The weary infantrymen were sitting quietly enough until the proprietress's baby started to cry – and cry – and cry.

The young soldiers' nerves were so on edge that one of them jumped to his feet and 'shouted out that if the baby didn't stop its screaming, he would bash its head in

A wounded American officer is loaded aboard a tank.

against the wall!'

The woman went white. She realised that the soldier was not joking; he was quite capable of killing her precious baby in the mood he was at that moment. She rushed the crying infant into a back room, trying to smother its cries with her apron.

McKee commented: 'I witnessed this incident and judged that her fear was justified . . . [but] no reporter could expect to get clapped on the back by his editor by writing that sort of a story.'[12]

Some men could not take the strain. They deserted, went 'on the trot' as the British soldier phrased it. Or they broke down, or became 'bomb happy', or simply would not fight whatever the threats levelled at them. Already back in Normandy, ten percent of British casualties – in the case of one veteran division, *nearly fifty percent* – were classified as suffering from 'battle exhaustion'.

As Brigadier Essame, an infantryman who had fought in both wars, wrote later: 'One of the greatest psychological problems was the way in which one or two neurotics could infect a whole formation. Sometimes this occurred when incompletely trained reinforcements were used as frontline troops, and panicked. Equally difficult to combat was the shock effect when really good officers were killed or gravely wounded.' Often, too, officers were suddenly called upon to take over in a crisis and found that they were not able to cope with the demands made upon them. An example of this kind of thing happened when a good commanding officer was wounded at the height of the battle and the second-in-command moved up from the rear to take over. At Brigade HQ he was given 'an erroneously optimistic view of the situation' and when 'faced by a desperate military situation which would have taxed the skill of the most experienced commander he became distraught, of course, and had to be removed.'[13]

Although desertions mounted again that January, Montgomery still stood out against the re-introduction of the death penalty for 'desertion in the face of the enemy' (it had been abolished in 1930). All the same, he forbade the sending of 'battle happy' soldiers back to the United Kingdom for treatment, where in most cases they managed to 'work their ticket', being released into civilian life to achieve there a remarkably swift recovery.

Instead Montgomery sanctioned the opening of 'exhaustion centres'. Here the men were interviewed by sympathetic psychiatrists and in due course returned to

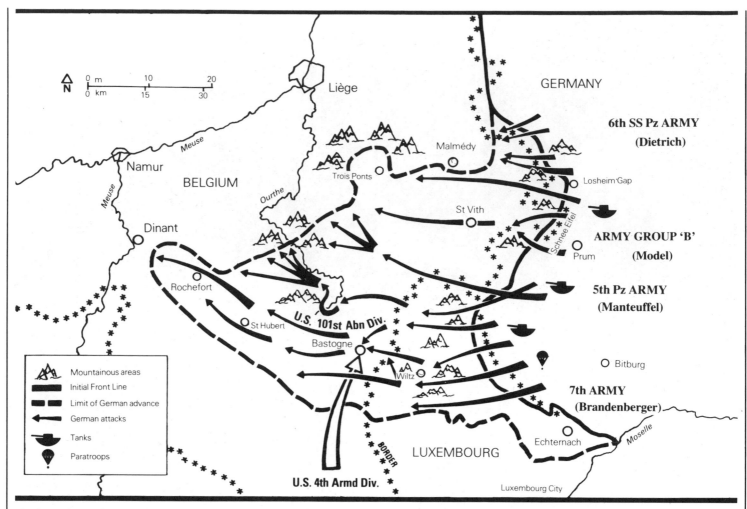

their units, where it was hoped that they would not run away again or crack up. Often it was just a pious hope.

In the US Army, which was bearing the brunt of the fighting that January, combat fatigue – or 'section eight', as the GIs called it* – was epidemic.

Pfc Lester Atwell, a medic attached to Patton's Third Army in the Ardennes, was dealing with a fresh bunch of wounded late one January afternoon when he was startled to see a soldier wandering about with wild, staring eyes and muttering to himself. He was talking in French for some reason, then repeating in English the one single long-drawn-out word: '*Noise . . . The N-o-i-s-e . . .*'

Finally, having dealt with the wounded, Atwell had a look at the strange, wandering GI and then told another medic to take him over to battalion headquarters: 'Tell them I said to let him rest up a few days around the kitchen. He'll be all right.'[14]

Atwell watched as the GI, who looked about twenty-four, was led past him, still whispering, '*The no-ise . . . the no-ise . . .*' The two figures went down the road and disappeared into the gloom. Atwell never saw the man again. Perhaps he had continued wandering, straight out of the kitchen.

Though it had now become unofficial policy, in many of the US divisions in the line, not to evacuate combat fatigue casualties, due to the fact that many outfits were simply running out of infantrymen, men still broke down, refused orders to fight, or simply ran away.

On January 4th, 1945, for example, the 6th US Armored Division decided to make a tactical withdrawal, the first it had ever made since it had landed in Normandy. By sheer chance, just as the tankers started to withdraw that gloomy icy afternoon, the Germans attacked. Panic broke out. In particular, the new replacements started to throw away their weapons and pelt towards the rear as the white-clad Germans came drifting out of the snow-bound forest, followed by German tanks. The withdrawal turned into something akin to a rout.

Colonel Hines, the son of a personal friend of Patton, in charge of the Division's combat Command A, ordered mines to be laid and flares to be attached to trip-wires scattered throughout the area, so that when the Germans stumbled into them the flares would expose the enemy – and also reveal the presence of those men retreating towards his command. Alarming reports started to filter in. Panic-stricken soldiers reported that whole outfits had been wiped out, that they were the sole survivors.

The survivors' claims were wildly exaggerated, but this was indeed the worst day in the history of the 6th

---

* 'Section eight' was the section on the US Army's official form allowing discharge for reasons of mental instability.

(Left) The Battle of the Bulge. December '44–January '45.

(Below) German troops lie in wait.

Armored. Finally, however, some semblance of order was restored and as night fell on the battlefield, Colonel Hines found himself in a stone cottage where the refugees were thawing out their frozen limbs and trying to steady their nerves.

One GI, his face covered with blood and dirt, his eyes two bitter holes, told Hines: 'I used to wonder what I was doing in the army. I didn't have anything personal against the Krauts, even if they were making me live in a frigging, freezing foxhole. But I learned something today. Now I want to kill every goddam Kraut in the world. You know why? *To save my own ass!*'

It was a sentiment that Colonel Hines, who was soon to suffer a horrendous wound which would blind and mutilate him, whole-heartedly approved of. But he knew that the lone soldier was in a minority. Morale was alarmingly low among the rest of the men. He didn't sleep too well that night.[15]

Neither did his boss, General 'Blood and Guts' Patton. That January 4th night, the usually optimistic and exuberant Third Army commander wrote sombrely in his diary: 'We can still lose this war . . .'[16]

Still the hard slog in the Ardennes continued. By now two and a half British divisions were also taking part in the fighting, side by side with the Americans. In the van were the Red Berets of the 6th Airborne Division, which had lost so heavily in the Normandy fighting. They were now being prepared for the airborne crossing of the Rhine.

Fighting for the village of Bure, one company lost its commander, two platoon commanders and the sergeant major, being reduced in one day to one officer and twenty men. Every company suffered similar casualties, losing over one quarter of its officers and men.

Mines and booby traps were another hazard, for buried beneath the deep snow their action was unpredictable and they were hard to spot. On one occasion during a patrol, the corporal in charge stood on a mine and was severely wounded. Another parachutist went to his assistance and was similarly hurt. The corporal sent back for help. Five medical orderlies arrived on the scene. Two of them were almost immediately blown up by mines when they went to the assistance of their comrades.

A little later the medical officer of the 13th Parachute Battalion, Captain D. J. Tibbs, MC, arrived. He gave strict instructions for everyone still capable of doing so to move back, and not to enter the minefield whatever happened until the sappers arrived with mine detectors. Thereupon he went into the minefield alone, moving from one wounded para to another, bandaging their wounds; when he reached the furthest one he stayed put. Miraculously he himself had not stepped on a mine. Despite the sub-zero temperatures he was by now in his shirt-sleeves, having placed his tunic round the worst of the wounded. At last the soldiers with the mine-detectors arrived and began to advance towards Captain Tibbs. As one of them, a Sergeant Carrier, reported later: 'We found him [Tibbs] supporting the man he was with in a sitting position. Sweeping the spot with the detector, we located a mine, where the man's shoulders would have been if he had been allowed to lie down – *and two more within a foot of the medical officer's feet!*'[17]

It was not only the German enemy that the Americans and their British allies had to fight in the rugged, hilly Ardennes; it was the weather, too. Back behind the front Belgian children were happily bombarding military policemen at the road junctions with snowballs. Toboggans were out and there was nothing sinister about the sleek snowy slopes of the many hills. But further up, closer to the front, the white loveliness of the landscape had become a menace, a horror that had to be fought against with every last ounce of a man's energy and strength.

For miles the wind had blown the soft snow into ridges across the roads. These ridges quickly hardened in the freezing temperatures, which made it necessary to manhandle trucks up the hills. Tracked vehicles slithered and went skidding into the ditches, to be left there till the thaw. Every driver became a bundle of nerves as he fought his vehicle forward, mile after relentless mile. Here and there, the crossroads were so deep in snow that bulldozers were useless and the trucks and tanks had to divert onto the ploughed fields, bouncing over the frost-hardened ruts in their effort to keep moving. And all the time the guns thundered, and men fought and died.

Captain Foley of a British tank regiment was leading his troop of lumbering Churchills forward down a lonely Ardennes road when they were struck by a tremendous snow blizzard. One of his Churchills slipped its track. Another was almost buried in the flying snow. 'With their tank suits zipped right up to the chin and their waterproof hoods fastened across their faces,' Foley wrote later, 'the crews looked like figures in an ancient film about arctic explorers' as they set about freeing and repairing their tanks.

Finally they had managed the task and, frozen and exhausted, they rested and enjoyed their reward, *one can of self-heating tomato soup!* Not Foley. He was worried. The sudden snow blizzard had obliterated every trace of the tanks that had gone on ahead of them, and there were no signposts. 'We were alone in a vast, unmarked expanse of whiteness.' Foley got down on his hands and knees. With the aid of his torch, he could just make out what appeared to be the kind of tracks that a tank leaves behind. But whether the tracks were those of the regiment's Churchills, he didn't know. He decided, however, to continue in the direction indicated by the faint tracks.

That night the lost Churchills rolled on and on through

Crocodile tank spits flame as British troops advance.

that lonely, wasted, snowbound country until finally 'like twin beacons of hope, I saw the white fingers of a pair of headlights on the horizon.' But were they the lights of a friendly vehicle or those of the enemy? Foley was taking no chances, not in the confused fighting of the snowbound Ardennes. With their turrets unlocked and all guns loaded, the little column of Churchills crawled down the snow-deep road towards the waiting vehicle, a barely glimpsed outline in the darkness.

'Shall I give him a burst just to warn him off, sir?' Foley's gunner asked.

Suddenly Foley recognised the vehicle. '*Christ, no!*' he exclaimed. '*It's the Colonel!*'

They had found safety at last. They had been on the road twenty-four hours, surviving on one can of soup. They had seen no sign of the enemy, but they were already exhausted – and on the morrow they must fight.[18]

Robert Barr, war correspondent with the BBC in the Ardennes, came across another lost company on the evening of January 13th. This time they were Americans, eating their first hot meal in five days, so the young officer in charge told the Englishman. Barr, standing there in the middle of the forest, noted in his dispatch that the lost Americans were grouped around a log fire on which 'there was a great cauldron and on the cauldron a great iron lid. It didn't fit too well and the steam hissed out all around the edges and the firelight made the steam turn scarlet. And in the midst of it all, a strange hunched figure with a long woollen stocking cap and a long brown beard sat with one hand poised over the great iron lid. In the other he held a ladle.'

Barr was so intrigued by these 'lost soldiers', camping out in the middle of the great snowbound forest, that he allowed himself to be talked into staying the night with them by the young captain in charge. 'We won't be here tomorrow,' the latter said, 'we've got a date with some panzers two miles east. Why don't you have some chow and see the beards come off? Let the war look after itself for one night, like we're doing!'

'It was such an unusual pantomime,' Barr told his radio listeners, 'the dark forest, the snow, the firelight, the long queues of little bearded men, the smell of good food and good coffee, I felt I had to see the whole show.'[19] So he told the captain he would join them for the night.

But in the dawn, by the grim, grey light of a new day of war, the idyll vanished, the beards came off, the men were short and sharp with one another, almost grumpy, and the young captain was no longer so expansive. That 'date with some panzers two miles east' was all too pressing. So they moved out, silent and morose, packed solid in the backs of their two-and-a-half ton trucks, leaving Barr and his engineer alone. Up front the guns began to thunder again.

At last the Germans in the Ardennes and the Alsace were beginning to retreat. Stubbornly they fought and retreated, stood again, fought, and then retreated yet again, their passing marked by the bloody faeces of dysentery – and their dead. Boys from the Hitler Youth Division found in cellars, defending their posts to the last, rifles frozen to their hands, faces black with putrifaction. Old men of fifty, their faces the colour of rich port wine. American dead, too, propped up by the roadside, frozen solid, eyebrows and hair white with hoar-frost, and telephone cable wire threaded through their rigid, outstretched hands in a kind of macabre joke played by the retreating enemy.

But most of them were far too miserable to play that kind of trick. The survivors staggered eastwards, women's shawls wrapped round their heads, feet bound with sacking, leaving behind them abandoned tanks and trucks, cast aside for lack of fuel. The wounded and sick hobbled desperately after them on makeshift crutches and sticks, anxious not to fall into the hands of the *Amis*, who were not taking prisoners this bitter January.

Noses red and bulbous with cold, pus running from their ears, bodies ridden with lice, they had only one thought in common – to cross the border of the Reich and achieve the safety of the West Wall.*

On January 16th, 1945, an American Army photographer, Sergeant Douglas Wood, was alerted to move up to the front. He was told the US First and Third Armies would be linking up just outside the Belgian frontier town of Houffalize. The 'Bulge' would be officially 'nipped out', and the month-long battle which had cost the Americans 80,000 casualties and the British

Sledges provide the answer as the front line is resupplied and returns its wounded men.

* Known to the Anglo-Americans as the Siegfried Line.

nearly 2,000 would be over. The historic moment would have to be recorded for the eager world Press.

Dutifully Wood went up to the front and, a little later, found himself crouching with some infantrymen of the US First Army on the northern bank of the River Ourthe, which still divided the two armies. About an hour after he arrived, a few cautious figures appeared on the other side. Were they the men of Patton's Third Army? Some of the First Army men waved. The soldiers on the other side took no notice. They disappeared again. Some while later, six men appeared and waded the knee-deep river. They were soaked and hungry and said they belonged to Patton's 11th US Armored Division. The link-up had taken place, and Wood dutifully photographed it. But he knew even as he posed his group that a picture of a 'bunch of ordinary doughs' wouldn't be good enough for a Press release back in the States. He decided to wait in case something more exciting turned up.

Then an officer, a senior one clearly, appeared. Wood poised with his camera. This was better. The officer introduced himself as Colonel Foy, from a reconnaissance battalion. He waded the river to where the tanks of Colonel O'Farrell's battalion of the 2nd Armored Division waited. Wood started clicking his shutter, crying to O'Farrell: 'Sir, there's a colonel here from the 11th Armored to see you!'

But if Wood had expected something dramatic, worthy of the great occasion – a kind of 'Doctor Livingstone, I presume' – he was disappointed.

O'Farrell popped his head out of the turret of his Sherman and Foy exclaimed, '*Well, Jesus Christ, if it isn't O'Farrell!* I didn't recognise you in a tank. Haven't seen you since Fort Knox.'[20] That was that. The link-up had taken place and the greatest battle the United States had fought in Europe in World War Two was over.*

Captain R. W. Thompson, the British war correspondent, was impressed by the 'feel' of Houffalize at that moment. There was, he felt, 'that kind of vacuum that seems to grip a place in the first moments: the enemy have gone; all that remains is dead; and there is this terrible silence that is as eerie a sensation as any I know.'[21]

From the heights above the town, Thompson stared down 'at the river winding amidst the ice deep in the gorge, the shattered trunks of the trees, the icicles veiling the outcropping rocks, the awful carcasses of homes shattered beyond all hope, all impressing themselves on my mind unforgettably.'

He walked down the hill and entered the town. The place seemed deserted. A lone cat scuttled away in front of him, disappearing into the snow-covered ruins. Finally after five minutes he encountered the first living

* There were other 'official' link-ups, but the one between Foy and O'Farrell is accepted as the first, at least between officers.

person. Next to a road-block, he spotted an old man toiling up the hill with the aid of a stick. When he came level with Thompson, he stopped; 'and his eyes, which were the saddest, most utterly hopeless sight I can remember, turned slowly to me, and he looked at me intently.'

'My daughter lived here,' the old man said, pointing to the ruins. Then his eyes moved away again and he plodded on once more.[22]

The tragedy of total war. The young men – those who had survived – would go away to fight new battles. Behind them they would leave death and destruction, and lasting sadness.

Now had come the time to pick up the pieces, pay off old scores, allot the blame for a defeat which had been barely turned into a victory – at the cost of 82,000 young lives, British and American, killed, maimed or taken prisoner.

In the 17th US Airborne Division area they started to collect the dead. Young Pfc Kurt Gabel volunteered to return to the point of attack on January 7th, where the Division's 513th Parachute Regiment had launched its initial push into the Bulge, and where the dead now lay beneath a white mantle of snow.

'Move out the same way you attacked,' Gabel and three other young volunteers were told by the Graves Registration men. 'As you come across bodies, group them together. If you find Germans, stack them separately.'

The four young paras began their slow, sad plod through the glistening snow. Almost immediately Gabel found six dead Americans on the route he had taken nearly two weeks before. He lined five of them up neatly. The sixth, he found, was impossible to stack. He was frozen stiff as a statue, curled up in the foetal position, hands clutching a gaping wound in his stomach.

At midday they had a break. They began to spoon out their K-rations from their cans in silence. Gabel found a piece of hard cheese and lay down to rest next to the bodies he had found. But somehow it seemed unfair to be alive and eating cheese next to these young men who were now dead. They seemed to be staring at him. On a sudden impulse he held out his cheese to the nearest corpse and said, '*Want a bite!*' He recovered himself almost immediately and pulled back his hand sharply. He continued to eat in broody silence, noting that the dead man's frozen face was beginning to thaw; the melting ice was running down his scarlet cheeks like tears.

A whistle blew. The volunteers and the Graves Registration men rose wearily to their feet to resume their labours. Open trucks arrived, bumping across the fields, and the Graves Registration men began to load the dead bodies of the paratroopers onto them. One grabbed the feet, the other the shoulders, with practised ease. 'One,

Winter freezes another corpse. Six German prisoners carry an American soldier.

two, three – *heave!'* they cried and flung the corpse onto the back of the truck.

Gabel stood watching them. He imagined himself dead and flung onto the 'deuce-and-a-half' as if he were a piece of wood.

Next to him one of his comrades blew up. His face ashen, eyes burning with hate, the volunteer advanced on the Graves Registration men loading the truck. 'You do that once more and I'll . . . *I'll blow your brains out!'*

The Graves Registration men said nothing. But they picked up the next dead para carefully and placed the corpse tenderly on the back of the truck – not as if it were a piece of wood, but the body of a man.[23]

In Malmedy, the scene of the 'massacre' of December 17th,* engineers of the 291st US Combat Engineers, who had been the first to hear of the shootings at that notorious crossroads above the little Belgian town, were also engaged in finding bodies.

The massacred soldiers – nearly a hundred of them – still lay where they had fallen, frozen now in their grotesque positions and covered with heavy snow. It was

a grim task, uncovering the stiff corpses, sweeping the snow from them with old-fashioned civilian brooms to reveal the horror of each one, and then placing a numbered marker on each body for the waiting photographers from the Inspector General's office. The entire field facing the burned down Café Bodarwé had to be swept thus to make sure that none of the victims were missed.

The photographs were duly taken, while the engineers rested on their shovels and brooms. Thereupon a group of black truckers loaded the corpses onto their vehicles to be taken back to Spa; there they would be viewed by the Inspector General and his court. The first step had been taken in what would be soon one of the most celebrated trials of the twentieth century, which would finally involve no less a person than the Supreme Commander, Eisenhower himself, and would help to smear the reputation of the whole United States Army.

But on this twenty-fifth day of January, 1945, the Americans were not concerned with such things. They wanted revenge.

Thirteen miles away from the place where the combat engineers laboured at their gruesome task, a squadron of US Thunderbolt fighter-bombers were sweeping in

* See '44 for details.

These photographs illustrate two stages of the Typhoons' attack on a German farmhouse.

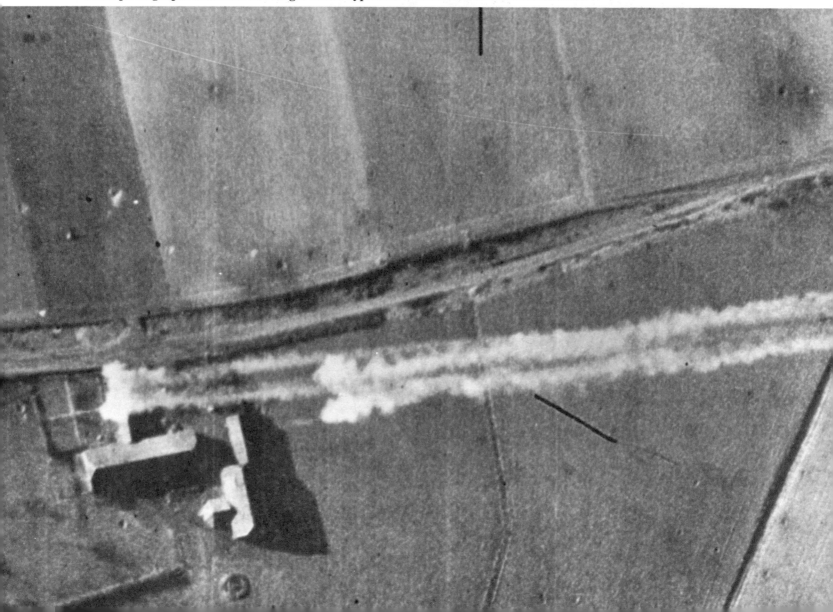

The lead aircraft fires its rockets while the second aircraft follows him in to complete the job.

low over St Vith, now razed to the ground since its capture by the Germans, heading for the little German town at the other side of the border: Prum.

As the squadron-leader in charge reported later:

To our surprise this road and others we could see were jammed with German vehicles of all kinds. Double columns, bumper to bumper. The concentrations were all retreating toward Prum, stretched ahead as far as the eye could see (in all my one hundred and eighteen missions I've never seen so much enemy equipment).

As I led the squadron down I found myself headed straight for a flak gun. I gave it a quick burst – and knocked it out. Then I took a quick look at the situation and decided to bomb first on the curve in the road. I dropped my two wing bombs on the curve, tore big holes in the road and knocked out six trucks. This stopped the whole column deader than a duck. Then we really went to work: bombed and strafed the column of tanks, half tracks, cargo-trucks and horse-drawn vehicles over an area of about five miles . . .

Hundreds of Jerries jumped from their vehicles and ran for cover; others started to pull their vehicles off the road in an attempt to hid them in the trees. But the ground was snow-covered so it didn't do them any good. We followed the tracks and bombed and strafed them in their hide-outs. After our bombs were all gone we worked back and forth on the column – and all hell began to break loose, as we'd knocked out the flak in the area and they were helpless. I've never seen so much confusion. The Jerries would run into the wood and then out again. They were like chickens with their heads cut off.[24]

Captain Wilfred Crutchfield of the USAF, who was that squadron-leader, was obviously a man who enjoyed his work. The fact that the 'chickens with their heads cut off' were human beings did not worry him that day. Killing had become impersonal. Revenge had to be taken. Soon nobody would dare to move by daylight on the German side of the border. Once the weather improved, the Allied fighter-bomber pilots in their feared *jabos*,* as the Germans called them, would shoot up anyone – soldier or civilian, man, woman or child – who dared show himself in that proscribed, accursed country of Germany.

To the rear in Allied territory life was getting back to normal once more, while across the border in Hitler's 'Thousand Year Reich' the country was slowly lapsing into chaos. But in those Eastern Cantons of Belgium which were mainly German-speaking, Malmedy, Eupen and St Vith, the Allies were still paying back real or imaginary scores.

Once again the feared partisans of the 'White Army' descended upon the villages and little towns of the area,

British infantry dug-in, awaiting attack near Stein, Germany.

38   * Short for *jagdbomber*.

plundering and terrorising the inhabitants, who had been German and then Belgian again, three times in the previous quarter of a century. Suspected by the American authorities as having collaborated with the German invaders of December 16th, 1944, they received no support from the US Civil Affairs officers. Hundreds of innocent people were beaten up and tortured. Thousands were denounced as traitors and spies, then packed off to such notorious prisons as the one in Antwerp, where the prisoners were housed in the cages that had once contained Antwerp's zoo. For one whole month, the Belgian government refused to send any supplies to their citizens in the Eastern Cantons, and the locals were forced to run the risk of mines and unexploded shells in order to scavenge the cans of food left behind by the advancing American troops and the beaten Germans. For nearly thirty years to come, the unfortunate 80,000-odd civilians of this remote border country would continue to suffer and be regarded as second-class citizens on account of their supposed role in the Battle of the Bulge.

Naturally the bitter Americans could not pay off all the old scores. Belgium itself had not played a very inspiring role during the great surprise counter-attack. The flags and the pictures of Churchill and Roosevelt which had greeted the 'liberators' of September 1944 had vanished immediately on that Saturday, December 16th, when the Germans had launched their offensive. Even the black market had closed down temporarily. No sensible Belgian wanted to be seen having anything to do with the Anglo-Americans now that the Gestapo was coming back. In towns just behind the front, such as Spa, the headquarters of the US First Army, the authorities immediately released all collaborators from the packed jails in order to make their peace with the Germans. Probably it was the wise thing to do in a country which had been invaded three times in the last thirty years. Yet it rankled. The 'liberators' had abruptly become unwanted foreigners to be shunned, at least in public, by those they had come so far and fought so hard to liberate.

Some of the men who had fought in the Ardennes were now being allowed to take short leaves once more in the big Belgian cities to the rear of the front. But the mood of the people – and the soldiers – had changed. The leave-men felt that everything had become commercialised; that all Belgian civilians – bar owners, pimps, prostitutes, the kind of people that soldiers came into contact with – were fleecing them; that they even begrudged the soldiers the privilege of free travel on their trams and trains.*

Corporal Dudley Anderson, a twenty-year-old veteran of the 6th Airborne who had fought in the Ardennes,

* During the Occupation, the Germans had claimed this right for themselves. When the Allies liberated Belgium, they took it over till the end of the war.

US tanks advance past battle-scarred trees outside Samree, Belgium.

WELCOME TO OUR

Allied liberators enter Antoine.

(Above) Bed sheets are used to camouflage 1st US Army soldiers as they patrol in the Ardennes.

(Right) Belgian girls await the opening of the 21 Dance Club in Brussels.

was granted twenty-four hours leave in Brussels after his battalion had been withdrawn from the line that January. After the luxury of a hot bath and a hot meal at the 'Montgomery Club', he and a comrade nicknamed 'Tombstone', the battalion's Casanova, set off to explore the Belgian capital. They had already been warned that brothels were out of bounds and that VD was epidemic in Brussels, but naturally it was in the brothel area behind the Gare du Nord that the two, now rather drunk, comrades ended up.

A pimp latched onto the two young men – 'Exhibition, sixty francs, gentlemen!' – and they found themselves in a small room packed with Allied servicemen, listening to a gramophone playing pre-war dance music and waiting for the 'exhibition'.

The 'exhibition' turned out to be two women in their thirties, thin, weary and hard-faced. They stripped and mimed the act of love in various ways for half an hour until finally the blonde one seized the beret from the head of a tank corps soldier, collected a handful of notes and coins from the assembly, and then squatted and took the money inside. The soldiers cheered wildly, whereupon she bent slightly and 'dropped the money, note by note, coin by coin, into the beret'. She offered the men their money back, but none of them wanted it; and Anderson noted that the tank corps trooper didn't put on his beret again.

Outside in the cold night once more, the pimp asked the two paras if they would like to visit a high-class brothel. They would. He led them into a nearby bar, with 'red plush velvet banquette seating around small coffee tables'. They guessed the bedrooms were upstairs, but as Anderson commented dolefully, 'We were not fated to get that far.'

Two pretty girls seated themselves next to the young paratroopers. Naturally they wanted champagne, which they drank rapidly and asked for more. Anderson asked what the price of a bottle was and was told it cost five pounds. That shocked him. A fiver was the equivalent of

two and a half weeks' pay! 'We can't afford any more,' he hissed in Tombstone's ear. 'We shall have to get them upstairs after this bottle.'

Of course, they hadn't a chance. Another bottle appeared and the two young paras began to get really drunk. Tombstone became amorous and started fondling his girl. But Anderson – who had taken part in two bayonet charges against the enemy in the last six months – was growing aggressive. He told Tombstone that the girls were 'taking us for a ride'. Tombstone's girl understood English. She leapt across the table and started to claw his face. 'To a Red Devil, accustomed to unarmed combat, a brothel girl was no opposition at all.' Anderson grabbed her and threw her across the table. Two bouncers appeared – which had 'a remarkably sobering effect on us'. The two chastened paras marched out with as much dignity as they could muster in the circumstances.

'Outside in the cold air, we looked at each other. Almost broke, there was nothing for us to do but to walk back to the hostel. The next day we spent as sober and respectable tourists, seeing the more conventional sights of Brussels . . . For us, the fleshpots of the city had priced themselves out of the market.'[25]

Corporal Anderson's experience was typical of many that winter. The liberators had outstayed their welcome. The civilians wanted to be rid of the soldiers and their war so that they could get on with their lives once again.

In France Colonel Charles Codman, Patton's personal aide, found that civilian life was rapidly returning to normal – despite the fact that there were still a couple of hundred thousand German soldiers on French soil, bottled up in the 'Colmar Pocket' and in the various Atlantic seaboard ports.

In the last week of January Codman attended a society wedding in Paris (before the war he had lived there). Afterwards he wrote to his wife to tell her about the

A welcome friend.

affair and in particular about a pre-war acquaintance who was also there: the Comte de Z., who had become a collaborator.

You ask about . . . Comte Y. de Z. and his collaborating activities. At the time of the Normandy landing he was reported, by the French, to have given us twenty-four hours before being pushed into the sea. A few days later he graciously extended our time allowance to a fortnight. At the expiration of said period, he ducked underground with the *maquis* hopefully on his trail. They failed to catch up with him, and if the following – overheard at the Coursier wedding reception – is a criterion, he appears to be on his way to a comeback.

Spirited young lady: 'If he should walk into the room now, I should cut him dead.'

Elderly gentleman: 'I know how you feel, my dear. He did appear at Monique's tea party last week. It was quite embarrassing. Out of courtesy to my hostess, I felt obliged to bow to him, slightly, but I did *not* shake hands.'

Lady of a certain age: 'Yes, I was there. Most uncomfortable. Monique being one of my oldest friends, I couldn't very well avoid speaking to him when he kissed my hand. However, I did *not* smile.'

'Next time for Monique's sake, she will presumably smile,' someone whispered. 'However, until the time after next, she may draw the line at hopping into bed with him . . .'[26]

French society in the middle of total war, January 1945!

Now the time had come to pay off the final score. In a ceremonial, deliberate, cold-blooded act, the top brass would show the ordinary 'dog-face' what would be his fate if he 'bugged out' and went 'over the hill' in the coming battle for Germany, as so many of them had done in the Ardennes. Far away from the peoples they had liberated (for they did not count now; liberation was over, and the conquest of the Reich was soon to commence) the US Army staged a drama of a kind not seen since the American Civil War nearly a hundred years previously. For the first time since 1865, the US Army in Europe was going to shoot a soldier for desertion.

On January 30th, the brass of the 28th Infantry Division – which would soon attack into the Colmar Pocket – took over the remote little mining town of Ste Marie-aux-Mincs, situated some five hundred metres above sea-level in the French Vosges, twenty miles or so from the River Rhine.

The locals, mostly mining folk or engaged in the local textile industry, were curious about this sudden invasion in that dour, German manner of theirs; for most of them were German-speaking, or even German-born. But the Americans generals and colonels who had commandeered all the key buildings and the mine-owners' villas situated just outside of town weren't giving anything away. Whatever their reason for being there, they weren't telling the 'Frogs' a thing.*

The American officers seemed, so the locals thought,[27] to be concentrating their attention on a house at the northern outskirts of Ste Marie, a nineteenth-century villa of three storeys and built of grey stone: Number 86, Rue de General Dourgeois. All day long, that snowy January 30th, 1945, US officers in jeeps came and went, and most of the afternoon there was the muffled sound of hammering and digging coming from behind the high wall that surrounded the villa. It seemed as if the Americans were digging for something in the garden.

That night, as a raging snow blizzard descended upon the Vosges mountains, cutting off many of the surrounding villages, the US XXI Corps Commander General Frank 'Shrimp' (on account of his size) Milburn gave a dinner party at his chateau at Ste Marie. With the wind howling outside and the shutters of the blackout rattling, the Corps Commander wined and dined those of his officers who would be leading the attack into the Colmar Pocket on the morrow. But the dinner was intended not only to hail the new offensive, which was aimed at finally driving the Germans back over the Rhine; it also served another purpose. For as General Milburn remarked to one of the two lowly colonels present, Colonel Edward Elson, the XXI Corps' senior chaplain, 'Chaplain, tomorrow morning the 28th Division are executing a private soldier by firing squad for desertion. I wish you would attend as my representative and give me a full report.'[28]

Elson agreed he would, and 'Shrimp' Milburn passed on to other matters. The bourbon and the good French champagne continued to circulate and the divisional generals' cheeks grew ruddy and glowed with good health and booze.

Roughly about the same time as the generals celebrated, an American weapons carrier labouring up the steep winding pass that leads to Ste Marie halted for a break. It was still snowing heavily and the MPs manning the vehicle thought they might get a warm-up in an isolated farmhouse just off the road. Two of them went inside to eat their sandwiches in front of the humble place's only fire and warm their frozen limbs. In due course, they came out and relieved the other two 'Snowdrops', as they were called on account of their white-painted helmets. Only the fifth man in the weapons carrier remained seated all the time, cold or not. But then he could not do otherwise, for his hands were chained and his ankles were bound.

He was a skinny American in his early twenties, his face pale from the long months he had spent in the stockade. Once he had been a replacement to the 28th Infantry Division but he had deserted during his first action and gone 'over the hill'.* Finally he had surrendered to the US authorities, confident that he would receive, at worst, a prison sentence at Leavenworth. But ex-Pfc Eddie Slovik, slight, sandy-haired and blue-eyed, had been wrong. Of all the many thousands of American soldiers who had deserted since the start of the war, of whom 2,864 were tried by general court-martial for the offence, only 49 had their death sentences approved. And of those 49, only one was to be shot – *Eddie Slovik*. Tomorrow he would face a firing squad composed of men from the Division he had deserted nearly six months before.

At last the MPs loosened his bonds and handed him a sandwich and a canteen of hot coffee. But the prisoner had little time for the food; he just toyed with it. Obviously his mind was on other things as he sat there in that remote place with the wind howling and the snow beating against the side of the freezing truck. 'Come on, fellers,' he said in the end, putting down his canteen, 'give me a break. Untie my feet and let me run out there in the snow. You shoot me with your carbines and get it over with.'

The big hefty MPs refused. One of them said, 'You're a good guy, but we can't do that. They've got a big party planned for you over in Ste Marie . . . the full-dress treatment. After they get through with you, those dog-faces are supposed to think twice before they take off. Just relax and drink your coffee . . . It won't be long.'[29]

Private Eddie Slovik nodded and drank his coffee, saying no more. As always he was obedient.

On the last day of January, 1945, the year of victory, Eddie Slovik was led out to his execution. He walked slowly and bareheaded into the courtyard of Number 86, saying the Act of Contrition, his breath fogging the icy mountain air. With him was the Catholic Chaplain Father Cummings, who walked with him to the post set up in the winter-wasted garden of the villa, erected the previous afternoon in front of the 'ricochet board'. He was stripped of all insignia. He seemed cold and a little shaky, but otherwise the only American to be shot for desertion since the Civil War was perfectly calm.

One by one the senior officers appeared, then the firing squad, all picked marksmen and all from the 109th Infantry Regiment, the regiment to which the condemned man had belonged. Its colonel, a lean, young Texan called James E. Rudder, came into the courtyard. After the execution, he would write a personal message to his soldiers in which he stated quite categorically:

---

* Nearly forty years later, researching the execution of Private Slovik, I discovered that the locals had only found out what happened in their town that January from a documentary film shown on German television (the town receives German TV from over the Rhine). As to the place where they shot Slovik, it is now covered by a block of flats.

* See '44 for the story of Slovik's desertion and the subsequent court-martial.

Today I had the most regrettable experience I have had since the war began. I saw a former soldier of the 109th Infantry, Private Eddie D. Slovik, shot to death by musketry by soldiers of this regiment. I pray that this man's death will be a lesson to each of us who have any doubt at any time about the price we must pay to win this war. The person that is not willing to fight and die, if need be, for his country *has no right to life* [author's italics].[30]

The sentiment was crystal-clear: fight or die.

Now General 'Dutch' Cota appeared, armed only with a black swagger stick. The General who had been dubbed 'the hero of Omaha Beach', and who had been wounded at St Lô, didn't believe in combat fatigue being regarded as a disease; nor did he believe in psychiatrists. As one of his divisional psychiatrists said after the war: 'Whenever he [Cota] found occasion to observe psychiatrists in action, the impression he got was not good: he relieved them, chewed them out, gave them a bad time.' General Cota was not the man, obviously, to understand the emotional problems of the son of poor Polish immigrants, who grew up on the wrong side of the tracks during the Depression, graduated to petty theft and was sent to jail, emerging only one year before he received those celebrated greetings from Uncle Sam. No sir!

Now the execution of Private Slovik could commence. They were all there.

It was all very formal. The firing squad lined up as Eddie was tied to the post. The witnesses, enlisted men from every unit in the 28th Division, were all assembled to the left; a similar collection of officers formed up to the right. There was no doubt that the whole affair was being staged by the top brass to have the maximum effect – not only in the 28th, but in the whole of the US Army. The rot had to be stopped. There had been too much indiscipline, cowardice, combat fatigue, desertion in the last six months. Soon the US Army would be moving over the frontier into Germany as conquerors. There was no room now for the silly weaknesses of democracy. The army which would conquer the Third Reich had to be hard and unyielding, not only to the foe, but to itself as well!

As Sergeant McKendrick tied the prisoner to the post with nylon parachute cord, Eddie told him: 'I'm okay. They're not shooting me for deserting the United States Army. Thousands of guys have done that. They just need to make an example out of somebody and I'm it, because I'm an ex-con. I used to steal things when I was a kid, and that's what they're shooting me for. They're shooting me for bread and chewing-gum I stole when I was twelve years old.'[31]

At nine fifty-six precisely, General Cota gave the command: '*Attention!*'

Captain Hummel, one of the witnesses who happened to be standing directly behind General Cota, said later: 'I don't think anybody who was there will ever forget one thing – the sharp crack of that volley echoing across the snow in those hills followed by an almost perfect silence. Not a sound . . .'[32]

But Eddie was not yet dead, although eleven bullets had struck him.* The shooting had been poor because the firing squad was nervous and all the slugs had missed Eddie's heart, marked by a white patch.

Doctor Rougelot, the surgeon in charge, examined Eddie and found he was dying. He tried to drag out his examination so that the shaken men of the firing squad would not have to fire again. But already the officer commanding the firing squad had ordered his men to reload.

This angered Rougelot and the Chaplain. 'Give him another volley if you like it so much!' the latter snapped.

Doctor Rougelot looked up from Eddie's limp body, supported at the post by his bonds, and said quietly: 'Take it easy, Padre. None of us is enjoying this.'

The Major in charge of the firing squad now asked Rougelot to pronounce Eddie dead or stand back for the second volley.

Rougelot slipped off his stethoscope. 'The second volley won't be necessary, Major,' he said softly. 'Private Slovik is dead.'[33]

While the Chaplain anointed the corpse with oil and the waiting Graves Registration men stood by with a mattress cover to slip the body in, Captain Hummel walked over to Sergeant McKendrick. He indicated the 'collapse board', which had been built the previous day to support Slovik in case he had not been able to stand upright. 'It turned out we didn't need that bit of apparatus, did we Mac,' he said thoughtfully.

'No, nor Slovik,' the NCO replied. 'I came nearer to needing it than he did. I can't figure that guy out. If he was a coward, he certainly didn't show it today.'

At ten-thirty on that last day of January, a high priority message was sent from Ste Marie-aux-Mines to Eisenhower's Supreme Headquarters at Versailles. It read:

TO: COMMANDING GENERAL ETOUSA.
FROM: HQ, 28TH INF. DIV.
PURSUANT TO GCMO 27 HEADQUARTERS ETOUSA 23 JAN 45, PRIVATE EDDIE D. SLOVIK 36896415, FORMERLY COMPANY G 109TH INF. WAS SHOT TO DEATH BY A FIRING SQUAD AT 1005 HOURS 31 JAN 45 AT STE MARIE-AUX-MINES, FRANCE.[34]

The month had ended the same way it began – in blood and sorrow and sudden death.

---

* As was customary, one man in the firing squad had been given a blank cartridge.

Troops of the 9th US Army dash forward under machine gun fire.

FEBRUARY

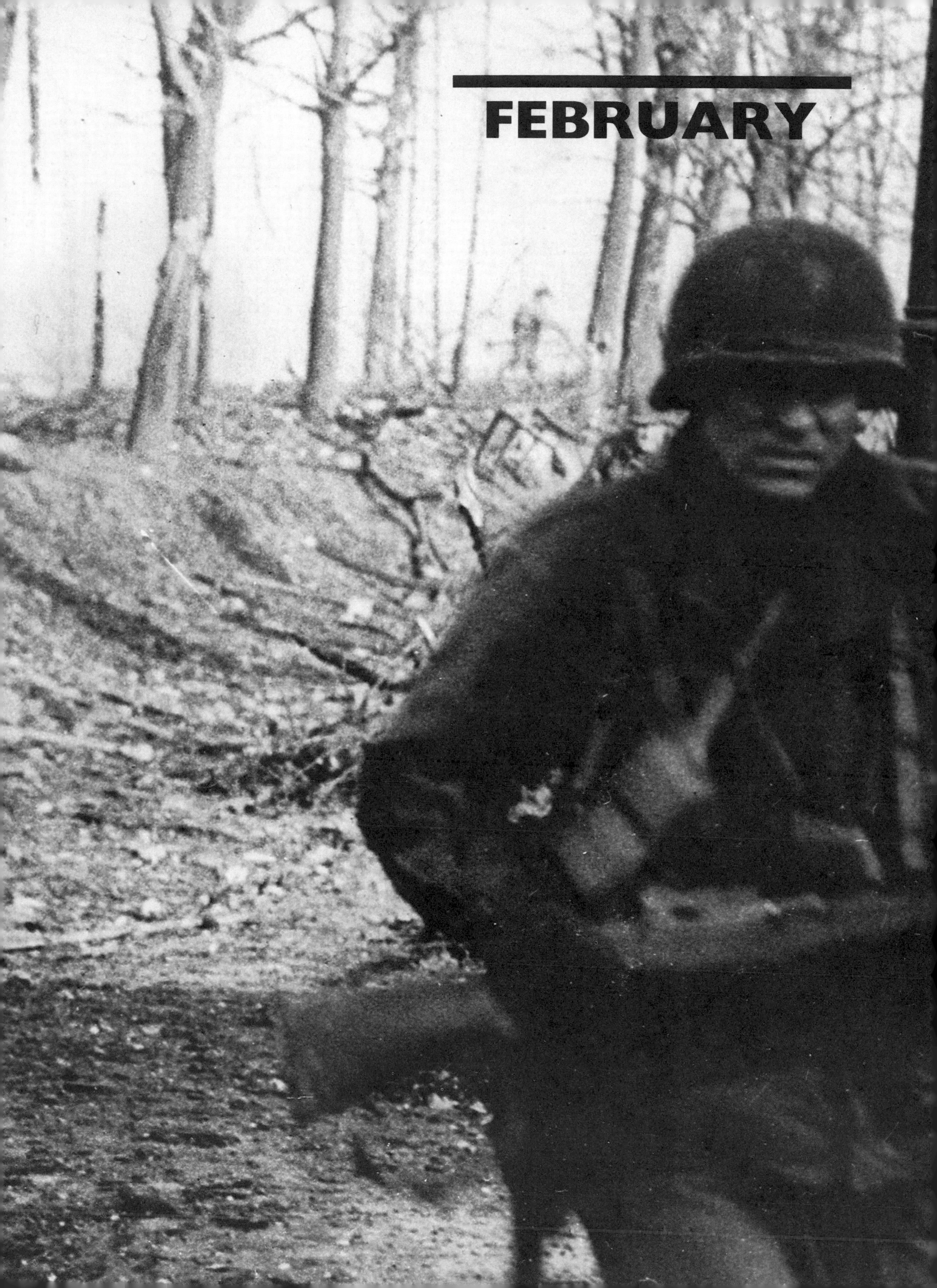

Through the Reichswald

Now while the Americans recovered from the ordeal of the Ardennes, it was the turn of Montgomery's British and Canadians. In this first week of February 1945, they would be called upon to pay the butcher's bill. They would launch the first attack across the border into Hitler's vaunted '1,000 Year Reich'. Two hundred thousand of them, in fact, grouped together in British General Horrocks' XXX Corps, as big as the whole of the pre-war British Army.

There would be five divisions of infantry in the first wave that would attack across the frontier into the German Reichswald, the huge state forest that lined the border between Germany and Holland. There would be the 51st Highland Division, known throughout the Army as the 'Highway Decorators' because they painted their 'HD' divisional insignia on anything and everything. With them there would be the 53rd Welsh and the 15th Scottish Divisions, plus the 2nd and 3rd Canadian Infantry Divisions, which so far had suffered the highest casualties of any of Montgomery's Divisions, nearly 120 percent. In support would be the ill-fated 43rd Infantry Division, which had already had a complete turn-around of its rifle companies due to their terrible losses, and the Guards Armoured Division, whose divisional sign was an eye; this, according to soldiers' legend, was supposed to wink when it saw a virgin. 'So far,' the big guardsmen were wont to quip, 'it ain't winked once on the continent!'

Now this massive array of men and *matériel* waited in the dripping cold rain on the Dutch-German border, facing the dark, sombre, somehow sinister firs of the Reichswald through which they must fight if they were to reach their objectives: the border towns of Goch, Cleves and Calcar, which lay behind the Siegfried Line. Since

A Churchill tank supports infantrymen as they advance through the Reichswald.

the previous September the Americans had fought without success to break through the massive fortifications of the Siegfried Line, with its thirty-six bunkers per kilometre. Now it was the turn of the British and Canadians, and they were determined to 'hang out the washing on the Siegfried Line', in the words of the popular song, just as they'd been boasting they would ever since 1939. But now they faced the reality – and it wasn't too inviting.

Some of the lucky ones were in billets, just across the border. Corporal Dudley Anderson was one of them. His post was in a hay barn off an abandoned farmhouse. To get to it, he and his comrades had to tunnel through twenty yards of hay, making a passage barely wide enough for two men to pass. If the barn had been set afire in an attack it would have been a death trap, but all was quiet save for an occasional shell. There were German patrols about but they never came near the paras' position. The most immediate hazard was rather different. 'I was sitting in my warm nest one night and felt something land on my head. It was so heavy that my head swayed to and fro', Anderson remembered forty years later. 'I realised that it must be a rat and a big one at that. I flicked my head and it scrambled off.' Later the paras found out that their comfy billet was infested with rats, but they did nothing about them. 'Live and let live was our attitude towards them, as long as they did not help themselves to our rations. We had enough killing on our hands without bothering about them.'[1]

But many of the waiting infantrymen were bivouacked in slit trenches, up to their ankles in freezing mud, in the worst winter in Europe in living memory. One subaltern in the Canadian North Nova Scotia Highlanders found himself 'living in caves and dugouts scooped out of the wooded hills':

There is a telephone in my dugout, hooked up so I can communicate with company headquarters, half a mile back, or with our forward artillery observation post, a quarter of a mile ahead of me. I often pick up the phone and listen in. The difference in voices! The people at HQ relaxed, unworried, loud (they shout over the phone), whistling, singing, joking, playing cards. The men in the observation post overlooking the enemy positions whisper into the phone. They try to end conversations as soon as possible and seem to be talking with their heads pulled down into their greatcoats. The strange dialogue goes on intermittently all night.[2]

The phone and the food brought up from the rear was the Canadian's only contact with the outside world. For days on end he and his comrades simply crouched in their holes. 'Some days we lie in the mud . . . We eat twice a day, morning and night. Food is brought down a slippery path, mined along the fringes, under darkness and between scattered bursts of enemy fire, for they know our habits.'

British troops rest near Udem.

So they waited for the big push, the veterans and the nervous teenage reinforcements, eating 'their armoured pig' (spam) and 'armoured dog' (sausages), spitting out, if they dared, the Vitamin C tablets which Army Command had now insisted they eat to keep them 'fighting fit' and which resulted in plenty of smelly 'green smoke' when they broke wind.

For the most part they were quiet, unaggressive men, save for the Canadians and the youngsters of those Scots regiments recruited in Glasgow and Edinburgh and brought up in the environment of street brawls and the 'razor gang' fights of the bitter, depressed thirties. Their opponents just across the border, mostly paratroopers of the First German Parachute Army, did not rate them very highly as offensive troops. Back in the previous summer, a captured German document reported that the morale of British infantry was 'not very great':

They rely largely on the artillery and air force support. In the case of well directed artillery fire by us they often abandon their position in flight. The enemy is extraordinarily nervous of close combat. Whenever the enemy infantry is energetically engaged they mostly retreat or surrender.[3]*

Later that year, General Bittrich – the one-legged commander of the SS Corps that recaptured Arnhem and destroyed the 1st British Airborne Division – told his staff:

We must remember that British soldiers do not act on their own initiative . . . when they are fighting in a town and when it consequently becomes difficult for officers to exercise control. They are amazing in defence, but we need not be afraid of their capabilities in attack.[4]

In essence Bittrich was right. For the most part the British 'squaddie', as he called himself, moved slowly and at a deliberate pace, doing only what was ordered of him – no more, no less. Why should he do otherwise? His attitude merely reflected that of the officers who led him into battle. The dead wood had been sorted out by now and most battalion commanders were in their mid-twenties – a couple of years younger than their American counterparts – and they were all very battle experienced. But they still cultivated their class habits, which made it appear unseemly to get excited or be in any haste. Everything had to be done at a calm, considered pace.

From top to bottom of the officers corps, it seemed that their concept of war was that it was some rather lethal form of sport. Montgomery invariably used racing or cricketing images in his orders and addresses to the troops. His officers aped him. They rarely *advanced* with

* There was naturally an element of propaganda in this – almost identical statements were made about American troops – but there was an element of sour grapes in it as well, for when the Germans lost they invariably attributed their defeat to Allied superiority in guns and planes.

British troops held in reserve move up to do battle in the Reichswald.

their tanks – they had a 'jolly good gallop forward'. Their spells in the line might be characterised as 'a jolly good (or bad) innings'. Sometimes they were lucky and 'knocked Jerry for six' or 'bowled him out' or captured 'a decidedly good bag of Hun prisoners'. In some of the better regiments, such as the Guards, they even kept game-books in which officers recorded how many Jerries they had bagged with their sniper rifles. Certain sections of the static front in Holland that winter were described as possessing 'excellent rough shooting' – and it was not pheasants that the officers-and-gentlemen were shooting.

These officers, who must never appear to 'flap', maintained a paternalistic attitude to their 'chaps', believing that the average Tommy was a simple soul, quite content as long as he had 'wallop', 'soccer' and 'fags' (fifty 'coffin nails' – *i.e.* Woodbines – a week, plus a handful of boiled sweets and two bars of bitter chocolate wrapped in blue paper and made by Rowntrees). Most of them were quite realistic about their men and their fighting ability. Infantry Brigadier H. Essame, commanding a brigade in the 43rd Infantry Division, knew that in combat 'their stock of courage could soon be exhausted, leaving them bankrupt and bereft of bravery'.[5] Those battalion commanders who had served in Normandy, and most of them had, knew about the unfortunate battalion of the 49th Division that had broken down under fire, many of the men going into hysterics or running away so that in the end the battalion was simply disbanded.* And that wasn't the only occasion when officers had been forced to draw their revolvers to keep their men in the line.

But all of these rather slow and pedantic officers felt they could rely on the regimental tradition, and on the ability and discipline of their senior NCOs to keep the men fighting. There would be no panic-stricken breakdown of whole regiments in the British Army as had been the case with the Americans in the Huertgen Forest and the Ardennes. All the same, these young officers were realistic enough to see that working-class resentment and stubbornness were too deeply engrained in the rank-and-file to make them do more than absolutely necessary. The tea-break and knocking-off-at-five mentality had been part and parcel of the ordinary Tommy's make-up since the end of the Great War. Even the Army with all its stringent punishments could not eradicate that.

Thus in these opening days of February 1945, the men of Horrocks' great corps waited for the attack on the Reichswald and their first 'bash' at the Siegfried Line, drinking their compo tea, smoking their Woodbines, cleaning their weapons – and their boots too, for this was the British Army after all; bull still reigned supreme, even in the line.

The veterans feigned indifference; they had seen it all before. Their only concession to what was to come was to change their underwear the night before the attack, for they knew the potential consequence of dirty linen being forced into an open wound: gas gangrene.

The reinforcements, naturally, were nervous. They placed their issue steel shaving mirrors carefully in the left-hand pocket of their blouses as a frail but sure means of protection. Some padded out their flies, for they had all heard the terrible tales of the 'bloke who had his goolies shot off'. And they asked questions – *how they asked questions*! – of those nineteen-year-old veterans. 'What's it like? . . . Go on, Corp, tell us, what's it like in battle?' But in the end they always received the same tired old cliché as an answer: 'The only way out of the infantry, my son, is on a stretcher – or six feet under.'

From the Corps Commander downwards, the officers were in no way sanguine about the task that lay ahead. Although Horrocks knew that months of preparation had gone into the coming battle, with 446 freight trains lifting a quarter of a million tons of stores, now spread over one hundred miles of new roads and 400 miles of reconditioned ones, with half a million men readied and thirty-five thousand vehicles, he too felt apprehensive.

Tall, lean, ascetic-looking, and very popular with his soldiers, the Corps Commander knew that to make a success of the biggest single operation ever fought by the British Army, he needed two things – 'complete surprise and good weather':

If the Germans got wind of our attack they would move up their reserves before the battle started. But the weather exerted the biggest influence of all because the ground was frozen hard and if only the frost would hold on until February 9th, our tanks and motor transport would be able to go everywhere across country without difficulty.[6]

His junior officers, brought up secretly to view the terrain across which they were going to attack, did not particularly like what they saw. Captain Foley of the Armoured Corps thought the Reichswald 'looked sombre and uninviting, the black trunks of the big trees as solid as if carved from granite'. 'There it is,' one of his fellow officers said to Foley quietly, 'our objective for the first day. The Germans think the forest is an anti-tank obstacle. Maybe it is, too. But you never know till you try. Personally I think we should be able to operate in there, providing we pick our trees carefully.' But another fellow officer, Captain Cunningham, wasn't so confident. 'We've got to reach it first,' he said dourly.[7]

Lieutenant Woollcombe of the 15th Scottish Division, just out of hospital and back with his old infantry battalion, was feeling equally uneasy. 'For at last it was the Siegfried Line and many of us felt a new fear . . . The Rhine may have stood for the mystique of our new enemies, but the Siegfried Line seemed their brute embodiment.'[8] And Major Bernard Fergusson of the Black Watch, a veteran of combat on three continents,

* See '44 for further details.

British soldiers move past German dead as they penetrate deeper into the forest.

hoped that the 'coming battle might be the last of the war'. But he concluded, 'The enemy would not lightly yield the Siegfried Line. He might well make his last stand in it.'[9]

Of course, the 'other ranks' were the last to know what their objective was going to be. Lance-Corporal R. M. Wingfield, for whom this would be the last battle, was assembled with the rest of his battalion of the Queen's Royal Regiment in the unit canteen, briefed by no less a person than the Brigadier himself. The officer pulled no punches:

This Reichswald Forest will be a tough nut to crack. Any of you who've done wood-clearing will know that they [the Canadians of the first wave] will probably lose a lot of casualties. The Forest can't be bypassed. It must be systematically and thoroughly cleared . . . The Reichswald Forest is a game-preserve owned by Uncle Hermann Goering. He's very touchy about his shooting rights, so at every entrance there are dirty great notices about what UHG will do if you're caught with a gun. *Watch out for the bloody gamekeepers!*[10]

Later that day the Queen's moved up to their front line positions. Wingfield's platoon had just moved into their billet when an officer of the local town-major's staff came blustering in, 'dripping with discipline and the fat of easy living'. 'Get out of this poxy bloody place!' the officer bellowed. There was a metallic click from the corner. One of Wingfield's pals raised his rifle deliber-

ately and pointed it at the fat officer. 'It's bastards like you who make me sick of the stupid war,' the soldier said through gritted teeth, finger white on his trigger. 'Get out of here, you greasy bastard!' The officer fled.

Now that the veterans knew what lay in store for them they didn't care. The 'base wallahs' would live to see the end of the war; they of the infantry probably wouldn't.

At one minute to five on the morning of February 8th, all was silent, tense, dark. No sound save the wind in the trees and the soft drip-drip of the fine rain. Five o'clock. With a tumultuous roar the greatest bombardment of World War Two commenced.

Horrocks was at the time stuck halfway up a tree on a platform that served as his command post. 'The noise was appalling and the sight awe-inspiring,' he wrote later.[11]

'It was a fantastic sight, never to be forgotten,' wrote the historian of the 4/7th Dragoon Guards, 'one moment silence and the next moment a terrific ear-splitting din, with every pitch of noise imaginable. Little bangs, big bangs, sharp cracks, the rattle of machine guns and the ripple of Bofors, intermingled with the periodic swish of a rocket battery. The night was lit by flashes of every colour and the tracer of the Bofors guns weaving fairy patterns in the sky as it streamed off towards the target.'[12]

'I was nearly blasted from my blankets by the deafening barrage of noise,' Captain Foley recalled years afterwards. 'The ground shook with the fury of the cannonade

59

and the walls of the sixty-pound tent whipped in and out like sparrows' wings.'[13]

The barrage woke young Lieutenant Woollcombe as he slept on the bare floor of the schoolroom which was his company's HQ. 'A hurricane lamp was burning. Around, huddled in their blankets on the bare boards, were the officers of A Company . . . There were also three subalterns, one of them awake, and I saw him there on his back with his hands pressed intently together, his lips moving ceaselessly at his prayers. Outside the windows, the continuous massed thunder.'[14]

All those who saw that tremendous barrage put up by nearly fifteen hundred guns were impressed, save war correspondent Captain R. W. Thompson, who had seen Monty's set-piece attacks before. He wrote that February: 'The most terrific barrage I have ever been under opened the Reichswald assault, and went on for about forty-eight hours. It was the most staggering, awe-inspiring display of fireworks the mind can carry.' The sting came in the tail: 'It killed about a dozen Germans!'[15]

The curtain of man-made fire, a terrible creeping inferno which incinerated everything in its path, swept forward at one hundred yards every four minutes. To mark the end of this four-minute period, when the guns would increase their range by another 300 yards, they all fired a round of yellow smoke. It was a tremendous technical achievement, co-ordinating the work of 1,500 guns link-ed only by wireless; and it exemplified the fact that, by this stage of the war, the British artillery was the best in the world.

Behind this massive barrage came the flail tanks beating a path through the minefields. They were followed by more of General Hobart's 'funnies': tanks with fas-cines on their backs, to bridge the great anti-tank ditch that ran for nearly three miles to the British front; flame-throwers, the feared 'crocodiles'; and 'kangaroos' (newly invented by the Canadians), which were tanks with their turrets removed and carrying the assault infantry.

Nothing like this had ever been seen before. Five infantry divisions advancing on a six-mile front, behind the fire of 1,500 guns, a solid armoured mass bulldozing all before it – for a while at least.

'Dead on the dot at ten-thirty,' Captain Foley related after the war, 'we emerged from our wood and headed for the Reichswald. In front of us the Black Watch moved purposefully forward; little groups of men hur-rying over the ground, while others spread-eagled them-selves behind what cover they could find and fired their rifles and Bren guns calmly and methodically.'[16]

Foley's Churchills pushed their way through the shat-tered trees, around steaming brown shellholes that looked like the work of giant moles, past bodies of the

Men of a Scottish regiment warily advance through the shattered Reichswald forest.

field-greys sprawled out in the dramatic postures of those who have met a violent death. And over it all hung the overpowering acrid smell of burnt explosive.

They came across a company commander of the Black Watch quietly smoking his pipe as he watched the action. 'With his little cane and red hackle at the side of his cap,' Foley recalled 'he might well have been taking a Sunday stroll down Aldershot High Street, except that vicious little spurts of dust were cracking about his heels.'

'Look here,' Foley called down from his turret, 'aren't you being shot at?'

'Oh, never mind that,' the Black Watch Major replied calmly, 'it's only got nuisance value!'

The Churchills trundled on. Suddenly Foley heard a noise 'like a small boy dragging a stick along some iron railings', and a line of sparks dotted the side of his tank. Hurriedly he dropped back inside his tank. 'They've woken up!' he cried. He peered through the periscope and saw that the Black Watch were rapidly 'melting into the landscape'.

The real battle had commenced at last.

Many vehicles – save for the Churchills with their broad tracks – were already floundering in the mud. The infantry had to go it alone. Aided by the reflection of searchlights shining on the low cloud ('Monty's moonlight', they called it), they moved on through the forest. Broken branches were strewn everywhere, leaving the trees looking like grotesque scarecrows. The Canadians of the 2nd Infantry Division ran into mines and machine-gun fire, but they carried their objectives. To their right, the 3rd Canadian Division had to contend not only with mines and minefields but also with flooding from the Rhine, which had been breached deliberately. Their infantry went into action on water, fighting their battles from their Buffaloes; soon they would be calling themselves the Water Rats, in imitation of Montgomery's famed Desert Rats of the Eighth Army.

Now it began to rain. Abruptly the mud became the worst enemy, bogging down supply transport, tanks and medical jeeps throughout the whole of the XXX Corps area. So bad did the situation become that one day the total ration for the 16,000-strong Highland Division was one tracked Weasel carrying a mere 500 tins of self-heating soup.

Private Barrance had been with the 53rd Division's Middlesex Regiment since Normandy, where he had had the strange experience of tossing a grenade back at a German soldier, who had thrown it from only yards away, and seeing the German smile slightly when it didn't go off the second time either. Now he was in the Reichswald Forest, facing the one thing he dreaded most: 'the thought of a track [of his bren-gun carrier] coming off under fire'. It happened on a trail 'in about a foot of mud with Jerry giving us about everything'. The hapless young driver was blocking the track, 'with high ranking officers, red and blue caps, Sherman tanks, AA guns all wanting to pass'.

'What's wrong?' someone shouted.

A harassed young Barrance yelled above the racket, 'The split pin has sheared from my track!'

The reply came back: 'You'd better fix the bloody thing, cos you're holding up the war!'

Forty years later Barrance wondered cynically: 'If the bloody thing hadn't sheared off, would the war have ended sooner?'

Hurriedly, he got off the road. Just in time. Suddenly, out of nowhere, six huge Tiger tanks trundled up the road. Barrance and his mates crouched lower and lower in the ditch, as one after the other the sixty-ton monsters rumbled by. Finally the last one had departed; they hadn't been spotted. 'All was okay. But where was my rifle? I found it some three hundred yards around the road, bent like a boomerang!'

Private Barrance had the devil's own time trying to get a replacement for that rifle. 'The Quartermaster thought I had done a Tarzan act to try and get out of the army.' Intelligence was convinced that there were no Tigers in that area. In the end Barrance did get a new rifle, 'but the memory of this is still with me and even today I sometimes wake up in a cold sweat.'[17]

Major Alexander Brodie, who seemed to make it a habit to serve with the 51st Highland Division, be wounded after a couple of weeks with them and then return home 'to have a good time as a wounded hero',* was back with the 'Highway Decorators' once more, this time with the Seaforth Highlanders. But not for long.

He and his company were involved in confused fighting for a collection of farm outhouses when suddenly he heard a plaintive voice say, 'Aber gib doch ein Antwort.' He had blundered right into the Germans!

Summoning up his German and in his 'best Bavarian accent' he replied, 'Ich bin der Otto' – and fired immediately. Then he ran madly for the cover of some rose bushes with the rest of his men.

One German threw a stick grenade. It exploded nearby, wounding Brodie in the throat; 'it tickled a bit but did not hurt much.'

But worse was to come. Firing broke out again in front and Brodie led a section forward in a charge, 'shouting and shooting from the hip'. They succeeded in chasing off the Germans. Then one of the feared enemy mortars opened up. Brodie was wounded again, 'in the leg and one or two other places . . . nothing serious.' By now the accident-prone Major was in shock, 'getting a bit delirious and shouting at soldiers who were only doing their job', so it was decided to evacuate him. Yet still his tribulations were not over. Just as he was staggering to

* See '44.

(Above) Infantrymen of the US Ninth Army crouch to avoid enemy fire in Julich, Germany.
(Right) The Reichswald, February '45.

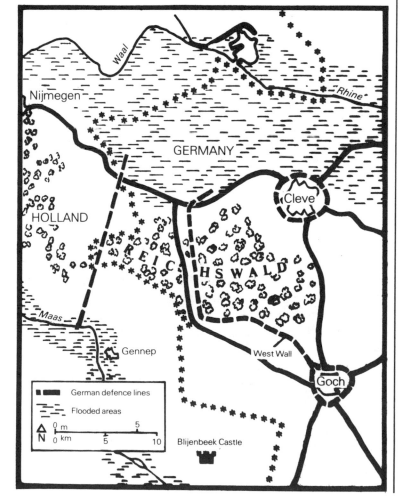

the field dressing station in the darkness, a shell came over 'and I fell down and was hit a nasty one on one foot where the toes join the foot'. His commanding officer decided that Brodie really had to be removed from the forward area, and ordered up a jeep. But on the way back the jeep 'skidded into a ditch full of icy water, which probably did my foot good'.[18]

Two days later Major Brodie was back in England once more, at the Queen Elizabeth Hospital, Birmingham. But he'd be back for more punishment before the war was done.

Corporal Wingfield of the Queen's Royal Regiment also found something tragi-comic about the fighting in the Reichswald, though the comic element wouldn't last long for him.

The Corporal's section had just taken a group of SS men prisoner when another burst out of hiding, 'hammering Schmeisser at his hip. He ran for a hayrick. Besa tracer stitched the air behind him. The earth at his heels boiled with dust. Now the Besa hit him and threw him into the haystack, which immediately brewed up.'

Two Germans and two British infantrymen rushed forward to save the trapped SS man, but the heat was too intense. They were forced back. The SS man burned to death.

The men of the Queen's pushed on. They passed a German who had been somehow blown on his head; he stood there upside-down, and very dead. They came to an anti-tank ditch. Wingfield realised to his alarm that it was defended. 'There was only one thing to do,' the young NCO recalled later. 'No one wanted to give the order. I gulped and turning to my section shouted: "Fix bayonets!" That seemed to bring us all to life. I heard the nasty snick of the bayonets locking home.' They broke into a run, a mad charge, screaming and yelling. One hundred yards away Wingfield saw that the lip of the ditch was lined with bits of white paper for some reason.

'So you're trying to pack up now, you bastards!' the men of the Queen's screamed as they charged forward. 'It's too bloody late!'

The trench was ten feet deep. Wingfield hit the bottom with a crash. Before him a bunch of ashen-faced men in field-grey loomed up. Germans! He pressed the trigger of his Sten gun. Nothing happened. It was jammed.

Before a frantic Wingfield could eject the stuck 9 mm cartridge and fire at the enemy, an angry voice cried in English, *What the fuck do you lot think you're doing?*

The young Corporal had charged his own B Company, together with a bunch of Germans ranging from the 'very dead' to those 'petrified with fright'![19]

That night the Germans opened the banks of the Rhine and started to swamp the rest of the battlefield, including the one road still available to XXX Corps. Horrocks threw in more reserves to speed up the advance before it was bogged down by the mounting flood. He unleashed his veteran 43rd Infantry Division – but this turned out to be 'one of the worst mistakes I made in the war':

The 15th Scottish had not got nearly so far as had been reported . . . There was already too much traffic on this one road and it was impossible to deploy across country owing to the boggy ground. The arrival of this extra division caused one of the worst traffic jams of the whole war . . . The language heard that night has seldom been equalled.[20]

By now the battle had become 'practically a naval action', as R. W. Thompson reported for the *Sunday Times*. Visiting Canadian infantry that week, he noted: 'The tops of houses, the turrets of derelict tanks, smitten tree trunks and the branches of telegraph poles and all the fearful garbage of war give shape to all this desolation of water. Otherwise it might almost be the sea.'[21]

Bereft of their armoured protection, the infantry was now encountering something worse than the mud – mines. The German paras had sown them thickly everywhere in the sodden fields and lanes, and they meant sudden death or terrible mutilation for the infantry.

Of all the weapons employed during World War Two, the mine was the most feared by the ordinary foot soldier, and no one was more efficient in employing them in a defensive position than the Germans. The anti-personnel mine usually contained an explosive charge, anything up to a mighty four pounds of high explosive, housed in a steel case. It was activated by a fuse, which set off this explosive charge by the application or release of pressure, by the pull of a trip-wire, by removal of tension, or by a delayed action mechanism. The enemy used many fiendish methods to ensure the death or maiming of the Allied soldier. And, as if that were not enough, the Germans often attached booby-traps. Mines were linked to other mines by hidden wires, so that even if the first one was successfully disarmed and lifted it would explode the second one.* Or a so-called 'matchbox fuse' would be hidden beneath the mine, and when the mine was defused in the normal way and lifted up, then the 'matchbox', a steel contraption held closed by a powerful metal spring, flew open and activated the second and concealed fuse. Result – another death or terrible disfigurement.

In the Reichswald the German para engineers had used all the ingenuity of their deadly trade. Not only were there the usual metal-cased mines, which could be

---

* To indicate the amount of lethal hardware used that winter in the Reichswald, the state of N-Rhine-Westphalia to which it belongs reported that 250,000 explosive items had been lifted *in 1980*. And during research for this book in 1983, the author went out with a local explosive clearing squad in the state of Rhineland-Palatinate. At the end of the afternoon the back of our truck was piled high with shells and mines – nearly forty years after they were laid.

detected by the British and Canadian sappers, but also mines housed in wood, glass and bakelite casings, which were undetectable – until it was too late. And yet another man would be lying sprawled in the smoking earth, face ashen with shock, staring at the bloody mess which had once been a foot or a leg.

'The minefields in the Reichswald were the worse sods I ever saw,' ex-engineer Corporal Alf Jones recalled nearly forty years later, the horror still evident in his voice. 'We couldn't get anywhere with the detectors – there were too many of the buggers. So the infantry had to go for them themselves, crawling through the muck and mire on their bellies, prodding for them with the point of their bayonets; then, when they had found them, digging into the earth underneath looking for booby traps and sweating like pigs as they did so. But that wasn't the worst of it. In the Reichswald, old Jerry always sited a machine gun to cover a minefield – and they had had all winter to prepare for our attack and they'd got everything covered. So the poor sods of the PBI had to do all this with the bullets cutting the air just above their noddles. It was a bugger!'[22]

Colonel Lindsay of thc 1st Gordons was leading his battalion through the positions of the Cameronians of Canada, guided through the thick yellow smoke of battle by the Canadians' pipes, when there was a loud bang. One of his officers named Danny dropped to the ground, moaning.

Lindsay, the veteran, knew immediately what had happened. They had blundered into a minefield. 'Everybody stand still, exactly where you are!' he bellowed above the racket, and then: 'Danny, how bad is it?'

Lindsay knew already that the young officer had either a shattered ankle or a whole foot blown off – what the medics called a 'traumatic amputation'. Either way Danny needed help immediately. 'Stretcher-bearer!' he roared to the Canadians to their rear, then turned his attention back to the young man. 'Never mind, Danny,' he called, 'the moonlight's lovely and I'll get you a bar to your MC for this day's work, you mark my words!'

Three quarters of an hour later, the first Canadian medics appeared on the scene – and promptly stepped on mines themselves. Finally things started to move and Colonel Lindsay, who had been standing on one leg for that whole period – 'I don't think I've ever felt so foolish in my life' – followed with the rest, all of them planting their feet exactly in the footprints of the Canadian pioneer sergeant who was leading them out of that deadly place.

When the time came for Lindsay to estimate the losses to his D Company that long day, it included four officers – or thirty percent officer casualties. 'I formed up the company and marched them back. I was dead tired and felt none of the elation to which I was entitled when I reported to Brigade that the road was now clear.'[23]

An engineer prepares to blow up enemy mines.

On that same day near Goch, Private Ferguson of the Highland Light Infantry – 'Hell's Last Issue' – was leading a Lloyd carrier through a path cleared across a minefield, in an attempt to bring up some six-pounder shells to an anti-tank section further forward. 'Wet Wullie was driving,' he recalled many years later. 'We called him "wet" because he once wet his bed. Anyway, Wullie was grinding along in first gear, working the tiller bars* as if he were wearing kid gloves, while I was keeping my eye on the white tapes which marked the edge of the Jerry minefield. All of a sudden there was one hell of a bang. I could feel the Lloyd heave under my hand where I was holding it. Wullie's face went awful pale and I could smell burning. We'd hit something, a mine I guessed. Sometimes the Jerries would mix anti-tank mines with anti-personnel mines, but at a deeper level so the PBI wouldn't spot and lift them. But Wullie seemed all right and I knew that, like a lot of the drivers, he'd lined the bottom of the carrier with sandbags as extra protection. So we went on with the shells. Finally Wullie pulls up where they're dug in and I go round the back to start unloading. Wullie doesn't move. So I shouts, "Don't be a lazy sod . . . Give a hand." I gets no

* The Lloyd carrier was steered by two tiller bars, which locked the track and thus allowed it to be steered to left or right.

Anti-tank mines are prepared for laying.

reply. I look inside. Wullie's slumped over the tillers. I crawl inside and there's poor Wet Wullie – dead! Both his legs had been blown off and the sandbags around the hole blown by the mine are red with his blood. God knows how he did it, but he had . . . If an officer had seen it they'd have given the old bed-wetter the Victoria Cross or something. Instead all he got, the poor sod, was three feet of German earth.'[24]

The sudden thaw brought not only mines, but the first spring flowers, too. Old sweat Corporal Arthur Hare, a sniper, wrote to his wife Elsie about that time:

I saw a little group of primroses today and they reminded me of the time we picked them together. When all this is over, I think I should like to become a gardener. It would be wonderful to be able to make something grow after all we've destroyed.[25]

Only twenty-four hours after he had written that letter, the would-be gardener was in position outside the small ruined German township of Borken. He spotted a German and lined him up in the calibrated circle of glass of his sight. Expert that he was, he kept his breathing controlled and took first and then second pressure. He hardly noticed the kick of the sniper's rifle in his shoulder, as the German did a 'kind of cartwheel' in his dying agony.

Later, Intelligence found a letter on the body of the dead German. It was addressed to his girlfriend, and it was all too poignant: 'Always thinking of you when I lie down at night . . .'*

'Let no one misconceive the severity of the fighting during these final months,' Lieutenant-Colonel Stacey, the Canadian combat historian, wrote afterwards. 'In this, the twilight of the Gods, the defenders of the Reich displayed the recklessness of fanaticism and the courage of despair. In the contests west of the Rhine, in particular, they fought with special ferocity, rendering the battles of the Reichswald and the Hochwald grimly memorable in the annals of this war.'[26]

This was certainly true for the Canadians of the 2nd and 3rd Infantry Divisions. Together with the British of Horrocks' XXX Corps they were going to lose nearly 17,000 men killed, wounded and captured in the Reichswald battle, and a similar number of non-battle casualties.

On the road to Calcar, a key objective for Horrocks, the French-Canadians fought for four long bitter days for the little village of Moyland, facing counter-attack

after counter-attack as the Germans threw in four fresh parachute regiments to stop the advance.

In the middle of the battle was a baroque eighteenth-century castle inhabited by a baroness, Ilsemarie Baronin Steengracht von Moyland. The castle was under constant attack by rocket-firing Typhoons, so the aged Baroness, with her servants and fifty villagers, took shelter in the deep cellars that had once housed the wine served to 'Old Fritz' (Frederick the Great of Prussia) when this was his favourite summer retreat.

Finally Moyland was taken and the German paras were driven from the shell-shattered castle. Its round towers, gashed and splattered by shrapnel as if with the symptoms of some loathsome skin disease, looked sadly down on the lawns beneath the dirty white flags that hung everywhere, trampled to mud by the infantry and the racing jeeps.

The Baroness greeted the Canadian conquerors with a protest. In spite of the white flags, the Canadians had continued firing. They replied they were sick of white flags; the German paras had used them often enough to lure unsuspecting Canadians into a trap. The Baroness sighed and muttered something under her breath about Nazis; then she sank into silence while a young French-Canadian infantry officer sat down at her grand piano and played that hit of 1939, the 'Warsaw Concerto', the dramatic emotional music of a world crashing down in flames. Among those present was R. W. Thompson, who watched the Baroness's face as she listened to the swell and flow of the music. To him she appeared occupied 'with the pageant of the years and of a distant past like a sumptuous tapestry of brilliant colour . . . All these dead things that she will never see again. All these things of a dead world . . .'[27]

Now at last the British and Canadians were paying the Germans back – not for Warsaw, but for Dunkirk and Dieppe; for the years of defeat, the starvation, the frustration, the bitter long path that had led them here, into the Reich itself; and for their dead.

But there were more dead to come for the Canadians. General Simonds, commanding the Canadian 2nd Corps, led his men into action on Horrocks' left flank. Again the slogging match among the mud, ruins and mines commenced. The Royal Winnipeg Rifles reported to Corps HQ that it was being subjected to the 'heaviest shelling the battalion has ever experienced', while the Regina Rifles recorded that the shelling was 'just as bad as anything encountered in Normandy'.[28] Old hands among the Canadians were comparing the fighting with Passchendaele and the shell-torn slopes of Vimy Ridge back in the Old War. The fact that Britain's highest decoration for bravery was awarded to several Canadian soldiers within a matter of days testifies to the savagery of the fighting in those waterlogged, muddy forests, filled with sudden death.

---

*Corporal Hare survived to be a gardener on a large estate. He never again took a rifle or shotgun into his hands, although he had ample opportunity to do so.

Sergeant Aubrey Cousins, for example, found himself with only four men surviving from his decimated platoon, just as German paras, in their rimless helmets and camouflaged smocks, started yet another counter-attack on the Canadian positions. Cousins ran through the thick of the fire to a stalled tank. He sprang aboard and, taking over, directed the gunner's fire on the advancing *fallschirmjaeger*. The German paras broke almost immediately, scuttling for cover in the forest. But after a few minutes their NCOs and officers rallied them. Once more they came running out of the firs on the attack. This time Cousins, fully exposed on the turret of the Sherman, directed the driver, who had got his engine running once more, to charge the Germans. The Sherman, all thirty tons of it, its guns blazing, sending up a flying wake of mud and earth, rammed right into the paras, sending them reeling to all sides in total confusion. Now Cousins, the one-man army, went over to the counter-attack himself. Dropping from the tank, he and his fellow survivors charged the nearest house at bayonet-point. They turfed out the frightened defenders, killing twenty of them and capturing many more.

At last, satisfied he had restored the Canadian position and that he could do no more, Sergeant Cousins consolidated his position in the captured house and told his exhausted men that he was going back to report to the CO. Five minutes later he was shot dead by a German sniper.[29]

Major Tiltson of the Canadian Essex Scottish was another Canadian who received the Empire's highest award that grim February. Leading his men in an attack over an open field and through a series of barbed-wire obstacles, he was shot in the head. He was confused for a little while, but still he continued at the head of his company, blood streaming down his pale face. A machine-gun nest loomed up out of the fog of battle. He silenced it with a hand grenade. He and his men pressed on to the German second line. He was hit again, this time in the hip. He collapsed to the ground, but continued directing his men as they cleared the German trenches in vicious hand-to-hand fighting, little groups of panting, cursing men in khaki and grey, swaying back and forth, giving no quarter and expecting none.

The German paras rallied and counter-attacked. Tiltson organised his survivors into a defensive position and slogged it out; by now the Canadian company was down to a quarter of its original strength. Again the Major was hit. Refusing all medical aid, he continued in combat, lying severely wounded in a shell-hole half filled with water. Finally the Germans were driven off – for the time being – and then, and only then, did Major Tiltson allow himself to be evacuated. He, too, won the Victoria Cross for his incredible courage. But the cost to the brave Canadian was very high: he lost both his legs.[30]

Grimly, doggedly, the British and Canadians continued

Riflemen run for cover in Goch while covered by a bazooka.

to advance against the fanatical resistance of those German paratroopers. But the strain was beginning to tell. Horrocks, as always up front, realised that his veterans had virtually all gone now; their places had been taken by teenagers. Everywhere he looked in the waterlogged foxholes and slit trenches he saw 'pale young faces . . . cold, miserable and hungry'. He knew they were reasonably safe in their holes, but as he told himself at the time: 'Soon they will have to emerge into the open to attack.' And Horrocks – who had had his share of suffering in two world wars, including being taken prisoner and being nearly mortally wounded – felt for them. For he knew 'they must force themselves forward with a sickening feeling in the pit of their stomachs, fighting an almost uncontrollable urge to fling themselves down as close to the earth as they can get. Even then they are still alone amidst all the fury, carrying their loneliness with them.'[31]

Every day another 1,500 men – the population of an average village – were killed or wounded. Of the original men who had landed with their battalions in Normandy eight months before, there was only a handful left. In the 2nd Battalion of the Gordon Highlanders, for example, B Company had only three men left out of the original 115 men. In Lieutenant Woollcombe's battalion of the King's Own Scottish Borderers, there was only Woollcombe and one other officer left who had come ashore in Normandy the previous June: 'The battalion had lost nearly sixty officers and had undergone a one hundred percent turnover of its war establishment.' In Woollcombe's own platoon only two men had survived.

It was not surprising that when Woollcombe was asked to leave the battalion that February, to become an instructor at the 15th Division's battle school back in Belgium, he went. 'You'd be a fool not to go,' his new commanding officer advised him.[32] So Lieutenant Woollcombe duly went, the last surviving officer who had landed with the KOSB at the start. A few days later his company commander who had advised him to go and 'take the cushy number' was killed in the woods outside of Goch, and the captain who had taken over his men was wounded by a shell and evacuated back to the UK.

Still the survivors soldiered on in the slaughterhouse of the Reichswald. In spite of the terrible conditions and horrendous casualties, there were very few cases of 'battle-happy' soldiers. The accepted theory was that there were few cases of combat exhaustion when men were on the defensive, but they mounted rapidly when they went on the offensive. In the Reichswald, however, there were fewer than two hundred men who were sent back for treatment, out of a force of nearly half a million men.

The young soldiers lived off the land, slaughtering many a fat German pig they had 'liberated', or looting the rich preserves – apples, pears, cherries, bottled in cheap brandy by the thrifty German *hausfrau* – found in the deep cellars of the shattered houses. They were a motley crew for the most part in their gumboots, leather jerkins and camouflaged netting scarves, their faces red and weather-beaten under their steel helmets; they looked more like farm labourers than soldiers. Their pleasures were simple that month: a looted feather-bed to sleep on in their dripping damp slit trenches, or a canteen of hot M & V stew washed down with a brew of compo tea. They were smelly and sticky, for they had done little but wash and shave their faces (this was the British Army after all) for days on end. It was too cold to strip off in a bowl of muddy water out in the open in the freezing air, so washing was limited to the places seen.

Private Barrance's platoon of the Manchesters was visited by one of their officers, who asked them when they had last had a bath – 'it must have been the smell.' 'Can't remember, sir,' Barrance replied. 'Right,' the officer snapped, 'baths laid on tomorrow at ten hundred hours.' The men weren't too pleased at the prospect. 'Have you ever waited in two foot of snow in a field lining up outside a marquis tent to have a bath?' ex-Private Barrance recalled forty years later. 'I think we all went in the front door and straight out the back without even getting our feet wet!'[33]

The soldiers in the line defecated in shell-holes, or, if they were under fire, in their own foxholes; there was no alternative. In the bitter rain they sheltered themselves by propping doors over their holes, or by stretching their ground sheets across the top, and huddled together with their mates (two men always to a hole) like lovers and tried to keep warm. They slept when they could, for they were always tired. At night there were always the constant alarms, the one-hour 'stag' or sentry duty they all had to do, and the morning dawn stand-to in case of an enemy attack. And every new day there was fresh pain, fresh misery – and always fresh dead.

R. W. Thompson, that most sensitive of war correspondents, who was still a serving soldier, felt for the young infantrymen. He watched a youthful colonel of infantry speaking to each of his boy soldiers as he passed them in their slit trenches. 'You've done fine . . . Good boys . . . It's been tough; going to get better now, much better . . .' He repeated the same soothing, encouraging words the whole length of the position. Thompson noted how the soldiers' faces 'look up at him from the wet earth of the woodland fringe, red boyish faces under the netted tin hats. The whites of their eyes are very white and their eyes shine. They are glad of his words. They call him "Two-Gun Pete".'

But as always in the blood-soaked, damned forest, the enemy guns roared and the shells came screaming in.

'Get yourselves well down!' Two-Gun Pete yelled above that baleful, malevolent howl.

Already it was too late. The shells exploded. Shrapnel flew among the boys in gleaming red-hot lethal chunks. They ripped apart the youthful flesh. Suddenly everything was 'great spouts of earth and smoke and flame' with 'jeeps skidding and twisting and bumping with the

Relics of the Nijmegen airborne landings stand in the background as troops in the new advance take a breather.

wounded and the RAMC men standing shielding the men on the stretchers with their arms and bodies and trying to hold them steady while the air is thick with flying metal'.

Thompson left the scene, cynically thinking that what had just happened to those unfortunate young men wouldn't be 'news' anyway. It would appear in the media as '*British infantry have occupied Kervenheim against stiff enemy opposition. Our men are now clearing the town.*'[34]

Nothing to reveal the heartbreak back home, the cost in human life of butchered young men, dead before they had had a chance to live . . .

Corporal Wingfield, one of the last of the Normandy veterans, was in the thick of it now. He was watching a bren gunner pour white tracer at the enemy positions a field away when he felt a searing pain in his left hip. It flashed agonisingly throughout his lower body. Somebody shouted. He fell down. A grenade exploded nearby in a blinding flash. Suddenly the English voices, full of anger, panic, agony, started to die away. The others were withdrawing, leaving Wingfield and the rest of the wounded behind. The Jerries were counter-attacking.

Wingfield panicked too. 'Christ, I've been hit!' he groaned to himself. For a moment he thought he had been hit internally. If so, he should be bleeding from the mouth. He coughed into his hand, as the German infantry surged forward. There was not that feared scarlet stain on his palm. It was dry. 'Thank God, I felt better.'

But Corporal Wingfield had a long and frightening night before him until he was finally picked up by the medics. As he and the other wounded lay there in the wet field, feigning dead, the Germans penetrated all around them. The Germans crept from man to man, calling softly to one another: '*Tod . . . Tod . . .*' ('Dead . . . Dead . . .') Suddenly the British artillery opened up. Obviously the survivors of the Queen's Royal Regiment's failed attack had reached their own lines. Now twenty-five pounder shells began to fall on both German and Englishman alike. A German was fatally hit and fell on top of Wingfield. All around the prostrate corporal, the wounded began to scream out: 'God – please, no more . . . *NO MORE!*' But God wasn't listening that cold dark night. Both friend and foe were ripped to pieces by the flying shell splinters. Wingfield was blown from side to side by the blast. One by one the wounded, German and British, stopped moaning. And as the shelling finally ceased, Wingfield, lying among the dead, thought he was the only one to have survived. 'Tearfully I poured out my thanks to God in an agony of relief.'

Leadenly the hours of darkness passed until finally, at dawn, the first Queen's stretcher-bearers entered the field, picking over the bodies, looking for the wounded. By this time Wingfield had blacked out. When he awoke it was to see the MO's face staring down at him, streaked with grime and sweat, and 'his nostrils were assailed by a strong hospital smell'. While he had been unconscious the MO had operated on him, digging out two tracer bullets from his lower body. He showed them to Wingfield, plus a tin which the Corporal had filled with cigarette-ends, one hundred and eighty of them, his most precious possession, just in case he ever ran out of a smoke.

'What do you want doing with this lot?' the doctor asked.

Wingfield told him he could throw them away; he would have no further use for them. He was right. He was being sent back to a field hospital for further treatment, and he'd never see his battalion again. His days as a fighting infantryman were over. *He* had escaped the six feet of earth of the cliché. *He* was going back on a stretcher.[35]

That day yet another veteran 'bought' it. Captain John Foley of the tanks was just reporting to his CO when a mortar bomb suddenly exploded. One of his men, a trooper named Riley, fell to the ground with a moan.

Foley rushed over to him. The Normandy veteran's legs were a 'tattered, bloody mess of khaki, tank-suit, woollen sock and raw flesh'. At first Foley could not make out what the 'polished white plastic' was in the middle of the red gore; then he felt 'slightly sick' when he realised that it was Riley's shin bone. He looked down at the wounded man's blue-chinned face and the 'unemotional eyes like transparent pieces of window glass'. Black mud streaked Riley's face and his cheeks were already turning a suet-colour due to the loss of blood.

'Hurt much, Riley?' he asked.

'Only when I laff,' Riley replied with a dead-pan expression.

'Probably the shock,' Foley said and prepared to give the trooper a morphia injection with the syringe that all tank crews carried.

Riley wasn't having it. 'Puts ye to sleep,' he growled, 'and the next thing ye know ye've no bloody leg.'

'Well, it's bloody enough now,' Foley remarked. Morphia was in short supply, however, and as Riley didn't seem to be in too much pain he put the syringe back in the first aid box.

'You'll be back in Blighty before morning, Riley,' a sergeant consoled the maimed man. 'Dead lucky, eh?'

A flicker of a smile crossed Riley's face. 'Shake the ole woman, that will,' he said.

Whether it did or not, Captain Foley never found out; for Riley never returned.[36]

One week later, on February 23rd, the bitterly fought for town of Calcar surrendered. Horrocks sent a personal message of congratulations to his weary, mud-caked troops. Now the end was near in the Reichswald. But still the German paras fought on desperately.

At Blijenbeek Castle, infantry of the 52nd Lowland Division had to launch a full-scale assault across the medieval castle's moat. Three times the paras defending the castle fought them off. One company of the Jocks was cut down, every last man, trying to scale the walls. The castle was finally taken only after the RAF had dropped nine 1,000-pound bombs directly on top of it.

A British casualty is borne away from the ruins of Goch.

Its garrison surrendered. *They numbered exactly fifteen paratroopers!*

Soon afterwards, the Germans' last bastion on that sector of the western bank of the Rhine – Xanten, the ancient Roman fortress – was abandoned, and the German paras trapped on the Allied side of the Rhine surrendered. As they marched back to their cages, dirty, ragged and exhausted, Brigadier Essame in charge of the 43rd Division's final assault ordered his staff to stand to attention as the German prisoners went past, and they duly did so, while the Brigadier saluted the former enemy. Later, in spite of criticism of his action in the British press, he described the German paratroopers as 'very gallant men'.[37]

It was over – and now the young soldiers took their spoils. John Prebble, the novelist, recalls entering Xanten through the medieval gateway, which still had an eagle and swastika hanging from its arch:

The streets were strewn with rubble . . . Men, dusty, sweating, grinning men with their arms and blouses full of jars of preserved fruits, mattresses, bedding, wireless sets and clothes, were everywhere. Canadians, Scots infantrymen and support troops were moving methodically from house to house . . . [amid] the wrenching of wood, the cracking of glass, shouts and jeers. There were no civilians anywhere.[38]

Prebble came across a soldier trying to cut the throat of a Friesian cow he had found in a barn, and not making a very good job of it: 'the green grass beneath its foam-flecked nostrils was slashed red.' Suddenly a German civilian appeared from nowhere. With his cropped hair and square fleshy neck, he looked like a caricature; Prebble wondered why he didn't have a 'Tyrolean hat complete with shaving brush'. The German took the knife from the hapless soldier and 'neatly cut the cow's throat' for him.

Even officers indulged in a little 'liberating'. Captain Foley had set his heart on a guitar that he had seen in a wrecked music shop in Goch. 'Looting or no looting,' he told himself, 'this I must have.' Rumbling back in the shattered Rhenish city in his Churchill, he told his driver to stop in front of the wrecked shop, but to keep the engine running.

'Going shopping, sir?' his driver queried, knowing exactly what the officer was after.

'That's right,' Foley replied. 'Sort of window-shopping in a way.'

But Foley never got his guitar. Among the ruins of buildings all around the music shop, he suddenly noticed some little red notices put up by the engineers, and they all read the same: 'BEWARE OF BOOBY TRAPS!' And then Foley remembered that the E-string of the guitar had apparently been broken and had curled to the rubble on the floor. The thought that he had nearly picked up an object which had obviously been booby-trapped sent a trickle of fear down his spine. Hastily he

74

The devastated town of Cleves is patrolled by British infantrymen.

turned and clambered back into his Churchill.[39]

As the other correspondents left the Reichswald to find more exciting stories elsewhere, now that the fighting was over, R. W. Thompson stayed behind. He wandered around the shattered town of Uden, noting how the German 'civilians offered food and drink to our men, as if they had liberated!' He decided to discover what the young replacements thought of the mass destruction all around them. It didn't take him long to find out. Suddenly he was confronted by the sight of plate after plate being thrown out of a window devoid of glass. A young soldier leaned out and remarked: 'The washing up, sir . . . You just chuck it out of the window!'

Thompson shook his head sadly. Nothing had any value any more, he told himself.[40]

Now it was all over – for a while. Yet the staff back at Montgomery's HQ were working against the clock to put the final touches to the last great set-piece battle that the British Army would fight in World War Two: an operation that they had been planning for the last six months. Even as the victors of the Reichswald got drunk, looted or simply slept, preparations for the last blood-letting were reaching the final stages. Already the reinforcement centres and hospitals in the 'rear echelon' were being combed for replacements to fill the gaps in the ranks of the assault regiments. Back in the United Kingdom, the barrel had been scraped clean. Churchill had even been forced to call up forty-five-year-olds, and he had ordered one division – the 5th Infantry – to be transferred from the Italian front, where it was badly needed, to meet Montgomery's requirements. There were simply no more 'bodies' left.

Captain Andrew Wilson was one such 'body'. After a spell in hospital he was returned to his old regiment in the Royal Armoured Corps, at the end of the Reichswald Battle. He was shocked to find there was no one left whom he still knew. All his old comrades were dead, wounded or missing. Wandering around miserably, he was finally spotted by an old acquaintance, a Major Duffy.

'Wilson!' Duffy called excitedly. 'Am I *frigging* right or *frigging* wrong?'

Wilson assured him that he was 'frigging' right; he was Andrew Wilson! Happy now to be back with his old unit after the impersonal boredom of the reinforcement holding unit, he attended his first 'O' group in a crowded cellar.

The radio was going in the corner. A German woman announcer, one of the English-speaking announcers employed in the propaganda broadcasts, directed by the arch traitor 'Lord Haw-Haw', to undermine the morale of the troops, was reading aloud from letters found on the bodies of dead British soldiers. Genuine or not they were full of 'homesickness and pathetic greetings'.

Here Wilson had a first real look at his new comrades.

The sight was not very reassuring. In their faces he saw 'weariness and resignation, foreboding and tension and numerous other emotions' which he hadn't suspected. The happy faces he remembered from before Christmas had vanished – and he soon discovered why. In exactly two weeks, he was informed, now that the Germans had finally collapsed in the Reichswald, Montgomery's Armies were going to make a full-scale crossing of Germany's last natural barrier – the Rhine. Suddenly everyone was looking at the newcomer while a senior officer explained where he fitted in. The 141st (Royal Tank) Regiment was going to take part in that great river assault, and because Wilson was a 'little fresher' than the others, he and his troop of tanks would lead the regiment.

Wilson's emotions are not recorded. Soon it would all start again . . .[41]

Throughout the Reichswald fighting, the advancing infantry had been 'supported' by the Lancasters and Halifaxes of Sir Arthur 'Bomber' Harris's RAF bomber squadrons. During the month of February, 'Bomber' (some preferred to call the tubby, bespectacled RAF hard-man *Butcher*) Harris's men had flown forty-two raids on the Reichswald, transforming the area into a wasteland. Unfortunately towns like Cleves and Goch were 'overbombed', turned into fortresses of rubble, just as Caen had been the previous June. Thanks to the RAF, the infantry thought bitterly, the defenders had been offered ideal defensive positions, in which they could easily hold out for days, even weeks.

Back in the United Kingdom before the Invasion, the Army had regarded the 'Brylcreem Boys', as the RAF was known, with a mixture of envy, contempt and admiration. To the 'brown jobs' (as the foot-sloggers were called by the fliers), the RAF seemed to have an easy life. Didn't even the 'erks' (lower-ranking RAF men) wear collars and ties, have cushy heated billets, and wear their hair much longer than they? (Hence the 'Brylcreem'.) They had been paying the butcher's bill for four long years while the majority of the Army was still training for the Invasion; they had lost over 56,000 officers and noncoms in the raids over Germany.

The ordinary American soldier's attitude was little different. He felt the USAAF 'flyboys' lived 'high on the hog', with 'plenty of dames and booze' and were promoted to high rank incredibly young. A famous Sergeant Maudlin cartoon summed up their attitude. It showed a bewildered, bearded, elderly infantryman somewhere in Italy being greeted by a freckle-faced boy in the uniform of the US Army Air Corps, with the stars of a 'bird colonel' on the shoulders of his leather jacket. He is crying, '*Hiya, Uncle Willie!*'

After the Invasion, however, that mixture of envy, contempt and admiration had rapidly changed. Now their feelings were almost of hatred. Time and time

A jeep carrying wounded passes through Goch on the way to a First Aid post.

again, the Americans had been bombed by their own air force; the US 9th TAC Air Force, for instance, was bitterly nicknamed the 'American Luftwaffe' because its planes had bombed US troops so many times. Cities such as Caen, St Lô and Cherbourg had been bombed indiscriminately, without any regard to civilian casualties, and had been transformed into fortresses stubbornly defended by the German survivors. Slowly the fighting soldier had come to realise that the RAF and the USAAF did not bomb solely military targets as they had been told back in the United Kingdom. Indeed, in many cases the pilots were doing just what the Germans had been claiming all the time; they were carrying out terror raids – attacks on non-military targets, looking for easy pickings, with the object of breaking down civilian morale.

At Caen, for example, the RAF killed 5,000 French civilians and *three Germans*. Corporal Alexander McKee, who was in Caen at the time, later wrote in his notebook:

Lisieux and Caen are examples of the inflexibility of the four-motor heavy bomber: it cannot block a road without bringing down a city. I'm not surprised that our troops advancing between Caen and Lisieux were fired upon by French civilians. No doubt many Frenchmen found it hard to be liberated by a people who seem, by their actions, to specialise in the mass murder of their friends.[42]

If France came as a shock to the ground soldier, the mass destruction of the first German cities they encountered across the border – Aachen, Dueron, Bitburg, for example – had an even greater effect. Even generals, not normally regarded as soft-hearted individuals, were appalled by the total devastation brought about by Harris's bombers and those of the US Army Air Corps. From Montgomery down to the level of brigadiers, they protested at Harris's high-handed manner and his total disregard of the civilians, friendly and enemy; plus the fact that his absurd 'overbombing', as they called it, made life harder and more dangerous for their attacking infantrymen.

Now, far away at his underground headquarters at High Wycombe, Harris and his staff were preparing to carry out the ultimate terror raid – *Operation Thunderclap*.

'Butcher' Harris – or, to give him his full title, Air Chief Marshal Sir Arthur T. Harris – chunky, energetic and now in his mid-fifties, was a 'colonial'. He had entered the Rhodesian Infantry as a bugler at the outbreak of World War One. After record, exhausting marches through German Southwest Africa, he swore he'd never march again. Thus he entered the Royal Flying Corps and received a permanent commission. In between the wars he saw service throughout the Empire and had been one of the first, as a squadron commander, to employ bombers against rebellious tribesmen. The success of those raids against primitively armed natives had encouraged him to believe in bombing as a sure means of ending wars rapidly, especially if the bombs destroyed the morale of the civilian populace. Now Harris wanted to turn the whole of his Bomber Command loose on the centres of communication and population in Eastern Germany. As Germany approached military collapse, he reasoned, heavy bombing of those cities might well bring about total surrender and make it unnecessary for Montgomery and the American commanders to make their assault crossing of the Rhine.

By the beginning of February, 1945, Harris's staff had picked four key cities for the attack – Berlin, Chemnitz, Leipzig and Dresden; though Harris's deputy Sir Robert Saundby had his qualms about the last city. In spite of the fact that it was a major rail centre, it had no industry to speak of, and it was packed with refugees and long columns of Allied prisoners-of-war passing through, heading south-west. It was also regarded as one of the most beautiful cities in Europe. Saundby wondered if the bombing of Dresden might not be another Cassino.*[43]

But in his usual aggressive manner Harris rode roughshod over all objections, taking his case for the bombing of Dresden and other cities right up to the Prime Minister himself. In the end Churchill cast aside his misgivings and gave his assent. Perhaps he wanted to impress the Russians with the power of his bombers at the Yalta Conference taking place that month; for the Russians would take Dresden. Whatever his motives, he would later regret that approval and quickly dissociate himself from Harris.

Now, as the Reichswald battle reached its highpoint, the planners in those underground headquarters waited only for favourable weather. On the morning of February 13th, a very unlucky date for Dresden, the weather was at last reported to be suitable and Harris gave the green light to his bomber groups. The RAF's Number 5 Group was ordered to attack Dresden that night. It would be followed by a combined force from four groups later. In all, 733 four-engine bombers would hit the beautiful eighteenth-century city with 2,659 tons of bombs. Early the next morning, 311 Flying Fortresses of the US Army Air Force would follow, dropping 771 tons of high explosive. The fate of Dresden had been sealed. The 'Florence of the Elbe' was to be obliterated.

That February, as the Red Army penetrated deeper and deeper into the Reich, driving a great flood of refugees and POWs in front of it through Dresden, it was

---

* The Allied destruction of the famous monastery at the town of that name, in Italy in 1944, is still an emotional issue in some quarters forty years later.

Men of the 9th Army.

Battered ruins of Cleves.

important to keep the city functioning. To do this, with so many thousand able-bodied men called up to the colours, the local authorities used labour from the east – *Ostarbeiter*, as they were called – some pressed and some volunteers, and Allied prisoners-of-war, working in outside *Kommandos* and housed on the outskirts of the city itself.

In the second week of that month, there were sixty-seven British and Commonwealth working parties in Dresden and seven larger American groups, all from Stalag IVb at Muehlberg, a huge multinational POW camp that supplied most of Saxony with labour.

One of the Americans was paratrooper Clyde Smith, captured on D-Day in Normandy. He reported later he worked twelve hours a day on a bowl of soup, some beetroot and a slice of bread. Every now and again the Americans of his group received a Red Cross parcel: 'You could take the cigarettes [from the parcel] and buy bread with them, if the guards didn't see you. Once, one of the men was caught stealing bread – he was taken to the hallway of the school we lived in, put in the middle of the circle of men and hit from one side to the other; after that no one was caught stealing.'[44]

Another American POW in Dresden that fateful night was future author Kurt Vonnegut – of German-speaking parents, ironically enough. Then a nineteen-year-old Private, he had been captured with the ill-fated 106th US Infantry Division, whose two regiments had surrendered in the Ardennes.* He and his fellow prisoners were billeted in *Schlachthof Fünf*, the public slaughterhouse that one day gave him the title for his most famous novel, *Slaughterhouse Five*.

Vonnegut worked in a syrup factory. He and his comrades were marched there every day to clean windows, do odd jobs – and steal the malt syrup, for the prisoners were constantly hungry. One dawn on the way to work Vonnegut saw the Germans hang a Polish farmworker whom they'd found guilty of having sexual intercourse with a German woman. Another day, forty-eight hours before Dresden was hit, Vonnegut and the rest were harangued by Howard W. Campbell Jr, wearing a ten-gallon hat and cowboy boots patterned with stars and swastikas, who tried to persuade his fellow Americans to join the SS's 'Free American Corps'.** Without success.[45]

But that terrible shaping experience of the budding writer's life and art was yet to come.

It was 'Crazy Tuesday' in Dresden. In peacetime this signalled the highpoint of the great Catholic carnival, which would end on the stroke of midnight when Lent would commence with Ash Wednesday. This particular Crazy Tuesday, due to the wartime restrictions, there

* See '44.
** The British equivalent was already in Dresden, constantly drunk in their fear that they were finally going to be sent to the front.

(Above) Bomber Harris.
(Right) German civilians survey their devastated town of Bitburg.

was no carnival. Still, the great city on the Elbe was crazy enough, its streets as packed as they would have been in peacetime. They were not the usual cheering, drunken citizens, however, wearing fancy-dress, but pathetic, shabbily dressed refugees from the east, hundreds of thousands of them, plus thousands of British and American prisoners-of-war. The railway stations and public buildings were jam-packed with fugitives. Even the city's lovely Grosser Garten, about the size of Central Park, had been turned into a makeshift camp housing about 200,000 refugees. As the sirens started to sound their dread warning and the *drahtfunk** indicated that the 'terror bombers' were close, it was estimated that there were some 1,300,000 people in the city.

Flying an unarmed Mosquito over Dresden that morning, 'Master Bomber' Wing Commander Smith broke radio silence for the first time and spoke to 'Marker Leader', asking if the green primary flares were in sight.

'Okay, I can see it,' the latter replied. 'The cloud is not very thick.'

Now Smith was flying right over the target, amazed to find not a single searchlight or burst of flak. He swept down lower over the shunting yards, and spotted Dresden's Central Station in the heart of the Altstadt (Old Town). 'Marker Leader, tallyho!' he cried exuberantly over the R/T and dived. At 800 feet, he released his 1,000 lb target-indicator bomb. It tumbled down like a fat ugly fish, leaving a brilliant red trail.

Minutes later 'Master Bomber' was calling over and over again to the main force of Lancasters, all 244 of them: '*Controller to Plate Rack . . . Controller to Plate Rack . . . Come in and bomb glow or red TIs as planned . . . Controller to Plate Rack . . .*'[46]

Dresden was about to die.

Sixteen-year-old Bodo Baumann was a member of a rescue convoy composed of 200 fellow schoolboys, ordered into the Old City to get people out of their cellars before they died of suffocation. By this time eleven square miles of the city centre had been turned into a raging furnace, caught in a firestorm, a meteorological phenomenon caused when many fires abruptly join to heat the air as high as 1,100°F. The tremendous heat caused a violent updraught which sucked fresh air into the centre of the blaze, and the suction in turn created a wind of tremendous searing velocity. The first firestorm had been noted in the July raids on Hamburg in July 1943. Now it was happening in Dresden, too.

Bodo Baumann's group were moving cautiously across a bridge, linked hand to hand, against a background of shattered blazing buildings which trembled and shivered like scenery in a theatre. Suddenly some-

* A signal system using national radio, which tracked the flight of enemy bombers across country to their target and warned those endangered.

one screamed; it was the man at the front of the human chain. He let go and was immediately sucked into the greedy flames of the firestorm. The boy behind him grabbed for something. In vain. He, too, was swallowed by the roaring flames. In panic the boys turned back, the flames hissing and howling like banshees deprived of their prey, running the way they had come.[47]

Not far away, a civilian by the name of Bruno E. Werner was caught in an agony of impotence as he watched the firestorm sweep across a military hospital in which were housed blinded or limbless soldiers from the Russian front. He saw wounded men jumping from the hospital windows, desperate to escape the flames: 'The fireworks were noisy and colourful, and in the midst of it hopped the one-legged in their blue-and-white striped hospital smocks, dragging along by their arms those who had lost both legs.'

Werner turned away, sickened, and bumped into a fire-engine that had been on its way to the hospital; the driver had been overcome by the flames and fumes. 'The motor was still running but the firemen had suffocated. Their uniforms crumbled in the baking air and they sat naked on their seats, lined up against the metal ladder, with straps round their brown bodies and helmets on their yellow skulls.' Behind him, the hospital patients in their striped smocks 'hopped bare-footed in the hissing embers, supporting themselves with crutches, spades and bars, and they limped or rolled, screaming and in flames . . . Outside the fence stood women in smouldering skirts trying to catch those who hurled themselves from the top of the towering fence . . .'[48]

Horror upon horror.

Margret Freyer, a beautiful twenty-four-year-old who had just escaped being imprisoned in a concentration camp, was running for her life, the firestorm hissing like a live thing behind her. Everywhere dead men and women lay on the burning pavements, suffocated due to lack of oxygen. In a frantic effort to survive Margret kept putting wet handkerchieves to her mouth, to keep out the searingly hot air. But she was running out of them, and she knew that if she fainted she would 'burn to cinders'. 'Insane fear grips me and from then on I repeat one simple sentence to myself – "I don't want to burn to death, no, no burning . . . *I don't want to burn!*"' She tripped, but managed to stumble on, crawling, pressing her last handkerchief to her mouth. 'I do not know how many people I fell over. I knew only one feeling: that I must not burn.' She ran out of handkerchieves and collapsed on the pavement, unable to go on. A soldier appeared out of nowhere. 'Please take me with you. I don't want to burn,' she croaked, her voice almost gone after screaming so much. But the soldier was too weak himself to help her. Instead, as if she were already dead, he laid her arms crosswise over her breast and disappeared.

Somehow Margret survived. As daylight came, she began to search for her missing fiancé among the dead. What she saw was so horrific that she hardly was able to describe it, even decades later:

Dead, dead, dead everywhere. Some completely black like charcoal. Others completely untouched, lying as if they were asleep. Women in aprons, women with children sitting in the prams as if they had just nodded off. Many women, many young girls, many small children, soldiers who were only identifiable as such by the metal buckles of their belts, almost all of them naked. Some clinging to each other in groups, as if they were clawing at each other.

From some of the debris poked arms, legs, shattered skulls. The static water tanks were filled to the top with dead human beings, with large pieces of masonry lying on top . . . Most people looked as if they had been inflated, with large yellow and brown stains on their bodies. People whose clothes still were glowing . . . I think I was incapable of absorbing the meaning of this cruelty any more, for there were also so many little babies, terribly mutilated; and all the people lying so close together that it looked as if someone had put them down there, street by street, deliberately . . .[49]

Even the animals in Dresden's large zoo were not spared. Otto Sailer-Jackson, a zoo inspector, was appalled to hear the 'spine-chilling screams' of his elephants when their house was hit. Together with others he rushed to rescue them and found 'a baby cow elephant lying on her back, legs up in the air . . . and a 90 cwt cow elephant flung clear across the barrier moat and the fence by some terrific blast wave'.

Loathing himself for doing so, Sailer-Jackson took up a pistol and began to shoot the animals – those that would be dangerous if they escaped and those that were already wounded. Terrified beasts were wandering around the ruins of the zoo – stags, hippos, red buffalo, bison, lions, tigers, bears. He came across one dangerous animal that had not moved, however: 'A female polar bear, which had been dreadfully burned and blinded by phosphorus incendiaries . . . Without making a sound, the mother kept the cubs pinned down with her huge paws so that they could not run away and out into the danger in the open.' Sailer-Jackson shot the bear and rescued the cubs, thinking they could be reared on the bottle later. 'But there was no milk in the ruins of Dresden and they soon after died of hunger.'[50]

After the bombers had finally departed, the German poet and writer Gerhart Hauptmann wrote an appeal to the world. Watching the destruction of Dresden from the surrounding hills he had suffered a stroke. He wrote:

He who has forgotten how to weep, learns again at Dresden's ruin. I know that in England and America there are enough good people to whom the glories such as the Sistine Madonna were well known. I am at end of my life and I envy my dead friends who have been saved this terrible sight. I weep and am not ashamed of my tears . . . I am nearly eighty-three years old and I am standing before God beseeching Him with my whole heart to show us His love more clearly, to show mankind how to purify ourselves, to show us how to reach salvation.[51]

But when the fires were finally put out in Dresden and they were able to count the dead – perhaps thirty-five thousand* – mankind in war-torn Germany was not interested in purifying itself. The conquerors were going to be as brutal as Harris's and Spaatz's airmen. They would have no mercy on the Germans; for the generals were in control now and they were going to punish the 'Kraut' or 'Hun' or 'Jerry' for what he had done in the past.

'There was Dresden,' Kurt Vonnegut could say forty years later, 'a beautiful city full of museums and zoos – man at his greatest. And when we came up, the city was gone . . . The raid didn't shorten the war by half a second, didn't weaken the German defence or attack anywhere, didn't free a single person from a death camp. Only one person benefited.'

'And who was that?' someone asked him.

'Me. I got several dollars for every person killed.** Imagine!'[52]

But that was many years after the war. In 1945, there was no room for irony or cynicism. As the Allies prepared to 'bounce the Rhine' in Montgomery's phrase, the generals ordered the Germans punished. Germany had sown the seed in the years of victory; in defeat, she was going to reap a bitter harvest.

---

* Some estimates of the dead have gone as high as 200,000. But that is a propaganda figure, in my opinion. Dresden is, after all, behind the Iron Curtain now and has always been used as a symbol of capitalist brutality.
** He meant the royalties for his book, *Slaughterhouse Five*, which details the number of dead.

MARCH

Winston Churchill and Monty with US General Simpson
reach the Wesel Bridge on the Rhine.

The crossing of the Rhine

Fraternising, British style.

'*The soldier who won't fuck,*' General George Patton once exclaimed in a moment of tipsy exuberance to his nephew Fred Ayres, '*won't fight!*'[1]

Patton's Third Army was beginning to cross Germany's frontier in strength, together with Hodges's First Army, sweeping into the wooded Eifel hills and heading for the Rhine. And his young soldiers were ready to do both.

For the first time these sex-starved GIs began to enter larger German communities, all of them decked out with white flags, sheets, towels, grandpa's underpants – anything that betokened surrender – and found most villages and townships still inhabited by children, old men, boys – and *women*!

The speed of Patton's advance had been too much for the German authorities. They had been unable to evacuate the civilians (who hadn't wanted to go in the first place) and carry out Hitler's vaunted 'scorched earth' policy. Suddenly those young Americans in their prime found themselves living side by side in the rough stone cottages and half-timbered farms of the Eifel with nubile young German females, often as sex-starved as they were. What were they to do? For the women were also the enemy, with menfolk still serving at the front: menfolk who might well be attempting to kill them the day after tomorrow. How were they to treat these women?

On the first day of March 1945, their Supreme Commander General Eisenhower made the position quite clear. In a printed folder, which he ordered to be handed out to each individual Allied soldier, he stated:

You are entering Germany, not as a liberator, but a victor. Do not keep smiling. Never offer a cigarette to a visitor whom you do not know well, nor offer him your hand. The

Germans will respect you as long as they see in you a successor to Hitler who never offered them *his* hand . . . . Forget the American habit of meeting everyone in an open way. Distrust everybody who has given you no proof of his honesty . . . Always wear a uniform, never wear civilian clothes . . . Never give way. Anything that is granted as a favor will be regarded by the German as his right and he will subsequently demand twice as much. He thinks fair play is cowardice. The only way to get along with the Germans is to make them respect you, to make them feel the hand of the master.[2]

Thus the concept of 'non-fraternisation' was born. Immediately the GIs adopted the word and shortened it. German 'frowleins' became 'frats' and the pursuit of them, in spite of the fact that anyone caught doing so could be fined or even imprisoned, was named 'fratting'.*

Patton thought the directive was nonsense. He knew his men. And as he once told Montgomery, 'As long as the soldier keeps his helmet on and his elbows on the ground, it ain't fraternisation – *it's fornication!*'[3] Montgomery was reported to have laughed.

That first week of March, the US Army newspaper *Stars & Stripes* carried out a survey of soldiers' opinions on this new edict. In its March 6th issue, it reported:

There are some, though objectively agreeing that fraternisation is a bad thing, subjectively long for non-GI companionship and find the Germans 'not so bad after all'.

There are others, too, who don't care – non-fraternisation is just a brass-imposed doctrine they say – and they'll talk to any German they 'feel like' so long as they think there's a good chance that they won't get caught and have to pay a sixty-five dollars fine, or be otherwise punished!

For officers and men in these categories – and though a minority, they are a considerable one – the current situation is a natural for fraternisation. There are a great many Germans around. At the moment they are friendly and the soldiers are lonely.

Lonely they certainly were, as far as females were concerned, and Paris and its 'Pig Alley' (Place Pigalle) was a long, long way away for the combat soldier. Tomorrow they might well be killed and they were going to have their pleasure – even if they had, sometimes, to take it by force.

Like the Spaniards, the Swedes, the English and the French before them who had passed through the Eifel and down the Moselle valley, plundering, burning and raping (and, incidentally, forcing many of the forefathers of these same young Americans to leave their homeland and emigrate to the United States), Patton's soldiers swept aside all opposition, taking what they wanted from the frightened civilians whether it was forbidden or not. Now the grandsons and great-grandsons of those humble folk who had fled their poverty-stricken villages for America – *Land der unbegrenzten Moglichkeiten* (land of unlimited possibilities) – came back to terrorise.

Young Susanna Sondag observed the entry of the US 6th Armored Division men into her native village Oberraden after two days of artillery bombardment that March:

They brought in the first ten German prisoners who had surrendered immediately the *Amis* had appeared. They were made to sit on the big wooden manure casks used for taking liquid manure to the fields. Then the sentry amused himself by firing at the feet of the terrified prisoners with his machine pistol . . . Meanwhile the inhabitants of the village, 140 of them, men, women and children, were packed into a house with one single lavatory, which couldn't be used on the guards' orders, although many of them were suffering from dysentery. Soon it became clear, even to those who had welcomed the Americans with smiles and cheers, that the GIs weren't exactly friendly.

During the afternoon the soldiers amused themselves by riding around on a little horse they had found and the children's cycles. In the end, the horse collapsed of exhaustion. Then they started to loot. Watches, money, blankets – they took the lot. One had three watches on the sleeve of his jacket. What they couldn't use they flung out of the windows into the streets below.

Towards evening they began to roast our chickens over open fires and shoot at stray dogs with their rifles. Slowly they got drunk with the spirits they had found in the cellars.[4]

All of which could perhaps be dismissed as mere youthful pranks, understandable in men who had been for so long caught up in the brutal savage reality of war. But now, with the drink, they began to turn much more dangerous.

We had all settled down to sleep for the night when we were awakened by the light of flashlights as two drunken soldiers staggered across the crowded floor, crying, 'Hello, frollein, hello!' Hurriedly the others pushed the young girls under the kitchen table and covered it with a long cloth. Fortunately the two *Amis* were too drunk to see the girls' shoes sticking out so they passed and we were saved – for this night at least.

Some young German women were less fortunate. In the little Eifel township of Wittlich, captured by the relatively inexperienced 76th Infantry Division on March 10th, the remaining 100-odd citizens were forced into the Marktplatz to hear a proclamation. While this was going on, their houses were broken into and looted; and two

---

* The Supreme Commander even imposed the death penalty on any German woman transmitting VD to an Allied soldier! In view of the epidemic of VD that broke out in the spring of 1945, it is highly unlikely that this drastic sentence was ever carried out.

Fraternising, GI style.

civilians who the GIs alleged had shot at them were taken away and executed. There was worse to come.

Four black soldiers, all volunteers for the infantry, for the 76th was one of the first mixed units in the US Army, seized the wife of a teacher at the local forestry school. They raped her in front of her terrified children. She never recovered and shortly after the war had to be placed in a mental home, where she died.

Frau Hilda Leitz, a young war widow in the same town, had better luck. A whole platoon of black Americans were billeted on her family. They did try to help out, but as she admitted much later: 'On Friday night when they got their pay and drink, my father used to make me go into the bedroom and lock the door behind me. Because on Friday night they always got drunk!'[5]

Of course it was not just the blacks who attacked the women. In the nearby village of Dudeldorf, also taken by the 76th, Frau Hoffmann – another war widow – was attacked in her bedroom in the night by a red-haired GI, although some newly released French POWs tried to stop him. Terrified out of her wits and even though she was stark naked, she dropped out of a window and ran for help. An American patrol found her and took her to the nearest HQ. The GI was arrested and Frau Hoffmann later heard that he had been shot by a firing squad.[6]

Further up the road to the Moselle, after a brisk fire fight which set the village of Bausendorf afire, GIs from the same division tried to force their way into the local inn, already ablaze. The two women inside were terrified. But before the GIs could break down the door, the blaze spread and the women were left to put it out with evil-smelling liquid manure; for the stream which ran just below the inn was filled with German and American dead.[7]

Of course, it wasn't all one-sided. There were plenty of 'Veronika Dankeschoens',* as the GIs called them, who were only too willing to engage in a little 'fratting' if the price was right – chocolates or cigarettes, perhaps, or even just for a little tenderness; after all, many German women had not seen their husbands or boyfriends for years.

Private Atwell, the American medic, was stationed in the Eifel village of Lissendorf for a few days that March. There he noted:

. . . one blonde girl who was richly curved with fat pallid cheeks, chapped lips and yellowish teeth. She wore a silk scarf wrapped around her head, a tightly fitting winter coat with a fur collar and boots that showed a few inches of plump silk legs. While we were trying to force our way through [the villagers] she brushed up against one another of us smiling

with her thick unpainted lips, showing her yellowish teeth.[8]

Sergeant Giles, the engineer, also noticed the 'frawleins' trying to make contact with the soldiers that month in the Eifel. Two young women had been ordered to clean up the men's billets, and Giles watched them curiously. 'They kept grinning at us and sort of rubbing around, trying to make time . . . One of them was a swell looker. Blonde with pretty long hair and very full bosomed. She made best possible use of herself, too.' But as Giles reported in a letter to his wife back in the States, 'There were no takers. If any of the boys have taken on anything since we got into Germany, I've not seen or heard of it.'[9]

Military statistics, however, seem to prove that there were plenty of 'takers', one way or another. General Betts, in charge of Eisenhower's legal affairs, wrote later: 'From the breakthrough at the Ruhr River in February 1945 until the cessation of hostilities, the trend [of crime against civilians] again shows a sudden rise, hardly proportionate to the number of troops engaged.'[10] From February to May, there were five hundred cases of *convicted* rape a month!

That March democracy came to Germany – at the end of a bayonet. In the Eifel township of Bitburg, from whence the US 4th Armored Division would start its race for the Rhine (and of which General Patton declared cynically that it was the 'most liberated town' he had ever seen – i.e. there were only three houses left standing), the population was rounded up in the yard of the local brewery to be told by Colonel George Peddy of Civil Affairs that they had to elect a burgomaster, because that was democracy. Who would volunteer? No one did. Every inch the conqueror, Peddy looked around the shabby crowd and pointed to the tallest man there, who was wearing some sort of official-looking cap. 'You're it,' he ordered. 'You're the new burgomaster of Bitburg.'[11] And with that he grandly departed, having appointed the local postmaster as burgomaster. Democracy – courtesy Patton's Third Army – had arrived in Bitburg.

Although General Patton did not believe in the non-fraternisation ban, he did believe in teaching the 'Kraut' a lesson. Every village on the route of his advancing troops received what he called 'the General Patton War Memorial': a preliminary artillery bombardment before the infantry took over, whether the place was defended or not. As Patton saw it, a few wrecked houses would always remind the Germans that his Third Army had passed this way.

But there were plenty of his men who needed no urging to punish the Germans. Seventy-one percent of all American soldiers polled that spring blamed 'all of the ordinary Germans for the war'. One bitter GI told the American writer John Dos Passos: 'First thing you

* Literally 'Veronica Thank-yous', shortened to the more significant initials: 'VD'!

German civilians experience the reality of defeat.

know we'll be apologising to the Germans for licking them . . . And they all hate our guts and it damn well serves us right!' Another said: 'The destruction is inconceivable. Unfortunately I can feel no compassion whatsoever for these folk.'[12]

There were many 'Kraut-haters' who believed in the dictum, 'The only good Kraut is a dead Kraut.' They looted houses wilfully and tossed unwanted items out of the windows into the streets. They burned superfluous Army rations or left-over food in front of the eyes of starving children. They dropped cigarette butts in front of old men who hadn't smoked for days, then ground them out deliberately with their heels. They were the ones who locked civilians into their houses without food or water for days on end. They were the haters, who decided at the flip of a coin whether a German prisoner would be shot or not.

Lester Atwell, now waiting with his section to cross the River Kyll, was present when a supposed German sniper was brought in by a crowd of shouting, jeering GIs, his arms twisted cruelly behind his back. He denied the charge, but General Purvis who had suddenly appeared did not believe the unfortunate man. He ordered his aide, Lieutenant Stuart Martindale, to beat the prisoner up. The unresisting German was duly beaten up. Then he was marched off, hands raised, stumbling as he went. An hour later Atwell heard he had been taken out of the village, 'ordered by General Purvis to dig his own grave and once he had done so, he was shot down into it.'[13]

Another story current among Atwell's outfit on the Kyll that month was that the advancing troops had been fired upon by a beautiful blonde sniper. Captured, she, too, had denied the charge, and indeed the GIs could find no weapon on her until their captain ripped open the front of her dress: 'And there she stands with the most beautiful pair of tits he had ever seen . . . And right there between them there's this little German pistol!'

'Well,' so the story went, 'he don't care how beautiful she is. He grabs the pistol and shoves it right against her heart, and he says, "You lousy sonofabitch!" and he lets her have it. One shot and she falls over, dead . . .'[14]

The killing continued. At Piesport on the American-occupied side of the River Moselle, small-time vintner Erich Mehs had his waterside premises taken over by Americans. They spent their days drinking his cellars dry and looking out for victims on the side still held by the Germans. They never saw any German soldiers because the latter were too wary and came out during the hours of darkness. It was different with the civilians.

Once, Mehs remembered later, the amateur snipers had spotted an old man, wrapped in a bed sheet to show that he was harmless, dragging a little wooden cart behind him. The drunken soldiers' aim wasn't too steady and it took four of them to finally bring the old man down. His body lay there by the side of the river for three days.[15]

In the village of Berscheid, the Americans arrived in the early afternoon after the customary artillery bombardment. Sixteen-year-old Alois Hermes went out to welcome them, carrying a makeshift white flag, leaving his mother behind, happy in the knowledge that her only son had been saved by the Americans; in a few weeks' time he would have been called up for the Wehrmacht.

Later all the villagers were rounded up and herded into a big farmhouse, all save Alois, his friend Josef and two Serbian prisoners-of-war. Frau Hermes took a look at her son as he was led away, 'not knowing that this would be the last time I saw him.'

Next morning at ten o'clock the guard outside the farmhouse was changed. He told the Germans that an American soldier and two civilians had been killed by German artillery fire. 'It took us some time to realise what had happened,' Frau Hermes recalled later. 'Our two boys Alois and Josef had gone from us. We cried and sobbed. We asked an American officer if we couldn't see them for one last time.'

'No,' the officer told the women. 'They've already been buried.'[16]

And that was the last poor Frau Hermes heard (she had already lost two sons killed in action in Russia). But in the village of Berscheid it was many long years before the rumours ceased about how exactly young Alois had met his death.

Alois Hermes was not the only young man to disappear without trace after his village had been captured by the Americans that first bitter week of March, which many of the older inhabitants of the Eifel and Moselle areas still call 'die Passionswoche' (Passion Week). Virtually every village and township had at least one disappearance to report.

The pattern was always the same. A handful of retreating German soldiers holding out for a few hours; the American artillery bombardment; the hurried withdrawal of the landsers, leaving the old men, women and children to face what was to come.

Cautiously the Shermans would edge their way towards the place, already bedecked with white flags. That meant nothing. They'd fire high explosive and incendiaries, while the infantry infiltrated, shooting at every fleeting shadow. Anyone who didn't stop on command was shot on the spot. 'Shoot first and ask questions afterwards!' was the motto of the nervous young infantrymen. Finally, when the GIs were satisfied that there were no more German soldiers in the place, the civilians would be collected. The older ones would be led off, while the younger men and boys were left standing there at the mercy of the victors.

(Right)
Bitter tears, as a German woman is forced to leave her home.

The house search would commence – often an excuse for looting. Thereafter the drinking would begin and, if the officers lost control of their men, the wild drunken shooting might start. Yet another young German would be reported dead 'due to German artillery fire' and the sorrowing relatives would never find the spot where the *Amis* had buried him.

The bitterness extended even to the smallest child. Fraulein Y. lived as a six-year-old child in a small hamlet just outside the town of Bitburg that March. She found herself in the front line for over a week, while the fighting ebbed back and forth. Her parents' house was turned into a dressing station for the wounded, first the Germans and then the Americans. Wounded men lay everywhere in the bloody straw of their candle-lit cellar, moaning and groaning. But the little girl with the adaptability of youth continued to play with her beloved pet dog in spite of the misery all around her. This, apparently, was too much for one of the American medics. He seized one of the rifles which the walking wounded had to deposit outside, grabbed the dog from the screaming child and shot it there and then. 'It took me years to forgive the *Amis* for that,' she recalled many years later, 'though the soldiers were always kind to me, giving me candy and chocolate. But my heart was broken and even much later when I looked for my first job, I refused an offer to go and work for them at the nearby American air base.'*[17]

Of course, all was not cruelty and revenge. A priest trying to cross no-man's-land with his flock was guided to safety 'by a grinning American, as big as a tree'. A boy dying of TB in a barn was given food and water by young GIs, who even went as far as putting a burning candle at his side and a crucifix on his skinny chest 'as if they were providing for both eventualities, life and death'.[18] A local voluntary fireman and his pump was taken away by the Americans, sure he was going to be shot; but instead he was asked to pump some water for a shower they had set up for themselves. 'The involuntary bathhouse attendant and plumber,' as the village chronicle put it, 'was rewarded by the generous *Amis* with Chesterfields and Camels.'[19] And forty years later, middle-aged Germans of the area who were then boys and girls remember the Negroes – '*die schwarzen Amis*' – with fond affection. For they, in those days, third-class citizens themselves, were always good for a hand-out, a bag of candy or a delightfully sweet Hershey bar. Yes, they still remember the black *Amis* in the 'awful Eifel' . . .

'It was the most romantic story of the campaign . . . enough to revive anyone's faith in life, even in war . . . What a wonderful play it will all make one day!'[20] So said war correspondent Alan Moorehead that March, when

* Eventually she did go and work for them, and happily, for many years.

96

A proud soldier of the 7th US Army guards a group of prisoners.

Remagen Bridge, captured intact March 7th 1945.

he heard the startling news that the whole direction of the war in Europe was changed. The Americans had captured a bridge across the Rhine.

But the Australian journalist did not then know the full extent of this 'romantic story'. For not only had a young lieutenant and a handful of brave American infantrymen captured the bridge across the Rhine at Remagen, and held it, but also their Army Commander General Bradley had made a snap decision to use the Remagen Bridge to take the wind out of the sails of Field Marshal Montgomery, his hated rival. Although the move was not part of the strategy for the final battle of Germany, Bradley would throw across five divisions within the next forty-eight hours.

But the supreme irony of this 'romantic story' was the fact that the officer who captured the Remagen Bridge was more German than American. Lieutenant Karl Timmermann had been born not a hundred kilometres from that celebrated bridge, the capture of which would alter the whole course of the last six weeks of the war. *Timmermann had been born in Germany!*

Timmermann's father, also of German descent, had been a doughboy in 1918, stationed at the nearby Rhenish town of Koblenz, when he had deserted, crossed the Rhine into unoccupied Germany, and married a girl from Frankfurt. Here his son Karl was born. For five years the Timmermanns lived in Germany, until, with the aid of the British Red Cross, they were finally allowed to go home by the American authorities. There at West Point, Nebraska, the young German-American grew up on the wrong side of the tracks.

On his eighteenth birthday, June 24th, 1940, the earliest possible date to do so, the tall skinny youth volunteered for the army from which his father had deserted. He joined, as he often joked to his buddy Lieutenant Swisher, 'because all the garbage can-lids froze down' and he wanted to eat. Commissioned, he went overseas with the 9th Armored Division and was wounded in his first action during the Battle of the Bulge when his division was badly mauled.

Now this first week of March, a newly appointed company commander in the 9th Armored's infantry, Timmermann, who had uncles serving in the Wehrmacht on the other side, had no illusions about war and

A bazooka is used to blast German snipers out from a house.

combat. As he wrote to his wife back in the States: 'There's no glory in war. Maybe those who have never been in battle find that a certain glory and glamour that doesn't exist. Perhaps they get it from the movies or the comic strips.'[21] Now, however, for a while before he sank back again into an obscurity that was ended by an early death, Karl Timmermann was going to achieve that glory. Soon he was to be the first American officer to cross the Rhine in battle.*

Late on the morning of March 7th, 1945, a grey drizzly day, Timmermann's A Company found themselves in an abandoned German Labour Corps camp on the Birresdorf road on the heights just above Remagen. One mile away, the Luddendorff Railway Bridge across the Rhine was still intact, with men and vehicles crossing it in a steady stream. For a while the senior officers of Timmermann's outfit considered shelling the bridge. Finally, however, General Hoge, the Division's assistant com-

mander, appeared. Stern-faced and angry, he 'chewed out' the soldiers for being so slow in capturing Remagen. Then, in a lower and more thoughtful tone, he went on: 'You know, it would be nice to get that bridge while we're at it.'[22] The idea of capturing the railway bridge had been born.

By two o'clock that afternoon, Timmermann's company had cleared out the opposition in Remagen and turned their attention to the double-track railway bridge, nearly 1,000 feet long, and at this moment the only surviving bridge across the Rhine. They started to snipe the place. Immediately the German defenders detonated the first of the explosive charges buried in and around the wrought-iron structure. They moved forward as far as a smoking shell crater which barred the road to tanks. At the other side men in field-grey scuttled around frantically, preparing to blow the remaining charges. Timmermann made his decision. 'We've got orders to cross,' he announced calmly, 'Alpha Company leading.'

Sergeant Sabia objected. 'It's a trap. Once we get in the middle they'll blow up the bridge.'

Timmermann hesitated only a moment. 'Orders are

* It is interesting to note that the first US soldier to enter Germany in World War Two, S/Sgt Werner Holzinger, was also of German extraction.

orders. We're told to go. All right, let's go!'[23]

There was no dramatic rush to capture the bridge. Unlike the virile heroes of the film made a quarter of a century later,* the bearded dirty GIs thought it looked like sudden death – and were hesitant. Their stomachs were queasy too, for some of them had been looting and drinking wine in the waterfront inns. But, strung out in platoons, they started to creep down the slight slope to the western entrance to the bridge, marked by two red-brick towers.**

As they moved off a Major Deevers cried after them, 'Come on fellers . . . I'll see you on the other side and we'll all have a chicken dinner!'[24]

His suggestion was met with many obscene remarks about what he could do with his chicken dinner.

Now, with Timmermann and his sergeants urging them on, the armoured infantrymen found the first explosive charges. Hastily they snipped through the connecting wire. Almost immediately machine guns opened up from the twin towers on the other side. The attack bogged down.

'Goddam, why let a couple of snipers hold up a whole battalion!' Sergeant De Lisio yelled angrily. 'Let's get off this damn bridge. If it goes, we *all* go!'[25]

He ran ahead, zigzagging wildly while the air sang with bullets. Sabia ran after him, telling himself the bridge seemed endless. He wasn't a good swimmer and he kept throwing glances at the swirling dirty water eighty feet below. He would go down like a brick, weighed down as he was with his heavy pack, he told himself fearfully.

Panting heavily, De Lisio rounded up five frightened Germans crouching over the jammed machine gun. Then he ran inside the tower and pelted up the stone stairs. A drunken officer and a soldier stood there. The officer staggered towards the detonating device in the corner. De Lisio fired a quick burst from his grease gun near his feet, vicious little blue sparks erupting from the stone floor. That did it. The two Germans gave up.

While this was going on, lanky young Alex Drabik was looking for his platoon leader De Lisio. Knowing how aggressive the Italo-American was, he reasoned he had gone ahead, into the railway tunnel. He cried, 'De Lisio must be over there, all alone. Let's go!'

Running so fast that his helmet fell off, Drabik raced for the tunnel, followed by a one-time plasterer from Minnesota, Marvin Jensen, who kept shouting, 'Holy crap, do you think we'll make it?'[26]

They did. Next moment Alex Drabik became the first American to cross the Rhine on active duty during World War Two. A few minutes later Karl Timmermann became the first US officer to do so. By nightfall a whole

* It was made in Czechoslovakia, prior to the Russian invasion. The latter made much of it as an attempt by Americans to seize power there prior to their entry.
** Today those same towers are defaced with peace slogans and demands for 'bread not war'.

Sherman tanks roll across the Remagen Bridge onto the East Bank of the Rhine.

division had started to pour across. By dawn a whole corps would be following. The Rhine had been crossed at last!

'It was a moment for history,' *Time* wrote that month. Associated Press cabled: 'It was the biggest military triumph since Normandy.' Fittingly, Karl Timmermann was awarded the DSC and lauded before he sank back once more into the obscurity from which he had come, not knowing that he had – indirectly – changed the face of Europe.

Now, with Churchill impotent and Roosevelt almost dead, the American top brass were running the war in Europe. They would ensure that Montgomery's great set-piece crossing of the Rhine would lose most of its strategic value. When it was successfully completed, the British Army and its attached US Ninth would *not* be given the vital task of racing to Berlin. The whole direction of the main Allied attack would be changed. Bavaria not Berlin would be the target, starting from the bridge at Remagen and those erected later in that general area of the Rhine.

As a result, Berlin, Vienna and Prague would be lost to the Western Allies. They would fall into Russian hands. Germany would be divided as a consequence – and remain divided into our own time. That was Karl Timmermann's legacy, a bitter one, but perhaps an apt one for a man who was rejected both by the country of his birth and by the one of his adoption. Now his senior commanders would line up to have their photographs taken, having 'a piss in the Rhine', regardless of the political consequences. 'To hell with the planners!' Eisenhower cried happily when he heard the news. Now he would let his generals have their head. That Tuesday afternoon in March, 1945, Karl Timmermann, who had six more years to live, helped to decide the fate of Western Europe.*

Late on the afternoon of March 23rd, 1945, Field Marshal Montgomery gave out the code-name for his great set-piece assault on the Rhine. It was 'Two if by Sea', puckishly borrowed – for some reason known only to the cocky little soldier – from the signal that sent Paul Revere riding through the New England countryside back in the eighteenth century to warn his fellow Americans that the 'Redcoats' were coming.

That night along the 22-mile length of the Rhine held by his armies, 3,500 guns, supported by 2,000 anti-aircraft cannon, many thousands of mortars and the Canadian-invented 'mattresses' (rocket-launchers massed in banks), thundered into action. For three long hours they poured fire onto the German-held side of the Rhine before the assault infantry began to cross.

* Unwelcome in his home town after the war, Timmermann rejoined the Army. He fought in Korea, but cancer struck him down and he died in an army hospital in 1951, aged thirty-one.

(Above) British troops clamber into their storm boats before crossing the Rhine.
(Right) The massive bombardment of the far side of the Rhine begins.

'The noise was so terrific that conversation in Battalion Headquarters was almost impossible,' the historian of the Lincolns recorded.[27] 'Our targets were preselected and the guns lost the paint from their barrels,' remembered R. Saunders of the 103rd Regiment Royal Artillery.[28] Captain Wilson, waiting to cross with his tanks, noted: 'East and west as far as I could see, the night was lit with gunfire; it flickered through the trees and flashed on the underside of the clouds. The ground shook ceaselessly and again there was a violent continuing explosion like a pack of cards being snapped.'[29]

In front of the thundering guns, the assault infantry waited. In the British sector they were the 51st Highland Division with the Canadian Highland Light Infantry Brigade attached, the 15th Scottish Division and the 1st Commando Brigade. In the American sector they were the veteran 30th and 79th Divisions.

Most of them, Canadian, British and American, were nervous. They told jokes 'at which no one would laugh ordinarily,' Wilson noted, 'wandering off frequently to the latrine' – a sure sign of nerves.[30] Eisenhower, visiting his soldiers, came across one GI who was silent and depressed. 'How you feeling, son?' he asked. 'General, I'm awful nervous,' the young GI confessed, 'I was wounded two months ago and just got back from hospital yesterday. I don't feel so good.' Eisenhower reassured him: 'Well, you and I are a good pair then, because I'm nervous too.'[31]

The British were none too happy with their assignment either. They knew that facing them were the best troops still left in the Wehrmacht, Student's paras, a whole corps of them, backed up by elements of two panzer divisions. Newsman Richard McMillan noted a young commando colonel drinking tea while he blacked his face. 'Wonder what Jerry's got on the other side?' he asked pensively.

It was a question that was worrying hundreds of young men in that first wave, as at nine o'clock in a hazy darkness, the four leading battalions of the 51st, the 5th and 7th Black Watch, the 7th Argylls and the 5/7th Gordons, slid into the Rhine in their Buffalo amphibians. Within a few minutes they were on the far bank, where an aptly named Colonel Jolly of the Royal Tanks planted his regimental flag; as always the British tried to do things in style. There was little resistance. At four minutes past nine precisely, their Corps Commander General Horrocks received a simple laconic message, which in its way was historic. It read, *The Black Watch has landed safely on the far bank.*

Now things happened swiftly. At ten o'clock the 1st Commando slipped across the Rhine at Wesel. Before them, 250 Lancasters had begun plastering the city, dropping 1,000 tons of bombs in a very short time. 'Arthur Harris & Company, House Removers', as the commandos called them, delivered a shattering blow to the defenders of the Rhenish city. As Major Bartholomew of the 1st Commando noted in his diary, 'It seemed as if more than mortal powers had been unleashed.'[32]

With their ears still echoing with that terrible bombardment, the green-bereted infantrymen scurried into the smoking ruins exactly fifteen minutes after the last bomber had disappeared. The anxiously waiting staff on the British side of the Rhine heard a 'voice literally purr(ing) over the wireless . . . "Noisy blighters, aren't they! We have taken the position . . . and have met no trouble . . ."'

Now it was the turn of the 15th Scottish. Wynford Vaughan-Thomas of the BBC went over with the assault wave, and later described the boats as 'racing for that hell on the other side . . . Now we're utterly alone it seems – right out in the midst of this whirling stream . . . waiting all the time for the enemy to open up . . . waiting all the time for them to spot us as we lie helpless.' But they weren't spotted. Finally they reached the other side, untouched.

There was an 'immense feeling of relief and excitement' throughout the little party as the CO of the assault battalion nodded to his piper. This historic moment had to be celebrated in true Scottish fashion. With due ceremony the piper raised his pipes to his lips and blew hard. Nothing happened. He tried again. Once more – nothing, just an 'agonising wail' from his instrument. As Thomas remarked when the red-faced piper tried unsuccessfully for the third time: 'If ever a man was near to tears, it was our piper.'

It was his great moment and now he cried in utter despair, 'Ma pipes, mon, they'll na play . . .'[33]

Now it was the turn of the veteran 30th US Infantry, which had been in the thick of the fighting since Normandy, and its running mate the 79th Infantry. They crossed with a mere forty casualties and thus by dawn Montgomery had three strong bridgeheads over the other side of the Rhine. Only in Rees and Wesel were the Germans still resisting obstinately, and at Rees the 51st was running into serious trouble as the German paras counter-attacked. Watching them, the Division's commander General Rennie had already fallen mortally wounded; and at the villages of Bienen and Speldrop his Black Watch had been driven back, with two companies trapped. Soon they would run out of ammunition. As yet, however, they were not prepared to surrender.

It was decided to send the Highland Light Infantry of Canada to their aid. In Normandy the Canadian formation had been almost wiped out. The same had happened once again in the Reichswald. Now, rested and brought up to strength, they were in a fighting mood as their war diary for March 23rd notes: 'Weather – clear. Vis. – unlimited. Morale – 100 per cent!'[34]

On one of the leading assault boats, Private Malcolm Buchanan noted how 'the whole sky seemed to light up as the guns commenced firing . . . On coming down to

The assault infantry lands on the east side of the Rhine.

get into the boat . . . I almost ran into a newsreel cameraman, who was taking pictures of the men as they came down the bank. As number one on the Bren, my position was in the front of the boat. At that point the river looked awfully wide, foggy and lonesome. I asked the operator of our boat why we had been singled out to have our pictures taken. "You," he said, "will be the first man to hit the shore. How do you like *that*?"

'Well, to tell the truth that answer kind of stunned me. Here I was loaded down like a horse. I thought, *"Boy, how am I going to move fast!"* '[35]

In the event, there was little fighting on the other side – at the start – and Buchanan made it. Most of the German prisoners seemed 'bomb happy', and the Canadian infantrymen took the opportunity of a lull to eat and grab a little sleep.

About noon, however, their Major King arrived 'with a roll of maps under one arm and a tommy gun under the other. As he approached we saw a big smile on his face, which caused one of the men to comment, "If Major King looks that happy, they must have dug up something real nasty for us." '[36]

They had. The Highland Light Infantry of Canada were to attack Speldrop and relieve the two companies of the Black Watch trapped there – if they were still alive.

German fire forces US infantrymen to stay low as they cross the Rhine. Some of them didn't make it.

That was not the only Canadian battalion in trouble that day. The HLI (Canada) had been followed across the Rhine by the North Nova Scotians, who had drawn a particularly unpleasant ticket from the lottery of battle: they were to attack elements of the 15th Panzer Division dug in at the crossroads near Bienen. It had been their mortar fire which had killed General Rennie – 'a guid general,' as one of his men said later, 'he wasna a shoutin' kind of man.'[37] They were to attack at noon.

'My platoon assaulted in a single extended wave,' one of their officers recalled after the war. 'Ten tumbled down, nailed in an instant by fire from two maybe three machine guns . . . The rest of us rolled or dropped into a shallow ditch, hardly more than a trough six inches deep, at the bottom of the dyke. The Bren gunners put their weapons to their shoulders but never got a shot away (I saw them after the battle, both dead, one still holding the aiming position) . . . A rifleman on my left took aim at a German weapons pit and with a spasm collapsed on my arm. His face turned almost instantly a faint green and bore a simple smile.'[38]

By nightfall the Nova Scotians held the northern part of the village at a cost of 115 men, 43 of them killed. Their casualties that single afternoon had been twenty per cent. The young officer quoted above went back to report to his CO. But after seven months of more or less continuous combat, he had reached the end of his tether. 'I hadn't any idea of how far gone I was emotionally. Instead of furnishing a coherent account, I simply stood in front of him weeping inarticulately, unable to construct a sentence, even to force a single word out of my mouth.'[39] Two days later he was on his way back to the United Kingdom, just as much a casualty of battle as if he had been wounded.

At five that afternoon the Canadian HLI lined up ready to assault Speldrop. A few surviving officers of the Black Watch assembled to watch the Canadian attack. They told the Canadians that their men were 'all dead or captured. Shoot anything that moves because it will be a Jerry. Don't take any chances, as too many have died there already.'[40]

The Canadians took a last drag at their cigarettes and a final drink from their second water bottle. Even the veterans were nervous. They were going to attack across open fields swept by German machine gun and artillery fire, with 800 yards to go before they reached the cover of the houses.

'We crossed the open in staggered intervals,' recalled Corporal Sam Dearden who was in a carrier. 'I rolled out into the open knowing that it would be rough even if the roads were mine-free. You could hear them shells crack as they passed overhead and beside you.' The German fire didn't seem to bother his platoon commander, Lieutenant Isner. He said calmly, 'I don't believe they like us here.'[41]

6th Commando personnel after capturing Wesel.

A German sniper is captured.

A Typhoon came roaring in at 400 mph. Angry blue lights flickered the length of its stubby wings. Somewhere ahead in the rolling smoke a German self-propelled gun scuttled for cover, but there was no escape. Fiery-red rockets, trailing a fury of sparks, zipped from the Typhoon. The SP was hit. It staggered and came to an abrupt halt, engulfed in flames.

Private Buchanan, on foot, doubled to keep up with their own barrage, which rolled forward only a hundred yards in front of the advancing infantrymen, churning up the wet ground in brown gouts of soil and pebbles, leaving huge smoking brown holes everywhere.* 'About 200 yards from the town,' Buchanan recalled later, 'we began to pass the Black Watch dead. There was one complete section of 8 to 10 men who had apparently been cut down by crossfire . . . As we came to about 150 yards of the town, the barrage *stopped*!'[42]

It was the SNAFU that Buchanan and the rest had been expecting all along. The Canadians hit the ground,

knowing what was to come. It came. With elemental savagery, the German guns roared into life. A moment later the din of heavy artillery was joined by the stomach-churning howl of their 'moaning minnies', multiple-barrel mortars. The German counter-barrage had commenced.

Lieutenant Isner jumped to his feet. 'Come on!' he yelled. 'If we're going to be killed, I'd sooner get it from our guns than theirs!'

Animated by the crazy logic of battle, Buchanan's platoon charged forward right into the fire of their own guns, which had started shelling once more. Isner was blown right into the air by an exploding shell. Buchanan was knocked to the ground by the blast. For a moment he was stunned, then he found to his surprise that he was all right. He grabbed his Bren and doubled across to where Isner lay. But as Buchanan remembered, 'He hadn't been as lucky as I. He was finished.'[43]

The survivors of Canadian HLI, gaps in their ranks everywhere, swept into the shattered village, crunching over the debris as they ran into the main street, firing as they did so. Buchanan let the first small house have a

* Forty years later, the only trace of that savage fighting at Speldrop is a series of shallow depressions, just visible when the sun is at the right angle.

burst. Like all German houses it had a cellar, with the cellar-window just protruding above the ground, making it an ideal ready-made bunker.* He kicked open the door and, like a western gun-slinger, sprayed the kitchen with bullets. He moved further in and changed his magazine. A dead German was slumped against the wall, mouth open foolishly. They had been waiting for him, but he had got there first. He was about to drop a .36 grenade into the cellar a moment later when a broad Scots voice suddenly stopped him: 'Don't shoot, for God's sake! Black Watch here!'

Hastily Buchanan stuck the cotter pin back in the grenade and yelled for the men to come out, one at a time. He was taking no chances. 'First up was a sergeant. He was a brave man to stand on those steps in the face of Bren gun fire. He said, "You've shot three of my men."'

Buchanan was horror-stricken. 'God, I'm sorry, mate!' he gasped. 'But your officers told us you lads were all dead or captured.'

Thereupon the sergeant explained how they had held off the Germans with their entrenching tools and bayonets, having run out of ammunition, even risking maiming by picking up the German grenades thrown at them and flinging them back.

A little way off, Corporal Dearden in his carrier also ran into some survivors of the Black Watch who had held off the panzer grenadiers all night. 'Don't stop here!' they yelled in warning. 'He shoots through these houses any time he feels like it. Leave your vehicle and join us in the trench.'[44]

Dearden took the warning. With the rest he abandoned the carrier and advanced on foot against stiff machine-gun fire. There were snipers everywhere in the wrecked brick houses. Dearden was hit in the pocket by a slug, but he carried on. 'Quite often we'd dodge from door to door, being fired on most of the time. The town was burning uncontrolled in some areas.' But the Canadians pressed on, 'mouse-holing', as it was called, from house to house, where officers were not fully in control and where friend killed not only foe, but each other. As Dearden recalled, 'In the confusion of the dark we lost men to the Black Watch and them to us, not knowing we were there.'

Buchanan was also involved in the costly business of house-clearing now. 'Not many prisoners were taken . . . If they did not surrender,' he recalled later, 'before we started on a house, they never had an opportunity afterwards.'

The Canadian HLI had been well trained in the highly lethal technique of house-clearing, a technique that demanded resolution and speed. A grenade tossed into a room, followed by a brave man going in full-tilt, spraying the interior with bullets. Then another room, then the next, and so on until the house was cleared – and always with a man posted at the top of the stairs in case the enemy made a last suicidal charge from the cellar. Skilled as they were, however, things still went wrong. Buchanan saw 'one man throw a grenade into a house, but before it exploded one of the new men went through the door. He was blown right back out. He had gotten excited and it had cost him his life.'

Now it was almost over. Sergeant Reidel now took over the survivors of Buchanan's platoon. He gathered them together and pointed out a squat group of buildings beyond an orchard from which heavy fire was coming. They could see angry scarlet flame stabbing the darkness at three separate points. Reidel told the weary Canadians: 'Get that objective and we have done the job.' Then he ordered them to attack.

They approached the enemy position from its blind side. Then, on the command from Reidel, they charged, 'throwing 36's, firing our weapons and doing a lot of yelling. . . . We were into them before they could turn their machine guns around on us. It was all over in a few minutes. They threw up their arms and yelled "Kamerad!"'

They had 'done the job'. But what they found in that last position made them shudder with fear. The defenders, all German paras, had outnumbered them two to one, and they had been heavily armed; they even had 75 mm cannon. And according to Buchanan, 'Beside each was a stock of HE, AP and what one man said was Canister.* No wonder the Black Watch was cut to pieces.'[45]

They attacked all night and most of the next day. Buchanan later recalled looking around at the survivors and thinking, 'We sure look like our regimental nickname suggests – "Hell's Last Issue".'

Finally they were pulled out and what was left of B Company was paraded in front of company commander Major King. The Company Sergeant Major snapped to attention in front of him and barked: 'Fifty-four men on parade, sir – all the rest accounted for, sir!'[46]

B Company had lost half its strength in those few hours on the far bank of the Rhine. But as Buchanan recalled proudly years later, they were all 'accounted for'. They had been either killed or wounded. None of them had been taken prisoner, for the men of 'Hell's Last Issue' were proud of the fact that they had never 'had a man taken prisoner, no one posted missing and no ground once taken ever lost' in all their fighting career in Europe.

---

* Most Allied soldiers thought these cellars were purpose-built bunkers. They weren't, of course, but German soldiers did make ready use of the civilians' cellars. The cellar of the house in which I write these words was used as such by German infantry in March '45, which might signify something, I suppose.

* High explosive, armour-piercing shells and anti-personnel fragmentation shells.

Next day the Highland Light Infantry of Canada were issued with fresh grenades and rifle ammunition, filled up with reinforcements, and sent back into the line yet again . . .

On the morning of Saturday March 24th, a fine cloudless day, the Top Brass assembled on a hill overlooking the Rhine. They were all there – Ike, Monty, 'Big Simp',* and naturally that 'former naval person', who wouldn't have missed this occasion for anything.

Churchill had suffered a series of minor mishaps to get here, where he really was not wanted. All the top brass were scared something might happen to him, for only a mile away on the other side of the great river severe fighting was still taking place. He had lost his false teeth; he had had his cap knocked off by the gun of an armoured car; he had had difficulty in finding the VIP latrine. But now he was here, dressed in the uniform of his old regiment, the Fourth Hussars, smoking a big cigar and happy to be present at this historic moment, confiding in the others, 'I should have liked to have deployed my men in red coats in the plain down there and ordered them to charge. But now my armies are too vast.' Suddenly the great man stopped his discourse and, springing to his feet, went running wildly a few yards down the hill, pointing to the sky and yelling, *'They're coming! . . . They're coming!'*[47]

They were. This time Montgomery was not risking another Arnhem fiasco. His airborne troops would drop *after* the land forces had gone in. So, promptly at ten o'clock, the airborne spectacle commenced. This was what had brought Churchill from London to the hill overlooking the Rhine. For three and a half hours, planes and gliders would come streaming in from the west in endless columns, bringing with them 26,000 British and American paratroops from the 6th British and 17th US Airborne Divisions. Perhaps the last mass paradrop in history had begun.

The US 17th Airborne, which had not previously made a combat jump, ate a good breakfast of steak and apple pie in their bases in Northern France before taking off. In the lead plane was Colonel Allen C. Miller; only five foot four, he was called 'Boots and Helmet' by his men because he seemed just that – all boots and helmet. Colonel Miller took a pill and promptly went to sleep.[48]

He was the exception. Most of his paras suffered from knotted stomachs and lumps in their throat that seemed to grow and grow, threatening to choke them. Even the veteran war correspondent Robert Capa, who maintained he had seen 'too many D-Days', was affected. In

* The commander of the US Ninth Army, General Simpson, tall and very bald. Incidentally, that hill is no longer there; it has since been virtually bulldozed away.

112

US paratroopers land in Germany.

Airborne troops watch another glider come down.

one of the gliders Howard Cowan, another correspondent, tried to forget the frighteningly vivid mental picture of the gliders coming in in Normandy and Holland and being torn apart. He closed his eyes on his neighbour who was vomiting noisily into his steel helmet.

The great armada started to approach its objective. The green lights began to flicker. The paras hooked up. On the German side of the Rhine, flak rumbled into action. Grey puffballs of drifting smoke came up to meet the transports.

Capa prepared to jump, telling himself that the time between the jump and the landing was 'twenty-four hours in any man's life'.[49] Now they started taking hits. Down below a British tank officer watched as a Fortress

'came lower and lower over our heads, glistening silver in the morning sunshine, the flames which streamed from one wing a deep orange against the azure blue. As it passed us parachutes blossomed from the side and we counted them anxiously and watched with horror as one failed to open and plunged straight to the ground in a white streak, the man kicking desperately up to the last moment, and we knew that remaining in that blazing plane, whether dead or alive, there was no one but the pilot.'[50]

In Colonel Miller's plane the command had just been given – *'Stand up . . . Hook up . . . Check your equipment . . .'* – when flak started to rip through the steel floor below the waiting paras.

to greet Capa was less poetic: 'Some of them who jumped with me landed in trees. A German machine gun opened up at the dangling men and they were murdered.'

Colonel Miller couldn't free himself from his harness. Slugs cut the grass all around him. In desperation he slashed through the shroud lines with his knife until they fell away. The firing was coming from a farmhouse. He pulled out his pistol and doubled towards it. He dropped down behind a shed. In that same moment, a big para vaulted the five-foot fence and slammed down next to him. Miller was so annoyed by the man's sudden appearance and his obvious funk that he booted him in the rear. Neither man said a word.

Now planes were coming in by the score and the casualties were mounting. Down below, Captain Thompson watched with horror as plane after plane was hit and fell to the ground 'in great spouts of fire and flying fragments of flame as wings and tails flew off like meteors . . . The thick pillars of smoke and flame were the funeral pyres of brave men.

'We who report this war,' Thompson thought, 'have a duty to the dead equally with the living, to tell things as they are, stripped at times of the glamour and the glory. If these terrible, charred and burning bodies that a moment ago were young men have a message – if they are not to have come to so shocking a death in vain – then the memory must be indelible in all our minds that this, too, is war . . .'[52]

Colonel Miller was alone again. The big paratrooper had vanished as abruptly as he had appeared. Miller pushed on by himself, stumbling over dead or badly wounded paras in the shell-holed fields. The carnage reminded him of old prints of the aftermath of Pickett's Charge during the Civil War.

Finally he collected a handful of men together and led them to a farmhouse, which was being used as an aid-post by the assistant battalion surgeon, Captain Fodor. Blood was running down the doctor's baggy pants as Miller entered. Calmly the doctor dropped his trousers and applied a tourniquet, saying in a matter of fact manner: 'I've just been shot in the ass.'

A moment later Colonel Jones, the paras' regimental commander, ran up to Miller with a handful of paras in tow. 'I want you to attack south from here with your left on the railroad!' he yelled, pointing to a field.

Almost as if on cue, machine-gun fire started from that direction. Hastily the paras hit the ground. All save Colonel Miller. He drew himself up to his full five foot four, the slugs cutting the air all around him, and shouted, '*Follow me!*'

Not a man moved.

'*Goddamit!*' he exploded. '*Get moving!*' He ran up and down the line of reluctant paras, yelling at them to

Several of them went down and the crew chief stumbled in to report the pilot had been badly wounded. The transport plane yawed violently to the left. Miller caught a glimpse of some railway tracks ahead. At least they were over the land, not the water. '*Jump!*' he yelled and, standing aside, let some of his panicking men go out first. Then taking a deep breath he launched himself out into space, the sky all around him blossoming out in white canopies, mingled with the red, blue and yellow chutes of their supplies. Above him the plane started to go into a dive, its left wing burning brightly.[51]

Capa's plane was hit too. Capa jumped in time and watched the dark figures of the paras transformed into 'silken flowers' as they drifted down. But the next image

Airborne troops preparing to attack Haminkeln.

move. Hesitantly two men rose. They started forward apprehensively. A few more followed. Finally Miller had them all on their feet, bodies bent as if they were facing a storm, advancing in a skirmish line. It was too much for the Germans. They turned and fled.[53]

Now it was the turn of General Matthew Ridgway, commander of the 17th Airborne Corps, to cross the Rhine. Not by air, but in an Alligator, manned by a British crew who fired bursts of machine-gun fire to their front every few yards. Ridgway, tall, hook-nosed and aggressive, clutching his World War One vintage rifle, the grenades he wore as a publicity gimmick attached to his webbing, dropped over the side and went forward, followed by an aide. He came across a German in a foxhole. The General stopped and stared. The German stared back. He was already dead.

They pushed on into a wood. A para raced up through the trees, mounted on a heavy farm horse and wearing a looted top hat. When he saw the general he didn't know whether to dismount, present arms, or take off his hat in greeting. Ridgway laughed and the mounted para laughed back.

Eventually Ridgway found 17th Airborne Division HQ, borrowed some jeeps, and moved out to find the British. Instead he found a fire-fight. Everywhere there was the angry snap and crackle of small arms.

Ridgway loosed off a couple of shots, and dropped out of the suddenly stalled jeep just as a grenade exploded underneath it. For a few moments he and his party just lay there. In the loud echoing silence after the sudden attack, Ridgway could hear men breathing heavily all around him, but he held his fire in case they were friends. Suddenly he saw some willows tremble. There was someone among them.

116

'Put your hands up, you son of a bitch!' he cried excitedly.

'Ah, go and shit in yer hat,' a very American voice replied contemptuously.[54]

This confused day, private soldiers knowing that they might not be living much longer were not too impressed by generals, however aggressive and far forward they might be . . .

Now the British Red Berets of the 6th Airborne Division had landed too. They had started from their fields in the Home Counties among exploding V-bombs and flown through them to the Rhine. Their first flights had arrived relatively unscathed, but the German flak was alerted by the time the second and third waves flew in. Casualties were high. Indeed, by the time the operation was over, the 6th would have lost thirty percent of its effectives (in comparison with the US 17th's ten percent).

Private James Byrom of the RAMC, who had dropped with the 6th in Normandy, found the usual confusion on the ground. One of the first sights to greet him was a group of German prisoners, 'white-faced and terrified, with an ugly Canadian paratrooper prodding the stragglers in the back'.[55] Wounded men were soon streaming in to the dressing station. The first aid and surgical teams sprang into action, cutting, sewing, excising, bandaging. But Byrom and the other medics could do nothing for one tough little Geordie whom Byrom had known back in Bulford. There his motto had been 'Follow the Crowd': Byrom remembered him saying, 'I've always followed the fucking crowd and I've always been reet.' Now he had followed the crowd for the last time, however. Another of his favourite phrases had been 'Whose side are ye on?' And this was his only articulate remark as he lay on the stretcher, mortally

117

wounded, listening to the medics' hollow assurances that everything would be 'all right'.

'He could already feel himself sinking into the anonymity of death and wished to be sure that we knew who he was,' Byrom wrote later. *Whose side are ye on?*

By now the 1st Canadian Parachute Battalion was engaged in heavy fighting with Germans dug in among the dank fir woods that ran parallel with the Rhine. Later they would call them the 'suicide woods'.*

Their Colonel, Jeff Nicklin, had already been shot dead as he dangled helplessly from a chute. Corporal Topham, nicknamed 'Toppy', was one of the medics tending the casualties; with two German prisoners under his command he was kept busy bringing in the wounded, although he had been shot in the nose. Together the three of them saved many Canadian lives that day, 'Toppy' ignoring the crude jokes being made about the state of his poor pulped nose. He would win the fourth Victoria Cross won by Canadians on the Rhine. The fate of his two German assistants is unknown.

For the Canadians were as hard in combat as ever. They were not too fussy about the niceties of the Rules of Land Warfare. Private Collins, in action for the first time, recalled later how they flushed out a sniper that day. 'He was running out with his hands locked over his helmet. Fortunately, or maybe purposely, he had missed us.' But the Canadians had little time for snipers, whether they shot to kill or not. 'One of the boys lifted him with a butt stroke of his sten. He was hit so hard we just left him there and moved on.'[56]

Now the gliderborne troops of the 6th Airborne were arriving in their large canvas and wood Hamilcar and Horsa gliders. Canadian correspondent Stanley Maxted, who had escaped from Arnhem the previous September, was just coming into land when his Hamilcar took a full burst of 20 mm anti-aircraft shells the length of its fuselage. 'There was an explosion that appeared to be in my head, the smell of burnt cordite. I went down on one knee. Something hot and sticky was dripping over my right eye and off my chin and all over my clothes.'[57] But the skinny middle-aged Canadian survived. Minutes later he was being attended to in a field dressing station.

One of the doctors at that station, Lieutenant-Colonel Watts saw the gliders sweeping into crash-land on the fields beyond. To him they 'looked rather like a fairground in process of closing down . . . Only the still figures of the dead gave a grim reality to the scene. Everywhere gliders were burning or tilted at impossible angles, their noses wrecked and smashed into the churned up earth.' Watts noted one such glider, an American-built Waco, with the charred bodies of the dead paras still strapped inside; it looked, he said, 'for all the world as if some monster had set a bird-cage on fire'.[58]

Slowly, gradually, the chaos and confusion gave way to order. The paras began to dig in to protect their dropping zones. Others began to attack. At the village of Haminkeln, which formed the division's frontline, nineteen-year-old Corporal Dudley Anderson of the Red Devons found himself taking part in his third bayonet charge of the war. As he described it later:

There was no command. Someone started to climb out of the ditch and the rest followed him. I found myself running with all the others towards the German trenches. I could see the Germans plainly now, still firing their rifles. . . . There was no time to swerve or dodge, just run, run as fast as your legs could carry you . . . and don't forget to yell and scream at the top of your voice. Never mind if some of your mates were falling or dropping behind. It was now just you or Jerry . . .

The German trenches were only twenty yards away . . . ten yards . . . five . . . I had picked out my German. Suddenly it was all over. The Germans were throwing down their arms and raising their hands. They had to be quick; some who were too late got shot. Not one of us had to use a bayonet, but no one, least of all the Germans, had any doubts about our intention of doing so.[59]

The Canadians had paused and now had time to rest and look at their surroundings. A shot-down Luftwaffe pilot was brought in. He was a cocky, thickset individual who so annoyed the Canadian paras that one of them challenged him to a fist fight. He accepted. Thus, in the middle of a battle, a Canadian sergeant and a German pilot went at it with their fists, hammer and tongs!

Private Collins, who was present at the time, later recalled how the German 'gave an excellent account of himself, but the sergeant knocked him down at last and he didn't wish to continue'.[60]

A little later, Wynford Vaughan-Thomas of the BBC came upon the Canadians in 'Suicide Wood'. He was impressed by

. . . that fantastic coloured landscape you always get after a big airborne landing, with parachutes dangling from the trees, green parachutes, yellow parachutes and containers scattered over the fields, gliders flung broadsides over the ploughed land. It looked as if a gigantic litter basket had been emptied over the whole countryside.[61]

Then the BBC man came across a small 'group of cowed and completely bewildered civilians . . . listening patiently while they were lectured by a paratrooper on how they were to behave in the future. They were giving no trouble, there were no desperate guerrilla fighters in this lot. They were only too eager to obey.'

Another future BBC television 'personality', then commanding 'C' Company of the 1st Ulster Rifles, a

* Today those same woods are a nature reserve, filled with wild pig and deer.

German prisoners captured on the East Bank of the Rhine.

glider unit, was moving forward through dead Americans of the 17th to link up with the American paras. One of the Ulstermen, Staff-Sergeant Cramer, a former policeman, recalled the scene:

I saw a figure in a long German greatcoat rise to his feet in the centre of a field and walk towards us with his hands up. The man was *Volkssturm*,* about fifty or sixty years of age, a long thin chap. Before we could do anything about it, three Americans let fly with their carbines and the figure fell. God, we were angry![62]

So was Major Wheldon, the future TV star.

'C' Company pushed on. Two more Germans surrendered to them, almost eagerly. They 'threw themselves down on their knees, and the older one was nearly crying', Cramer reported. He was not impressed by them. 'They were in baggy uniforms, trousers reinforced at the seat, and instead of lovely jackboots they wore thin canvas gaiters like us.'

And Cramer was not the only one to feel a certain disappointment at these specimens of the German Army. When he delivered his prisoners at the divisional cage, the glider pilot in charge cried: 'Christ – can't you do better than *this*?'

* The German Home Guard.

But in spite of the poor quality of the opposition, old men and young boys of the *Volkssturm* could still cause casualties. At the end of the day, when the Ulstermen started to count heads, they found they had lost 16 officers and 243 other ranks – nearly a third of the battalion. Similar losses were suffered throughout the Division, which, by dawn one day later, would have helped to throw back two strong German counterattacks and would, together with the US 17th Airborne, partially have destroyed the 7th and 8th German Parachute Divisions and the 84th Infantry Division.

The bridgehead on the eastern bank of the Rhine was firmly established by now, not as a mere toehold, but as a continuous front line with men and supplies pouring into it from the other side of the river. As Wynford Vaughan-Thomas reported that day:

All the way from the river bank, the roads are full of new troops moving up and infantry marching through the dust, and the farmhouses being taken over as headquarters, ration dumps being set up in the fields . . . all the signs of the army moving in, in a big way.[63]

Prime Minister Churchill thought so, too. In spite of the protests of his generals, he insisted on taking a short cruise along the other side of the Rhine to see for himself how the battle was progressing. This would be his first

(Above) **Members of the 6th Airborne man an anti-tank gun near Haminkeln.**

trip on the great river since he had sailed along it in a motor torpedo boat at the end of World War One.

At Wesel he scrambled ashore near a railway bridge, which had been partially destroyed and was still under enemy shellfire. Shells were now falling closer and closer, sending up great spouts of wild white water.

An anxious junior officer approached his Army Commander, General Simpson. 'We're bracketed in already, sir,' he said. 'One or two more tries and they may hit us!'

So 'Big Simp' caught up with the great man and said, 'Prime Minister, there are snipers in front of you. They are shelling both sides of the bridge and now they have started shelling the road behind you. I cannot accept the responsibility for your being here and must ask you to come away.'[64]

The look on Churchill's moonlike face at that moment reminded Chief of Imperial General Staff Alan Brooke of a small boy being dragged away from 'a sand castle on the beach'. Grasping a girder of the bridge with both hands, Churchill flung a glance over his shoulder at Simpson, as if daring him to pry him loose from it. Then, to everyone's relief, he let go and reluctantly walked back to the boat. Watching him go, the bespectacled, bird-watching Brooke thought of the remark that Churchill had so often made to him in the past: 'The way to die is to pass out fighting when your blood is up and you feel nothing.' As that moment Brooke thought Churchill really did wish to die at the front, as though he considered it a suitable end to his career, or a way to be freed of the uncertainties, the worries, the bitterness and defeats of the years to come.

But that wasn't to be. Churchill would live to a great age and would die in bed. Not so, many of his 'redcoats'. In the six weeks that were left of the war, many more of them would die a violent premature death.

(Below) Field Marshal Sir Alan Brooke, Monty, Churchill and General Simpson on the Siegfried Line.

US troops of the 14th Armored Division, 7th US Army advance past burning buildings in Gemunden.

APRIL

The rat race

It was a crazy time. The British called it 'swanning'; the Americans called it 'the rat race'. Both phrases meant that Allied armour had an almost free run on the other side of the Rhine. The Shermans and Churchills no longer fanned out over the countryside, as in France and Belgium, but went straight down one or two parallel roads, bypassing towns, leaving the infantry to mop up behind them. As a result, there were still vast tracts of countryside to left and right of the roads that were still in German hands.

For the Allied tankers, this type of tactic involved the reconnaissance elements crawling forward, 'daring' the enemy to reveal his position by firing at them. At point there would be one lone armoured car or tank, linked by radio to another one half a mile behind, which in turn was in visual contact with the armoured infantry in their half tracks further back. Sooner or later the unfortunate men at point, who knew they were 'in for the chop', as they phrased it, would run into a roadblock covered by anti-tank mines, *panzerfausts*, the deadly German rocket-launchers, and machine guns. Sometimes there might even be some last-ditch flak crew using their feared cannon in a ground role. Then the fun would start, and the men at the point would die. Immediately the armoured infantry, alerted by the second tank, would speed up the road, rolling expertly over the sides of their vehicles, fanning out to left and right of the roadblock, and begin to 'winkle out the Jerries', as the parlance of the day had it, with their bayonets.

Wynford Vaughan-Thomas of the BBC, watching a British armoured group advancing out of the Rhine bridgehead in that first week of April 1945, saw how they seemed 'to probe and stop and hesitate around corners, moving by little fits and starts'.[1] As he explained to his

radio audience back home, although the countryside seemed deserted, it wasn't. 'Being in the lead tank is one of the war's most uncomfortable jobs,' he went on, accurate as ever. For the retreating Germans played cruel and lethal tricks on the advancing Allies, making them pay for every yard of ground captured. They took, for instance, to chopping down the trees that normally fringed the Continental roads, then using them as road-blocks. In the end the tankers would get sick of approaching each tree cautiously in case it was booby-trapped. The lead tank would simply sweep it to one side – until the retreating Germans added a new dimension. They placed a gun crew immediately behind the felled treetrunk, hidden from sight by the foliage, who would get off one shell at point-blank range before fleeing for their lives, leaving behind another shattered Sherman and its dead crew.

Barriers would be covered by anti-personnel mines placed in the fields to both sides, so that when the armoured infantry bailed out to outflank their position they would find themselves stepping on 'bouncing Bet-tys' or 'deballockers' with horrifying results.

'Swanning' brought other problems, too. Apart from the ever present nightmare of supplies – how to get fuel and food up to the tankers, who were now advancing at the rate of up to twenty miles a day – there was the problem of prisoners. What was to be done with these thousands of shabbily-clad men of the Wehrmacht, whose sole possession now that they had lain down their arms was their *brotbeutel*, the cloth bag in which they carried their *Kommisbrot*, their iron-hard black bread?

Wynford Vaughan-Thomas, following up the 'swan', thought they were

. . . most polite and the most helpful of prisoners I've ever seen. One gentleman who spoke reasonable English stopped me on the road and inquired, 'Please. Where is your prison?' I told him it was about twenty miles to the rear. And he said, 'Oh but please, that is too far. You have not got one a little nearer?' I told him that if he waited a few days we'd have one right on his doorstep. But the irony was wasted on him. All he said was, 'Good. Now I will tell my friends. They are all tired, too.' And off he went into a wood to fetch out twenty more extremely shabby supermen who meekly lined up and awaited orders.[2]

Not all prisoners, however, were treated so consider-ately during that April. To the south, Patton's Third Army had cut off what was left of the 6th SS Mountain Division, which Patton's men had been fighting ever since February. In the confused fighting with large areas still in German hands, two thousand of the SS mountain-eers began to work their way around the American rear positions and thus escape the trap.

During the course of this withdrawal, the Germans captured a US field hospital complete with doctors and

Two young German soldiers caught attempting to ambush British tanks. Note the bazookas on their bicycles.

female nurses. The SS remained in possession of the hospital for one night only, moving out the next day without having harmed the medical personnel in any way. But, due to the nature of the 'rat-race', rumours spread faster than facts. Soldiers of Patton's 5th and 71st Infantry Divisions heard that the SS men had killed the male medical staff and raped the American nurses. Their revenge was terrible. That week there was an unspoken agreement among American troops not to take SS prisoners. As a result, 500 SS men were killed in cold blood before the surviving 800 of the 6th SS Mountain Division were allowed to surrender. The village chronicles of Hesse and Wurttemberg are filled with grisly stories of the *Amis* slaughtering any SS man they came across.

And not only SS men. At Aschaffenburg, the advancing Americans found German officers who had advocated surrender hanging from lamp posts in the streets. And according to General Bradley: 'Women and children lined the roof tops to pelt our troops with hand grenades. And from five nearby hospitals wounded German veterans limped in to join the battle.'[3] Whatever the truth was, any resistance left in Aschaffenburg was speedily brought to an end. The American infantry were ordered to withdraw and the bombers were whistled up.

'After the city's rubble had settled over the bodies of the dead,' General Bradley wrote in his account of the war, 'the Nazi commander Major von Lambert walked meekly out of a bunker carrying a white flag.'

There were tragic mistakes made too. Near the wooded ridges of the Teutoburger Wald just beyond the city of Bielefeld, which were held by NCOs of a nearby training school, the 2nd US Armored Division – the famed 'Hell on Wheels', created by Patton himself – was unable to advance any further.

Staff Sergeant Clyde Cooley, one of the few surviving veterans – he had been with the Division since North Africa – had just knocked out a German tank at fifteen hundred yards' range. 'All hell broke loose as everybody opened up,' he recalled later. 'Just as the fight started to end, a German truck filled with what appeared to be soldiers barrelled towards the tankers.'[4]

Major Hollingsworth, in charge of Cooley's battalion, ordered his gunners to wait till the truck was within range. They did so and then every tank gunner opened up with his half-inch machine gun. The truck caught fire and lurched to a stop, overturning and pitching its occupants out onto the road. Most of them had been killed by the gunners' bullets, but some were still alive, screaming in agony and fear. Their screams sounded high-pitched, somehow feminine . . .

Cautiously Hollingsworth and Cooley crept forward to investigate. To their horror they discovered that they had shot up a truckload of what the German soldier cynically called 'officers' mattresses' – female auxiliaries of the Wehrmacht.

(Above) German SS trooper who tried to surrender was hanged by his comrades.
(Right) Tiger tanks fording a river.

But the futility and tragedy of war were not all one-sided that April. Colonel Hines, who was now a veteran armoured commander, had crossed the Rhine and was busy with his tanks fighting retreating German infantry at what is today Frankfurt's International Airport. After the war he recalled:

I was standing in the turret of my tank talking on the radio telephone. The tank was swung round so that its tail end was towards Frankfurt . . . A shell which I did not see coming hit the deck of my tank . . . I remember seeing the explosion and trying to pull down the hatch with my left hand, only to discover that I had lost the fingers of it. I remember dropping down into the tank and finding that I was choking from bone and shrapnel fragments in my throat and scooping them out with the fingers of my right hand. I then remember trying to call to report our situation and to have someone take my place, but I am confused as to whom I called or what I said.[5]

It is not surprising that the young Colonel was confused. He had been blinded and had lost his nose, upper jaw and several fingers. In fact, Colonel Hines got through to his divisional commander, made his report correctly, and then added almost as an afterthought: 'You'd better replace me, sir. I'm wounded . . .'

Private or colonel, there were no distinctions made by Mars the God of War that month; he swallowed them all in his greedy maw, taking 'greenhorns' and veterans alike with equal cruelty.

Dudley Anderson, the nineteen-year-old para veteran who had survived Normandy, the Ardennes and the Rhine, had just reached the River Weser with his company of the 'Red Devons' when it happened to him.

Five German tanks, four of them the monstrous 60-ton Tigers, seemed to appear from nowhere and started beating up the paras. One of the paras scored a direct hit with the only anti-tank weapon they possessed, the Piat.* The paras cheered. But not for long. The other tanks were still coming at them. The Piat gunner fired again and again. In the end he scored seven direct hits and used up all his ammunition. The paras had only their rifles and bayonets left now. Helplessly they cowered in their trenches as the metal monsters rumbled towards them. They were trapped. Beneath the weight of those giant tanks, the soil would crumble into the trenches and bury them. One by one the men surrendered.

Anderson decided to stick it out. He buried his loot – a swastika flag, an SS officer's dagger and pistol – in the bottom of his foxhole, hoping to be missed. That wasn't to be. As his comrades filed off into captivity, they glanced at Anderson's hole, 'presumably to say a last farewell, thinking I was dead'.

The looks didn't go unnoticed. The last tank in the column stopped and the German tank commander climbed down. Pointing his pistol at the cowering Red Beret he said in perfect English: 'For you the war is over.'[6]

Even generals could not escape. Not far from where Colonel Hines suffered his terrible wounds, General Rose's 3rd US Armored Division was battling north across the wooded Hessian hills, in darkness and fog, in an attempt to link up with the American 2nd Armored on the other side of an area soon to be known as the Ruhr Pocket.

At first the 3rd's drive north was something of a drunken fiasco, the start of a tragi-comedy. Leading the column on foot through a particularly bad patch of fog, Lieutenant-Colonel Richardson found the first tank was getting closer and closer. When it finally nudged him in the back, he thought it wiser to jump into a ditch. Obediently the 30-ton monster followed him into the ditch, and stalled. Thereafter tank after tank bumped into the one in front of it, the drivers all stalling their engines. Richardson clambered out of the ditch and shouted angrily up at the first tank outlined stark black against the fog, 'What the hell happened to the tank commander? . . . What's going on?'

One of his young officers clambered up the turret and peered inside. 'Something's wrong, sir,' he called down in a shaken voice. 'There's champagne all over the floor of the tank, sir.'[7]

Five minutes later Richardson discovered why. The column had looted a whole warehouse full of champagne, back at the ski resort of Brilon. They had been drinking all night, ever since leaving Brilon. (In fact, it seems that everybody was getting drunk during the drive north; in the neighbouring resort town of Winterberg, American troops fought SS men up and down the corridors of the town's best pre-war hotel – slinging empty champagne bottles at each other!)

An angry Colonel Richardson radioed back to Brilon, telling his executive officer to turf the rest of the tank force out of town and move up front. 'Throw the champagne out and keep all the hatches open!' he ordered, reasoning that the cold damp fog would soon sober up his drunks. Then, walking back to his jeep, he passed an ambulance that somehow or other had found itself up at point. A familiar figure grinned down at him inanely from the cab and said thickly, 'Colonel, we ought to go back to Brilon . . .' It was the MO, nicknamed 'Doctor Scattergood'; he was the one who had instigated the looting of the champagne.

Richardson's reply is not recorded.

The more or less sober column pushed on. About one hour later it bumped into a group of determined young SS tank trainees at the Wehrmacht's big tank range outside Paderborne. The comedy was over now. It was time for the tragedy to begin.

Just as the firing commenced, Richardson received a message by radio stating that 'Big Six' was coming up to visit him. At that particular moment Richardson could have done without 'Big Six'; he had other problems on his hands. But there was nothing he could do about it. 'Big Six' always believed in commanding from the front – hadn't he been trained by Patton? – and nothing was going to stop him.

'Big Six' was the code-name for General Maurice Rose, the son of a rabbi, who had worked his way up from private to general – no mean feat in the prejudiced pre-war US Regular Army. He was not a likeable man; he was too ambitious and very hard on his officers, having them court-martialled at the drop of a hat. But he was an excellent fighting soldier, who did not shrink from the danger of battle.

This night he got it. Although Richardson radioed back, 'Don't send Big Six this way,' Rose was already on the road and had bumped into the expected trouble. As was typical in the confused fighting of the 'rat race', German tanks had cut off the end of Richardson's column. Now in the foggy darkness, General Rose's party stumbled into the Germans blocking the road, but somehow managed to escape. In spite of the near disaster, the General ordered his party – two jeeps, an armoured car and a motorcycle – to take a side road and

* A crude spring-loaded weapon, which had a punch like a mule and was often more dangerous to the operator than to the enemy.

130

An American tank supports infantry as they dash for cover.

continue northwards. This little convoy had just breasted a rise when out of the gloom a big tank appeared. Some of the Americans thought it was the big new Pershing, which had just been introduced into the European theatre, and were urging that the General should close up to its protection. Then one of the officers identified the squat metal monster standing there in the fog. 'It's a Tiger!' he yelled in sudden alarm.

Immediately there was hasty confusion. The drivers gunned their engines and started to flee. Not Rose's driver. In the lurid flames of a red flare, he could see one of the Tiger's guns starting to train on General Rose's jeep.

A German stuck his head out of the Tiger's turret and indicated with a jerk of his machine pistol that the Americans should surrender.

'I think they want our guns,' Rose said miserably.

Reluctantly Major Bellinger, Rose's aide, and T/5 Shaunce, the driver, started to unbuckle their shoulder holsters. Rose, however, who stood between the two men, had to reach down to his waist to unfasten his pistol.

The nervous young SS tank commander misunderstood the movement. He pressed his trigger, the Schmeisser chattered, the General was hit. He crumpled to the ground, his chest ripped open. Bellinger flipped backwards into a ditch and Shaunce leapt behind the tank out of the line of fire. Both were saved, but General Maurice Rose was dead.

On the following morning, two 3rd Armored Sergeants, Owen and Hauschild – who had also been ambushed but had escaped, taking with them one hundred German prisoners – reported back to the Division. There they were ordered to return to the scene of the ambushes and try to find the Commanding General's body.

They did. Rose had been left lying where he had fallen, his maps and pistol untouched, as if the SS had not realised they had killed a general. Sergeant Owen pocketed the pistol for the General's family back in the States, while Hauschild found a blanket. Roping the body into the blanket and placing the helmet on the chest as a mark of respect, they started to drag the dead General back to their own lines.

Here they were confronted by a green replacement lieutenant who asked the weary men what the hell they thought they were doing, treating a two-star general with such disrespect.

Owen flared up. He had left several friends back there, lying dead on the road. He wasn't taking any smart talk from a 'shave-tail second looey'. He told the young officer off, in no uncertain manner. He was promptly arrested and turned in for a court-martial.

To some of the doughs of the 3rd Armored it seemed a fitting end to the whole affair. After all Rose had been a feared martinet all his fighting career.

Eisenhower for his part, hearing of General Maurice Rose's death, ordered that the Ruhr Pocket which Rose had helped to win that April Fool's Day should be renamed in the dead man's honour 'the Rose Pocket'.

There were humorous moments too in the great 'swan' that month. Islands of Allies were being surrounded by vast numbers of enemy civilians. For now the Allies were pushing deep into the heart of the Ruhr, one of Germany's most thickly populated areas, from which the war-weary civilians had refused to be evacuated at the Party's orders.

One British infantry battalion, for example, attacked a large sugar factory on the outskirts of the town of Rheine, cleared it of the enemy (or so they thought) and then, as was the universal custom, began to look for loot and souvenirs. This time the 'loot' turned out to be on the hoof, in the shape of several buxom Russian women who had been working in the factory and had hidden in its cellars during the fighting. The hated fraternisation ban did not apply; the Russians were allies, after all, for the time being anyway, and the women were willing, very willing. The delighted infantrymen wasted no time.

A small orgy had just commenced in the cellars when there was a fresh outburst of firing. German snipers had concealed themselves in the cellars, just waiting for an opportunity like this. They caught the Tommies with their trousers down, figuratively and literally. The soldiers and the women scattered madly for cover. But some were not fast enough. They were hit.

One of them, a sergeant, was later being carried up the stairs from the cellar on a stretcher, lying face-down, his khaki trousers down about his ankles, a nasty red flesh wound scoring his pale buttocks. 'Shot on the job,' he moaned to the unsympathetic soldiers. 'What a bloody war!'*[8]

Speeding up a German road at his usual breakneck speed, Patton came upon two GIs 'breathing down the necks of two German girls'. 'Stop!' he barked at Mims, his driver. There was a screech of protesting rubber as the vehicle shuddered to a halt. *What the so-and-so do you mean by fraternising with those so-and-so German so-and-sos?*' (thus Colonel Codman recorded his boss exploding).

One of the GIs unwound himself from his partner. 'Sir,' he said easily, 'these here are two Russian ladies who have lost their way, sir. We are trying to learn their language, sir, so as to direct them properly.'

For a moment Patton gave the GI the full benefit of his 'War Face, Number Two'. Then he relaxed. 'Okay,' he

said, 'you win!' and turning to his driver he snapped, 'Go ahead, Mims.'

But once out of earshot he shook his head in wonder at the audacity of the man, murmuring: 'That really is a new one . . .'[9]

Captain Foley, whose first attempt at looting had ended abortively in Goch, was strolling around the farm in which his troops was billeted for the night. Suddenly he stopped, hardly able to believe his luck 'as I saw, nestling warmly in a bed of straw, a delectable speckled brown egg!'

After years of Army powdered eggs, and the one egg per week *per-haps* back in England, he was beaming with pride as he showed it to his men. He was immediately surrounded by 'an admiring throng of whistling tank crews'.

'How would you like it, sir?' one of his men asked cheekily. 'Boiled, fried, scrambled or poached?'

'I think I'd like it boiled,' Foley answered nonchalantly, 'with a little brown bread and butter.' But he had to settle for hard-tack ration biscuits.

Everyone watched the delicacy being prepared. Four separate watches timed it and a sprocket spanner, normally used to tighten tank tracks, was found to serve as an egg cup. Finally it was done to perfection. Foley spread out his 'fairly clean' khaki handkerchief like a napkin. The others looked on enviously. The feast could commence.

'With a great flourish, I tapped the end with my spoon and was rewarded with a resonant and crystal-clear "ding".' Foley frowned and tried again. The same thing happened.

A stunned silence had descended upon his men. Suddenly one of them flung his head back and yelled, '*It's a pot-egg!*'

There was a roar of laugher on all sides; 'people who had been cursing each other the previous day slung their arms around one another and wept tears of merriment'. As for Foley, he glared at his pot egg and thought it a 'typical example of German thoroughness'.[10]

But even if the majority of the soldiers found these antics funny, there were some who were sickened by the behaviour of their comrades, looting, wrecking, seducing, using their cigarettes, chocolate and coffee to entrap the Germans, especially the women, who had not seen such things for years.

In Private Atwell's section of medics, for example, the supply sergeant Joe Mortara was constantly trying to tempt German women into bed with him. Holding out half a bar of chocolate he would murmur enticingly, '*Schlafen . . . Schlafen . . .*'

'Now that's a goddam shame,' protested Phil, one of Atwell's buddies, 'to tempt women with little kids who

---

* After the war, the division to which this sergeant belonged was given a bulk award of Dutch medals. It was decided to give them to soldiers who had been wounded three times – and he fell into this category. So for the rest of his army career he had to bear the sneer: 'When yer kids ask one day "How did you win yer medal, Dad?" yer'll never be able to tell 'em, Sarge!'

Comrades throw bottles down to fellow looters.

haven't enough to eat!'

One morning – the same morning that it was announced there would be a fine of sixty-five dollars for any GI who spoke to a German civilian – the men lined up to receive an orange each, the first fruit they had received for weeks. They were watched by a thin, sickly-looking woman holding a skinny baby in her arms. Phil took his precious orange and gave it to the woman.

'They want to fine me, court-martial me, let them,' he said. 'I don't care who they are and what they've done. It's a woman and a child and they're hungry. They can have half of anything I've got.'

Later that same day, when Sergeant Mortara tried the same old trick with his chocolate on the sick-looking woman, Phil exploded. He had just received four parcels from home. Now he put together a bundle of goods from them and placed them in front of the woman. '*Fer der kinder,*' he said in broken German. '*Mit obgekochter Wasser. Suppe.*'*

The German woman broke into tears and tried to kiss Phil's hand.

Joe Mortara wasn't so pleased. 'Hey, what's the matter with you?' he asked angrily. 'Here I am, I got the chocolate bar all ready, and you come along and spoil everything.'

'I'm sorry, Joe,' Phil answered, 'but I'm going to continue spoiling it for you. If they want to go to you voluntarily, well and good. That's their business. If it's through hunger, *no*!'

'Jeeze, you don't have to be *so* friendly with them,'

Mortara moaned; and Atwell noted that he wrapped up the Hershey bar 'for use some other time'.[11]

By now superior commanders had virtually lost control over their far-ranging units. Previously the men had mostly lived and fought in empty countryside, their bed for the night a hole or at best a barn. Now they were in villages, towns, large cities, taking just what they pleased, doing whatever they wanted without anyone to stop them. The only control now was in the hands of NCOs or younger officers who were often too inexperienced to exercise it.

As US General Franklin Davis, then a major, wrote later, 'There were new benefits to being victors.' They were conquering enemy territory now, instead of liberating the countries of the Allies. They often slept in houses, apartments, taverns, hotels, even sumptuous villas. Once a town fell to them, their billeting parties had only to select a good spot, tell the German inhabitants '*Raus!*' and they were in.[12]

But discipline was becoming a problem. Many GIs violated the orders against looting; they stole and mailed home cameras, silverware, assorted bric-a-brac. Incidents of rape by GIs were on the increase.

Discipline in the British and Canadian armies was stricter, but Montgomery's frontline troops did their share of looting too. German prisoners-of-war *expected* to be searched and have their possessions taken from them. They would advance on their captors, pale and scared, already taking out their wallets and unstrapping their wrist-watches. '*Tick-tock fuer Tommy!*' they would

* 'For the children. With boiled water. Soup.'

133

cry. They thought it was one way of ensuring they weren't shot on the spot.

But the ordinary civilians were not prepared for the brutal manner in which rough, tough soldiers took over their homes: breaking down doors or hammering on them with the butts of their rifles; or simply throwing the whole weeping and wailing family out onto the street, while they 'searched' the house. Mostly the infantry took silly 'souvenirs' – top-hats, dress swords, German policemen's leather *shakos* – things they would sooner or later be forced to abandon because they had to carry everything on their already overladen backs.

The rear-echelon troops were different. They had vehicles and they had permits, which got them through the 'stop-lines' thrown across the roads to the rear by Redcaps to stop looting and desertion. The rear-echelon men went in for looting on a grand scale. Wild rumours circulated among frontline troops of base colonels, even generals, shipping back Mercedes, fine china, Oriental carpets and the like all the way to England. There was even the tale of a well-known air marshal who salted away a fortune in looted German goods on a small Greek island. *

In April that year, frontline vehicles returning to the rear to pick up supplies were all equipped with a small wooden Priority board in the windscreen: 'PRIORITY – CARRYING LOOT' some jokers scrawled on them. But the drivers weren't always joking.

In the American Army, where looting was almost universal, not even the military police could be relied on to remain honest. And among frontline troops they were known as the 'lootwaffe' – a pun on the name of the German Air Force, the Luftwaffe.

Atwell, becoming progressively sicker of what was happening in Germany, was on the move again. His company pulled in at a 'higgledy-piggledy village' that looked 'like a page from Mother Goose'. The men dropped from their 'deuce-and-halfs' and immediately began breaking into the thatched, timbered houses. Atwell went into an old woman's kitchen to sit down and have a rest. Suddenly two infantrymen battered down the kitchen door, which was open all the time.

'Has this place been looted yet?' they cried.

The old woman began to weep, covering her wrinkled face with her apron.

'Hey, get her the hell outa here!' one of the infantrymen yelled. 'What's she bitching about anyway? Go on, ya old bastard, get out!'

* There are undoubtedly old men alive today in the UK and USA who are still sitting on a fortune in looted art works, such as the Hohenzollern crown jewels. Even as I write this, a work of art which disappeared in 1945 turns up and is auctioned off for a fortune at Christie's, New York. There are others, still prominent in business, who started up back in the late forties with the loot they had smuggled out of beaten Nazi Germany.

Soldiers of the 9th Army turn a blind eye to looters in Lippstadt.

The woman fled.

Atwell went out into the yard but he hardly noticed the sun streaming down. Suddenly he was overwhelmed with misery. 'God,' he told himself, 'I'm tired of this, tired of the war, of human beings – *of everything* . . .'[13]

As for the top brass this April, they were scrambling over each other in their last eager efforts to win as much personal prestige as possible before it all ended. They vied with each other to capture well-known German towns. The banner headlines in the newspapers back home – *'Patton Captures X', 'Hodges' First On the Rampage in Saxony'* and the like – would soon be over. They would have to return to the drab obscurity of the peacetime army once more, stationed in some remote camp where the highpoint of their existence would be the bourbon-and-poker session at the officers' club on Saturday nights. They had all experienced the same thing as young officers at the end of World War One. Now they were fighting another sort of battle – the battle to win prestige.

That month the most important town in Hodges' First Army area was the Saxon capital, Leipzig. Courtney Hodges, who had seen himself reduced in rank from Lieutenant-Colonel to lowly Captain in 1918, was determined his Army would capture the place before the Russians took over. The task was given to the veteran 2nd US Infantry Division, under the twenty-two-year-old Captain Charles MacDonald.

After being wounded in the Bulge and four months of solid combat, in such a state that he could become tearful 'at the drop of a hat', MacDonald was in the middle of a fire-fight with some retreating Germans when he was asked by one of his subordinates, Lieutenant Whitman, accompanied for some reason by a German officer, 'Want to capture Leipzig?'

'Do I want to do *what*?' MacDonald gasped incredulously.

'Just what I said,' Whitman grinned. 'This is an Oberleutnant from Leipzig and his CG wants to surrender the city . . . without a fight.'

A spontaneous cheer went up from MacDonald's weary begrimed company. They had been fighting Leipzig's defenders for a week now; this was great news.

MacDonald hesitated. A mere captain of US infantry did not simply go in and capture one of Europe's greatest cities just like that. This would have to go through 'channels'. It did. From battalion to regiment, from regiment to division, right up to Corps and then to Army itself. Later MacDonald wondered if Eisenhower himself had not been informed. In the end, however, the lowly captain received permission from the regimental executive officer, who merely said: 'All right. Keep in touch with your battalion and go ahead. Let me know how you come out.' MacDonald was flabbergasted.

As he later recorded: 'Now that I had the necessary authority, I almost wished they had refused. But there would be no refusing the excited soldiers around me. They rushed to get seats in the two jeeps.'

So the young Captain and his men set off to capture the great Saxon city, last taken by no less a person than the great Napoleon himself. As they drove into Leipzig they found themselves surrounded by teeming crowds. Thousands of armed Germans simply stood and stared as they passed. They were cheered by British and American prisoners-of-war, some on crutches, with tears streaming down their faces 'as the GIs smothered them with cigarettes and K-rations'.

Finally Captain MacDonald and his happy band of excited GIs were ushered into the presence of Police General von Grolman. There ensued a somewhat confused discussion in a mixture of German and English – which wasn't helped much by the liberal quantities of cognac offered to the Americans. The Police General said he would surrender his police, but he could not guarantee what the soldiers of the Wehrmacht might do then. More cognac circulated. Somehow the subject of surrender got forgotten. The Police General asked what the divisional patch of the 2nd Infantry Division signified – it was an Indian head. So the Americans started leaping round the room in an approximation of an Indian war dance, complete with much whooping. Lieutenant Whitman, who was now very plastered, draped a blanket around his shoulders, stuck his fingers behind his head like feathers and cried, 'Me Indian! Me Indian – woo..woo..woo!'

The Germans loved it. More cognac was served. Whitman produced K-rations and tossed an extra box to the Germans. 'A prize in every package!' he cried drunkenly. They were wild with delight at the contents of the US Army rations. More cognac appeared – only this time it was served by a pretty girl in a starched white apron and short skirt. MacDonald's eyes wandered to her shapely legs. The civilian who was serving as a very poor interpreter noticed MacDonald's reaction and said in broken English, with much rolling of his eyes, 'You like Fraulein, no?'

Hastily, trying to save face, MacDonald declined.

A toast was proposed. After so much cognac, MacDonald neither knew nor cared 'whether it was long life to Adolf or not'. The crazy discussion went on . . .

MacDonald somehow got back to Battalion for further instructions, fearing for his life at the hands of the trigger-happy black soldiers who were now serving with the 2nd. He was ordered to pull his men out. He made the dangerous journey back into Leipzig once more.

A lot more cognac had flowed under the bridge in his absence. A real binge was taking place, in fact. Whitman had taken a fancy to a pretty blonde who happened to be the mistress of one of the officers present at the crazy party. *'Fraulein schlafen mit der Leutnant,'* he kept insisting drunkenly. Finally one of the German officers ordered the girl to do so. But just as she was preparing to

US troopers hunt for snipers in the rubble of Waldenburg.

sacrifice her virtue for peace and international understanding, Lieutenant Whitman passed out.

In the end MacDonald did manage to get his men back to their own lines, whereupon they all crawled straight into their sleeping bags. But MacDonald could not get to sleep at first. His mind was too full of the events of that night, 'which seemed ridiculous and unreal and I wondered how they could really have happened. I saw the headlines which I had envisioned when we first started on the zany mission fading away into nothing.' As he finally drifted into sleep he thought, 'Perhaps later in the day we would attack the city and enter like civilised soldiers, not like fugitives from a lunatic asylum.'

It was a pious hope. Next day they marched into Leipzig to discover that the US 69th Infantry Division had taken it. While MacDonald and his men had been drinking cognac in the Town Hall, the 69th had been engaged in a bitter fire-fight close by, with three American tanks being knocked out during the engagement. It was typical of the 'rat race'.

Later MacDonald's men discovered 2,000 cases of champagne. The result was predictable. As MacDonald related after the war:

To the casual observer, the Gohlis section of Leipzig might have been a dead city, but I knew that behind those blackout curtains, a host of GIs were having riotous celebrations . . . The more attractive *frauleins*, it had been found, had not been evacuated. Non-fraternisation rules were forgotten behind the anonymity of the blackout curtains. Every GI was a king for a night and his kingdom consisted of girls and champagne and wonderful soft beds and a roof over his head.

One man slept with a German opera singer![14]

While the GIs enjoyed their victory, another world was ending for some behind those same blackout curtains. For those deeply involved in that National Socialist dream of a '1,000 Year Reich', there was no future. For them there was only the cut-throat razor, the bullet, the L-Pill.

Edward Ward, one of the two correspondents who had entered Leipzig with the 2nd Division, searched the town that same day looking for a good story for the BBC. He found it in the Town Hall:

In one room, which had been the *Oberburgermeister*'s council room, was a grisly spectacle. Three Volksturmers lay sprawled dead over the tables, with pools of blood on the floor – they had committed suicide. By the side of one was a bottle of cognac and a half-empty glass. He'd evidently needed courage.[15]

The caretaker led Ward and the others to the Chief-Mayor's own office, opening the door with a bunch of keys hanging from his belt. Ward went in. 'Anyone there?' he shouted. There was no reply. He penetrated

deeper into the luxuriously furnished, panelled room. There he found them. 'Seated at a large desk was *Oberburgermeister* Freyberg, his hands on the table, head tilted back.' He was dead. Opposite, in the armchair, sat his wife. She too was dead, as was the third member of the *Oberburgermeister*'s family, a flaxen-haired, twenty-year-old girl wearing glasses. On the desk was a phial, with its stopper lying beside it – the poison with which the three of them had killed themselves the previous day.

The caretaker opened another locked door, where 'Chief City Treasurer Doktor Lisso lay slumped on his desk'. On the sofa opposite sat Lisso's wife. Once again, they and their daughter, wearing a nurse's uniform, had committed suicide rather than face the years to come when they would have to answer for the cruelty of the regime that they had supported so whole-heartedly.

Alfred Freyburg, Mayor of Leipzig, lay sprawled across his desk after committing suicide.

Ward shook his head. He had his story, but it wasn't a pleasant one, even if these dead Germans – and there were more of them throughout the building – were the enemy. He ordered the caretaker to lock the doors once more. Let the Germans clean up their own mess. Silently and thoughtfully, he walked back out into the spring sunshine.

But it was not only American generals who sought to capture prestige objects in that last week of April, 1945. The French Army had been the last army to cross the River Rhine. One month before, General de Gaulle had sent a telegram to his First French Army commander:

My dear General, you must cross the Rhine even if the Americans are not agreeable and even if you have to cross it in boats. It is a matter of the greatest national interest. Karlsruhe and Stuttgart await you, even if they do not want you.[16]

So, at two thirty on the morning of March 31st, a single rubber dinghy paddled by a Sergeant Bertout and ten men of the 3 Régiment de Tirailleurs Algeriens crossed the Rhine at Speyer.*

Thereafter the French had raced through Southern Germany spreading terror, just as they had done in the days of the Sun King and Napoleon the Great. More, they captured prestige objectives that had been assigned to the US Army. Freudenstadt, a pretty resort in the Black Forest, was seized and set on fire, and then for

* Of all the score of crossing sites over the great river that I have visited for this book, the smallest and last, i.e. the French one, is the only one recorded today by a permanent memorial (at Speyer).

three days was subjected to systematic rape and looting. Stuttgart, which had been assigned to the US Army, was captured by the French and held against protest, until Eisenhower finally stepped in and threatened to cut off all supplies to the First French Army. Only then did they withdraw.

But in this last week of April, there was one objective that the French were determined to secure for themselves, although again they would be poaching on the territory of the US Army. This time their aim was to seize the ultimate prestige objective of all. It had absolutely no military value, but it did have tremendous symbolic value for de Gaulle and his shaky military government back in France. It was Hitler's own home, *Der Berghof*, situated high in the mountains above the resort town of Berchtesgaden.

The task was given – unofficially, of course – to General Leclerc's 2nd French Armoured Division, which didn't belong to the First French Army but to General Haislip's US XVth Corps, part of Patton's Third Army.

Now Leclerc, who had fought his way through Africa, France and Germany for four long years, broke off all contact with Haislip and set off through Bavaria in an attempt to beat other American units to capture Hitler's mountain retreat.

Opposition was minimal – from the Germans, at least. As Gaston Eve, son of an English father and French mother who was serving with the 2nd, recalled after the war: 'We kept rushing on, day after day. A few shots were fired at us here and there, but there was little fight left in the Germans.'

Emil Fray, another half-Englishman, remembers, 'We pushed on very fast in competition with the Americans. We were operating in groups again and ours had a pretty straight run through, with only odd spots of opposition. The destruction in all the German towns was tremendous and delighted us . . . Everybody seemed to be waving white flags and nobody knew anything about Hitler.'

But if the Germans offered little opposition to these Frenchmen, going it alone and without orders, the Americans did. Both the 101st Airborne Division and the US 3rd Infantry Division, commanded by John 'Iron Mike' O'Daniel, wanted the honour of capturing Berchtesgaden, too. Indeed O'Daniel had ordered, without any authority from higher up, that all approach bridges across the Saalach River, which effectively formed a barrier against anyone trying to reach Hitler's home, should be guarded and that no vehicles except those of the 3rd be allowed to cross.

Now, however, French troops had appeared out of nowhere and were blocking *his* approach. As Haislip recalled after the war, 'I soon lost him [Leclerc] in Germany. Suddenly there was a phone call from the divisional commander [O'Daniel] complaining the French had appeared and were getting in the way. I said, "Just *you* block the roads and that will stop them." '

Frightened civilians hurry through the streets of wartorn Bamberg.

The last known photograph of Hitler as he is rewarding his young troops.

In his turn, the thin aristocratic French General now appealed to Haislip, only to be told by the American: 'You aren't supposed to be there at all. You've had Paris and you've had Strasbourg, you can't expect Berchtesgaden as well.'[17]

Naturally enough, this did not satisfy Leclerc – not when the glory of France was at stake. He ordered his men to go all out for Berchtesgaden and damn the Americans! Driving with Leclerc in his jeep, Colonel Chatel remembers, 'I was racing ahead with the General . . . when, on two separate occasions, American military police on traffic control tried to stop us. He wanted to go, go, go and he told me to drive right at them and make them jump. I did and they did!'

After pausing to shoot some renegade young Frenchmen who had fought in the SS for the Germans,* Leclerc finally found himself stopped by 'Iron Mike' O'Daniel's sentries on the River Saalach. Leclerc demanded to see 'Iron Mike'. The American refused to see him, the loyal ally, but ordered his sentries to let Leclerc pass, though not his vehicles. Again the sour-faced Frenchman insisted he should be allowed to see his opposite number. O'Daniel stalled until he was certain that the *Berghof* was actually in the hands of his 3rd Division, while the French fumed below in Berchtesgaden; then he allowed the vehicles of the 2nd French Armoured to cross the Saalach.

Now Leclerc turned the tables neatly on O'Daniel. On the morning after the capture of the *Berghof* – or the 'Eagle's Nest', as the triumphant Americans preferred to call it – O'Daniel decided to hold a formal ceremony up on the mountain top. For representatives of such a great democracy, American generals were curiously fond of pomp and circumstance.

Only a few days before, O'Daniel's Corps Commander Haislip had held a full-scale review of his troops at newly captured Nuremberg. As the Army newspaper *Stars and Stripes* reported: 'The General stood under the Stars and Stripes – a flag of freedom replacing the swastika, the symbol of slavery – and watched his veteran troops parade through the square of the Nazi shrine city where Hitler ranted to his uniformed fanatics at annual party conventions.' Now 'Iron Mike' O'Daniel thought he could go one better.

Unfortunately for him, French troops of Leclerc's Division now held the approach roads to Hitler's home and they weren't allowing any Americans to pass. It was the Saalach River business all over again, with the French holding the trumps.

O'Daniel fumed. A long and heated discussion followed. Finally the two generals reached a compromise. Both the French and American flags would be raised above the ruins of the 'Eagle's Nest' at a joint ceremony.

---

* Their graves are still there – ironically enough, the only memento of the absurd French race to Berchtesgaden.

American and French troops mingle at Hitler's mountain retreat, the Berghof.

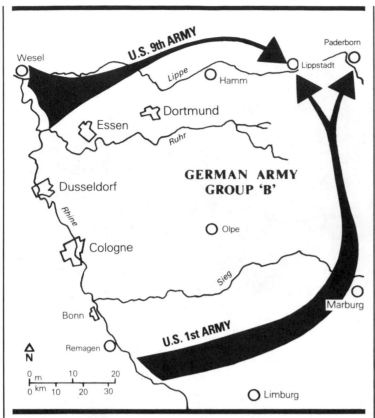

The Rose Pocket, the encirclement of Field Marshal Model's Army.

But even now things went wrong. After the ceremonial raising of the flags, the presenting of arms and saluting, the French flag fell down, leaving the Stars and Stripes alone to wave over the *Berghof*.

But O'Daniel's triumph was short-lived. Eisenhower personally stepped in and ordered him to get back to capturing his original objective – Salzburg, just across the border in Austria. Thus the French were left in possession until the US 101st Airborne arrived to take over.

French honour had been satisfied. A cynical, somewhat sad Leclerc – who knew, even if the American generals didn't, that the days of glory were over – allowed himself to be toasted in Goering's champagne. He gave the toast: '*Et maintenant, prenons une mentalité de baigneurs . . .*'* Dutifully his senior officers echoed his words. It was over. The generals had had their day.

In the second week of April, German Sergeant Walter Maxeiner was trying to make his way home. The thrice-wounded veteran of the campaign in Russia had fought his last battle. Now, trapped by the Americans in the 'Rose Pocket', he had discharged himself from Field Marshal Model's Army Group B and with some comrades was attempting to break through the American

* Literally: 'And now let's imagine we're holiday-making on the beach' (*baigneur* being a contemptuous word for those who laze around and prefer to be idle).

cordon. During the course of this attempt, he and his comrades came across a strange group of high-ranking officers standing about in a field, as if they did not know quite what to do with themselves.

Curious, Maxeiner went over to find out who they were. Almost immediately he recognised one of the officers, who sat on the barrel of an 88 mm cannon swinging his legs. The ex-sergeant stopped and stared in awe at the broad-faced officer with his jaunty cap and monocle. For it was no other than the legendary officer who had once been called 'the Führer's Fire Brigade', the man who had snatched victory out of defeat time and time again. It was Field Marshal Model, his former army commander!

'When Field Marshal Model, for that is who it was, saw us, he beckoned us over,' Maxeiner recalled long afterwards, 'and asked where our homes were, our age and military careers. For some time he discussed my tour of duty on the Eastern Front with me. It turned out that I had been in a unit under his command at the time.'[18]

Maxeiner plucked up enough courage to ask his former chief what he should do now. Model, trapped in the 'Rose Pocket', smiled sadly and said, 'Go home, boys. The war is over for us.' With a serious mien he shook hands with the sergeant and said, 'Good luck on your trip home and tell your men not to lose courage and continue to remain decent boys.'

Maxeiner saluted for the last time and went off, not knowing he would be one of the last people to see the legendary little Field Marshal alive.

Model moved on, too, wandering around the woods of the Sauerland area accompanied by a few aides, knowing that the Americans were hunting for him. Indeed, General Bradley had promised the bronze star to any US soldier who brought him in. No longer did he command great armies, where decisions had to be made instantly. Now he was plagued by indecision. What was he going to do next? He was haunted by thoughts of Field Marshal Paulus who had surrendered with his Sixth Army at Stalingrad. More than once he remarked to the others, 'A German field marshal does not surrender.' But what was the alternative?

On April 21st, Model reached a wood near the Ruhr industrial town of Duisburg, only a week before bitter street-to-street fighting broke out. His party was weary and despondent. One adjutant, Colonel Pilling, heard Model ask in quiet despair, 'What is left to a commander in defeat?' Then he answered his own question: 'In ancient times they took poison.'

A staff officer urged Model to surrender, just as some 400,000 of his men, including a score of generals, were currently doing in the Pocket. Model refused. 'I simply cannot do it,' he said without pathos. 'The Russians have branded me as a war criminal and the Americans would be sure to turn me over to them for hanging.'[19]

Late that same afternoon, accompanied only by Pilling, Model went deeper into the forest. 'My hour has come,' he told Pilling. 'Follow me.' In a secluded glade, he stopped and pulled out his pistol. 'You will bury me here,' he commanded.* Then he shot himself without any further comment. Field Marshal Model had followed Field Marshals von Kluge and Rommel into that special Valhalla which Hitler had reserved for his finest commanders. Suicide had claimed yet another of those generals who had brought Germany victory after victory in the great years.

Now his soldiers and the soldiers of all the other armies surrendering to the *Amis* in the south-west started to file dutifully into the POW cages in their thousands and hundreds of thousands. They were in for a shock.

Five months before, on Christmas Eve 1944, a German prisoner-of-war in Camp Hampton Roads, Virginia, noted that the Christmas Eve dinner given to him and his fellow prisoners by the Americans consisted of 'turkey filled with sage and onions, turkey giblets in gravy, cranberry sauce, mashed potatoes, candied sweet potatoes, green beans, asparagus tips, fruit cocktail, mixed pickles, rolls and butter, apple pie with cheese, ice cream'.[20] And this repast was served at the height of the Battle of the Bulge on the other side of the Atlantic!

Now, however, as Germany was brought to her knees, things had changed for the weary men in shabby field-grey uniforms as they entered the mass cages hastily erected the length of the west bank of the Rhine. Belsen, Buchenwald and Dachau had been discovered. Patton had vomited. Eisenhower had sworn revenge. These new prisoners were in for trouble.

Fourteen-year-olds and sixty-year-olds, some clad in shorts and some in pyjamas, a few naked save for underpants, without boots, without anything save perhaps a tin to hold whatever food the guards deigned to give them, they were herded behind the wire by soldiers yelling '*Mak schnell . . . mak schnell!*' It was a command that would haunt many of them, the survivors, for years to come.

In most cases the new camps were nothing more than open fields surrounded by concertina wire, guarded by aggressive young American replacements toting machine pistols. There was no accommodation. The prisoners' only cover from the wind and rain of April and the blazing sun of May were holes in the ground which they scraped with empty tins, cans, forks, even with their bare hands. Forced together with as many as 3,000 men packed in a square hectare, they were hopelessly over-crowded, standing next to each other in miserable, groaning ranks, some of them sinking from exhaustion into the sea of water faeces – for there were no latrines at

A German prisoner faces defeat.

first and many of the men had what they called 'thin shits'.

In the US Cage at Bad Kreuznach, not far from the Rhine – the 'Hell of Kreuznach', as it soon began to be called by its occupants – 560,000 men were incarcerated in an area intended for 45,000. Marzel Oberneder, a prisoner there, reported later to the post-war West German Committee of Investigation:* 'The ground was a sea of mud, one's toes squelching in wet boots.' Another POW in the same camp testified: 'Two comrades leaned against one another forming a kind of pyramid, coats over their heads against the rain. They stood there all night trying to keep dry.' Another reported: 'An old man stood next to me, suffering from a high temperature . . . Finally he sank down into the mud. Every time he turned, he slipped deeper and deeper into it until finally his faced was covered by it. He must have suffocated.'

More and more men were thrust into the camps by guards wielding pick-axe handles. Amputees were beaten with their own crutches. Food started to run out. Ex-Corporal Hans Friedrich of the Grossdeutschland

---

* Today he is buried at Vossenack War Cemetery near Germany's border with Belgium, along with thousands of the soldiers who died at his command in the bitter frontier battles.

* The Committee's report, *Bericht des Wissenschaftlichen Kommission der Bundesregierung z. Geschichte der deutschen Kriegsgefangen des 2ten Krieges*, is so revealing that the West German government has never dared to publish it in full for fear of offending their NATO allies.

Division, an elite formation, testified: 'For a long time the only food was biscuits. Four tarpaulins full of them for every 1,000 men. Some men got only a handful of crumbs to last them all day.' Another ex-POW reported to the Investigators that the daily ration at his camp was 'three spoonsful of vegetables, a spoonful of fish, two prunes, one spoonful of jam and four biscuits' – and that for weeks on end.

Next to the great cage of Rheinbach, guarded suitably enough by men from the 106th Division, three-quarters of which had 'gone into the bag' the previous December during the Battle of the Bulge,* there was a field of clover when the camp was first set up. The starving prisoners ate it bare. Then they started on the field of grass next to it. Ex-Lieutenant Willers reported: 'We rubbed the leaves and shoots of the hedges into a powder and ate it. After fourteen days, the hedges looked like skeletons. We did, too.'

At Rheinbach, Willers recalled how 'the Americans used to fry steaks and pour the used fat into a hole in the earth, just outside the wire, perhaps to torment us. We made long sticks, stuck them through the barbed wire, dipped up the fat and licked it off the sticks. The *Amis* thought that great fun.'

Their bellies were bloated. Their teeth fell out. The camps became huge latrines. 'Rheinbach,' one of them recalled later, 'was simply a sea of urine from end to end.' Prisoners started to die. The American figures are that 3,053 prisoners-of-war died in those Rhenish camps in their first few weeks of imprisonment. The Germans, naturally, give much higher figures. Ex-Lieutenant Willers, for instance, maintains that in his camp alone two hundred men died daily.

The much vaunted German discipline and comradeship was fast breaking down, especially where men came from different units.** It was dog eat dog; every man for himself. Helmut Leitz, an eighteen-year-old who had just had one foot and a leg amputated at the knee, had to crawl back and forth through the mud to the water-point.[21] Not one single prisoner ever helped him in that painful progress. Other crippled soldiers made themselves little boards which they tied to their hands so that they could move through the mire more easily to the water and the latrine holes. Some who could not balance themselves on the poles suspended above the faeces tumbled in and drowned there horribly.

The rain was followed now by burning heat and there wasn't enough water. The strongest and fittest took their share and devil take the hindmost. One witness who had been imprisoned in the Kreuznach Camp reported that a great water container arrived one day. It was rushed by

* See '44.
** The British interned their one and a half million prisoners as complete units, leaving internal camp organisation and discipline in the hands of their officers. This saved much hardship.

A sentry of the US 15th Army stands over the German prisoners captured in the Ruhr Pocket.

the parched prisoners and overturned. That didn't stop the POWs. They crawled inside to lap up the precious fluid, 'boots hanging out of what looked like a gigantic overturned flower vase, licking the sides and grunting like animals while others wandered off sadly without a drop to drink'.

Ex-POW Josef Nowak recalled, 'The queue for water started at ten in the morning. Any who left his place had to start all over again at the end of a line of 30,000 men. Those who sat down and went to sleep were dragged forward by the collar by their comrades. Once, after standing in line for sixteen hours, I managed to reach the taps and started to fill my little tin. I poured the water down my parched throat from it and attempted to fill it again. But I received a great kick in the rear from the next man in line for my pains. I moved on hurriedly.'[22]

Corruption flourished. The prisoners sold everything to their guards for food – their watches, their medals, even their wedding rings. The internal staff who were now Germans – 'kitchen bulls', as they were called in the slang of the Wehrmacht – were equally corrupt. These 'capitalists', as they became known, had to be protected from the rest of their fellow prisoners. They were housed and protected in a special cage, for they were hated by the rest.

Officer-Cadet Tins recalled: 'Their meals were five times as big as ours . . . and they were terrible crooks, asking for rings and watches in exchange for a handful of biscuits. They wanted a hundred marks for a loaf of bread, a precious fountain-pen for three potatoes, and so on.'[23] Another prisoner at Rheinbach remembers the 'capitalists' having only three set phrases: '*What do you want? Where are you going? Get out!*'

Naturally, whenever the ordinary prisoners managed to get their hands on these *Kapitalistem*, justice was swift and rough. They were either beaten to death or drowned in the stinking mess of the latrines. When they were released from the camps after the war, they made sure they 'took a quick dive', in the parlance of their time; for they lived in fear of violent retaliation from their fellow ex-prisoners. It was wiser to change one's identity and move to another zone of occupation than the one where one had been a *Kapitalist*.

But outside the camps in Occupied Germany, life went on as if nothing had happened. Benno Tins, imprisoned at Koblenz-Lutzel, noted bitterly how on the street outside the wire 'well-dressed civilians, women and children and one single man, pass without a single glance in our direction'. Marzel Oberneder at his camp observed how 'girls dressed in white, driving in coaches, decorated with roses, hurry to the Corpus Christi celebrations . . . They didn't look at us.'

Now that the German *landser* was virtually beaten, nobody, particularly his own people, had much time for him. The civilians thought that these half-starved, filthy, lousy wretches in their dirty field-grey tatters had lost the war for them. They compared the prisoners unfavourably with the healthy vigorous Americans, who were the victors.

Predictably the prisoners turned sour and blamed their defeat on the Allies' overwhelming matériel superiority, their tanks, their planes, their guns. The 'terror raids' had weakened the will of the conscripts, who were a rabble of old men and young boys. As always in that nation, divided traditionally even in its own soul, everyone was to blame but themselves. Anything to avoid the truth – which was that most of them had simply lost the will to fight and had surrendered.

But not all of them gave up so easily. There were still approximately two million German soldiers under arms in the West and many of them were prepared to sell their lives dearly. In the last two days of April, 1945, three soldiers from the US 3rd Division alone won the Medal of Honor, for example, for feats of arms beyond the normal call of duty. And this was despite the situation reported by Fred Olsen, the *Time-Life* war correspondent: 'When the commanding generals of the 3rd and 45th Divisions impatiently phone the regiments to get their tails busting and move forward faster, the colonels and the majors and the captains merely smile tolerantly and take their time.'

Private Joseph Merrill of the 3rd Division's 15th Infantry Regiment did not take his time the day he won the Medal of Honor, his last day on this earth. Finding his company pinned down, he made a hundred-yard dash across open country under intense machine-gun fire. Firing his rifle at point blank range, he killed four Germans armed with sub-machine guns. He started for the nearest gun-pit. A grenade exploded and shattered his rifle. He continued, armed only with three grenades. Zigzagging violently to avoid the bullets cutting the air all around him, he heaved two grenades into the gun-pit, grabbed a German's pistol, and finished off the survivors.

Re-armed, he set off for the next machine-gun post, thirty yards away. He killed four more Germans in a trench. Suddenly his luck ran out. A bullet slammed into his belly and wounded him critically. But even this did not stop him. He staggered on, blood streaming from his shattered stomach. He heaved his last grenade into the gun-pit, finishing off the survivors with his captured pistol. In that same instant he was ripped apart by a vicious burst of fire at close range. He died instantly, a mere boy of twenty.

German resistance was so hard and desperate in places that, even at this late stage of the war, veterans cracked up under the strain. Staff-Sergeant Giles, who had survived the whole long campaign, was caught in a surprise artillery bombardment on the Danube. One of his best buddies was killed, a man named Hall.

Retribution on a German foreman by forced foreign workers.

It was too much for Giles, who had joined the US Army before Pearl Harbor and was one of the few real older soldiers of the US Army in Europe. 'Well,' as he wrote later to his wife, 'Jesus Christ, I just caved in. Just plain caved in. I began bawling and couldn't quit and couldn't help myself. Just sat there and shook and bawled.'

Another of Giles's company, an engineer called Jeff Elliott, was also there when the mortar bomb exploded and killed Hall. He watched in horror as 'the blood ran out of the bottom of the truck into a red pool on the ground . . . When I saw Hall's blood, I thought it was mine and I thought I was a goner.' He and another man named Diez decided to remove the body of the dead man. But he couldn't. 'The blood was still pouring out of him. I had to turn away and puke and then I started crying. I couldn't lay a hand on him . . . I was very ashamed after it was over. I liked Hall very much. I thought I would write to his wife, but I went and got drunk instead.'[24]

Desperate enemy troops still held the so-called Graebbe Line in Northern Holland. There were 120,000 of them and, ironically enough, nearly half of them were Dutch, whom the Allies had come to liberate. These Dutchmen of the 34th SS Division (Landsturm Nederland) knew there would be no future for them in liberated Holland,

so they were fighting bitterly to the very last. Although they were green and inexperienced, the Dutchmen were fighting over country they knew intimately and they made the Allies pay dearly for their gains.

Canadian Captain MacDonald of the 11th Armoured was racing into action with his Sherman when he saw the Dutchmen to his front get up and run. 'But one had the guts to stay behind with his bazooka near a railway embankment.' This lone SS man, still fighting on when most Germans were surrendering, fired his hollow-charge bomb, which whacked and boomed against the side of the Sherman. Fortunately for MacDonald, the British infantry packed on the deck of the 30-ton tank took the full blast of the bomb. When he pulled up to have a look at the bloody carnage of what was left of an entire infantry section, he was appalled and sickened. 'Holy catfish,' he recalled years later, 'what a mess!'[25]

In the third week of April, the enemy soldiers holding the Graebbe Line made a determined counter-attack on the Canadians holding the little town of Otterloo. Unable to resist the obvious pun, Matthew Halton of CBS radio called it the 'Battle of Otterloo'. He described how the enemy rushed a battery of Canadian artillerymen:

The gunners jumped to their field pieces and fired them over open sights at the oncoming Germans. When the enemy overran the guns, the gunners dug themselves in and went on fighting from their slit trenches with Sten guns, rifles and pistols. Not a single gunner surrendered and not a single gun was captured, but the Germans surged past the gun area and into Otterloo.[26]

They did not get through. The headquarters staff turned out to stop them. A desperate little battle developed in the narrow streets of the town. The Canadians' Colonel, firing from his hiding place beneath his caravan, shot two. His batman killed three. Nearly every member of the headquarters staff had 'at least one notch to carve on his gun. Some have as many as ten,' Halton reported to his listeners back home.

At the height of the battle, four Wasp flame-throwing carriers trundled into Otterloo. They rattled up a road along which more Germans were pouring, shouting at the top of their voices. Great tongues of flame spouted from the Wasps' cannon. The running Germans were engulfed in oily blue flame, and their yells of triumph turned into screams of agony. Later Halton counted '105 German dead, all terribly burned'.

Not far away, the British 49th Infantry Division – which had been in Holland so long that it was nicknamed the 'Nymegen Home Guard' – was also fighting its last desperate battles in that country. Moving through a shattered Arnhem, which Montgomery had failed to capture so many months before, the British infantry prepared to meet a counter-attack by Dutch SS.

One of those who moved out with them was nineteen-year-old Reg Dunkley, one of the seven surviving members of his company who had been in the fighting ever since Normandy. As he plodded through the ruins of the outskirts of Arnhem with the green replacements, Dunkley felt an eerie sensation, as if 'you had no right to be there and that someone was watching you in case you did something you shouldn't. You were looking over your shoulder all the time. The other lads felt it too.'[27]

That night Dunkley's 'D' Company successfully beat off the Dutch SS's attack, driving the survivors into a small wood where they dug in. Now Dunkley and a handful of his comrades were ordered to 'recce' the wood before the company attacked. They were all veterans, who had been in the fighting from the very start. 'So off we went, seven of us line abreast,' Dunkley recalled nearly forty years later, 'mostly armed with automatics . . .'

We had gone about 150 yards when the stonk opened up just like that. A distinct whistle of shells. No word of command was given to retreat. We just turned and ran like the dickens. The sergeant in charge was killed by the same shell which fell close to me.

I knew I was wounded. There was a stinging and a ringing in my ears. I knew my right kneecap had gone. You know at the dentist's, you can feel the grating of the instrument on the bone – so I could feel my kneecap grating . . . I couldn't

British troops patrol after the second battle of Arnhem.

speak and I thought I'd bought it because they were still shelling. I saw one of our chaps only the length of a small garden away from me, bending down. I shouted to him but I could make no sound.

How long it took the stretcher-bearers to come, I don't know. Not long, perhaps ten minutes. I didn't know the sergeant had been clunked behind me until I heard the stretcher-bearers say, 'Let's get Dunkley away first. The sergeant's gone for a chop.'[28]

So now there were only five left of the original Normandy veterans. *

* Reg Dunkley lost a leg, and twenty years later he developed epilepsy as a direct result of his wounds. Today, four decades after the war, he still suffers from what happened in that Dutch wood in April 1945.

Not far from where Dunkley lay seriously wounded on the edge of that wood, Private Bob Day of the 1st Leicesters was advancing with the rest of his battalion when he too came under a tremendous, frightening artillery bombardment. He had already been wounded the previous year by a mortar bomb at Salerno, but he had never experienced anything like *this* in his combat career in Italy.

Great jagged bits of metal were flying all over the place. When mercifully the firing ceased, I looked up in a daze, scarcely believing I was alive. Then I heard screams coming from the other side of the dell and I could see a young officer with one of his arms nearly severed. The poor chap was obliviously delirious and several of my section did what they could to comfort him before he was taken away on a stretcher.

I turned to have a word with the Bren gunner and saw that he was still leaning against the bank with his head bent forward. He appeared to be asleep so I nudged him. But he was dead. There was a tiny hole in his back and he must have been killed instantly.

The irony of it all was that the barrage hadn't come from the Jerry guns, but from our own. I can't remember his name, but he was a quiet, pleasant fellow who had told me only the day before that his wife had just had a baby.[29]

Yet another young man had died violently, never to see the child he had sired.

But the slaughter was slowly coming to an end. In the south, the Americans had already crossed the border into Czechoslovakia, while further north their comrades had crossed the Elbe and were pushing into what was now a kind of no-man's-land. Still further north, Montgomery's men had also crossed that river and were racing for the coast against token opposition. Soon they would link up with that other ally and it would be all over. Soon they would meet the Russians.

MAY

Elements of the 9th Armored Division of the US First Army roll into the burning town of Limburg in Germany.

Liberation

The first elements of the British 6th Airborne Division – eleven light tanks laden with Canadian paratroopers – reached the Baltic port of Wismar at one o'clock on the afternoon of May 1st, 1945. Before them lay two undamaged bridges carrying roads that led into the north-western part of the city. The paras hesitated. Were the bridges mined? As they considered what to do, a German officer strolled up and offered to guide them into the city.

Still they hesitated. Was the German officer going to lead them into a trap? In the end his calmness convinced them. They started to rumble forward. The 6th Airborne had thus reached the Baltic city before the Russians and effectively sealed off Schleswig-Holstein and Denmark from the Red Army.

Sporadic fighting broke out in the streets. German jets screeched in low. The Red Devils were forced to take cover. Were the Germans going to make a fight for Wismar after all?

Suddenly a bedraggled German officer came running up, hands raised over his head. 'Sorry we fired on you,' he gasped. 'We thought you were the Russians . . . Give us five minutes and we'll surrender.'[1]

The paras let him go again and rumbled on in their tanks towards the edge of the local Luftwaffe field, which was packed with planes. A light plane started to take off. One of the tanks sped after it. Carried away by the thrill of the chase, the British gunner pumped shell after shell at the German plane. But it seemed to bear a charmed life. As the tank braked at the end of the tarmac to avoid rolling into a drainage ditch, the plane took off and escaped. Moments later the bedraggled officer re-emerged from his bunker, bringing with him two hundred prisoners, who had surrendered willingly now that

Reduced to horse transport the last remnants of the German Army move on to Luneburg to surrender.

they realised they were not going to fall into Russian hands. As one tanker exclaimed, 'This is a proper Fred Karno's, this is!'*[2]

But the battle for Wismar was not all comedy. That same afternoon, Major Watts, a doctor with the 6th, was with a small convoy of jeeps driving through the outskirts of town when he came across a column of German wounded. Men being dragged along on carts; men stumbling forward on foot; men with blood seeping through their paper bandages, helping each other along, obviously in fear of their lives. Watts stopped his convoy. He spotted a nurse who was tending some amputees on the carts, and asked what was happening. She told him that they had been travelling in a troop train, heading west, which had run out of coal. As they were considering what to do next, the train had been attacked by a Cossack patrol. The Russians had sacked the train, robbing even the dying, shooting anyone who had attempted to resist. Before they left, they had swept the whole train with machine-gun fire.

Watts ordered his men to select the worst cases and put them on the stretchers fixed on the jeeps. He told the nurses and the rest to stay where they were until he could bring help. Five minutes later he returned from the Luftwaffe hospital, where he had unloaded the stretchers, to find the column vanished. Their fear of the approaching Russians had obviously been too great.

Now the paras had reached the centre of Wismar. Driving through the silent street, the young Red Berets could nevertheless sense those anxious civilians hidden in the shuttered, locked houses, hearts thumping with fear, wondering if the tanks were Russian.

In the lead, the 3rd Para Engineer Squadron secured the port installations. They rushed the port captain's office and commanded the Germans they found there to surrender. All of them, soldiers, sailors and civilians, obediently unbuckled their weapons and shot up their hands – all save one fourteen-year-old wearing the uniform of the Hitler Youth. '*Heil Hitler!*' he shouted defiantly and added in poor English, 'We will win the war!'

One of the paras, Sapper Jones, tried to make him stop shouting. In vain. Eventually he and a couple of others seized the lad by his bare legs, up-ended him, stuck his head in the nearest lavatory bowl, and flushed. That put an end to his defiant ranting.[3]

Now with the city centre and port in their hands, the paras began to push eastwards. They knew that the Russians could not be far off now, and they were cautious. They did not want any trouble with their unknown allies.

Shortly before nine, a group of the paras spotted two motorcycle combinations, followed by two lease-lend American scout cars containing seven ragged soldiers

and one buxom female soldier armed with a tommy-gun. As the paras came closer, they could see the eight strangers were ready for trouble, fingers crooked around the triggers of their weapons.

Suddenly they relaxed. They had recognised the British uniforms. There was much shaking of hands and mutual back-slapping. Bottles of vodka were passed around amid exaggerated expressions of goodwill and eternal friendship. Then abruptly they turned, as if at an unspoken command. They climbed back into their shabby rundown vehicles and returned the way they had come.

One hour later as the paras, exhausted by now and not a little drunk, stretched out on their requisitioned beds in the newly captured city, the Russians commenced

* World War I expression for a military mess (after the famous comedian); what the Americans called a 'snafu'.

The British 6th Airborne Division's first contact with Russian troops.

building a monstrous roadblock on the outskirts of Wismar. The Iron Curtain had already begun to descend.

American General Ridgway, commander of XVIII Airborne Corps to which the Red Devils belonged, was also worried about his men's dealings with the Russians. He didn't want them accidentally firing on one another. He needed to know exactly where the Russians were.

The only really mobile force that Ridgway had at his disposal was the US 7th Armored Division. He ordered them to send out a patrol to find the Red Army, which, according to Intelligence reports, was 'somewhere to the east – between fifty and a hundred miles according to

rumor'. So it was that a recent West Point graduate, twenty-two-year-old William Knowlton, set off that day with a small force of eleven armoured cars and twenty jeeps to find the Russians. With him he carried half a dozen bottles of looted Hennessy cognac, which he was to give to the first senior Red Army officer he met in order to persuade him to return with the Americans to Ridgway's lines.

From time to time Knowlton's patrol encountered little knots of German soldiers, but they threw away their arms when they saw the Americans and volunteered to go into captivity – without an escort. Knowlton let them go.

The Americans entered the small town of Parchim. There they were met by cheering civilians, standing six deep along the roads. German military policemen with sub-machine guns slung across their chests saluted smartly as they passed. Knowlton had the impression that the Germans regarded his force more as liberators than conquerors. Later he learned the Germans thought that the Americans were driving east to *fight* the Russians!

By nightfall Knowlton had still not met the Russians, so he decided to set up his command post for the night at a little inn at the village of Luebz and carry on the following morning. But unknown to him his presence had been reported to no less a person than General von Tippelskirch, commanding the 200,000-man 21st Army. Von Tippelskirch sent some staff officers to meet the young ex-West Pointer. A little later one of them radioed his divisional commander, General von Jungenfeld, that he had met 'an American captain' who was 'in command of twenty tanks'. That meeting must have been a very liquid one, for the unknown officer concluded his message to von Jungenfeld thus:

Both of us are tank leaders. With forty good tanks, we request you personally order an attack against the East, to start the morning of 4 May. We believe that with Hitler dead, it is the moment finally to defeat and crush the Russians and thereby Communism. Therefore we request you and expect from you a clear order of attack against the East and we are convinced that we will defeat and drive out the Russians and we are also sure that everywhere other comrades will immediately follow our example.[4]

Knowlton and his unknown German drinking-companion never did fight the Russians, though Knowlton later helped to bring about the surrender of von Tippelskirch's massive army to the US 82nd Airborne Division. However, that same evening, some Allied troops did actually fight their allies – the men of the 6th Airborne, the captors of Wismar.

The situation in the German port was chaotic. Hundreds of shabby Wehrmacht soldiers were milling around on the streets, wondering how and to whom they were going to surrender. In the port itself, among the scores of German Army vehicles abandoned on the quaysides, the displaced persons – Poles, Czechs and Russians – were looting happily. In the main square, the bodies of half a dozen German civilians dangled from the bandstand, hanged for firing on British troops. And everywhere the happy Red Devils were celebrating their victory with looted schnapps – and whenever their officers looked the other way, with 'bits of frat'.

The Russians from the other end of town were out looking for women too. That night twenty-odd of them appeared outside the big Luftwaffe hospital to which Major Watts had taken the seriously wounded Germans the previous day. One of the paras guarding the hospital

told them to go away, but the Russians had spotted the nurses standing at the window next to the paras. 'Frau . . . Frau komm . . .' they shouted, swaying unsteadily, for they had been drinking a mixture of V-1 fuel and looted potato schnapps. Then they became more threatening, waving their tommy-guns and yelling, 'Davai, davai! Frau komm!'[5]

Another para told them to 'bugger off' and waved his sten at them. Suddenly a shot rang out – and then another, then the rattle of a sten-gun . . . The Russians scattered as the fire-fight developed.

It didn't last long. Speedily the 6th Airborne officers restored order. But by the time they had done so, there were six or seven dead Russians sprawled out on the cobbles of the square below. The first fight between the erstwhile allies had taken place.

A great flood of German civilians and soldiers was desperately fleeing westwards, trying to reach the lines of the Western Allies before being overtaken by the feared Red Army. In those first days of May, there were nearly two million of them trudging westwards, carrying their pathetic bundles with them, all that they had been able to save from a lifetime of work, reaping a bitter harvest from the seed which Hitler had sown.

Many of them were hoping to make their escape by sea. Every available seaworthy craft had been pressed into service to transport these frantic refugees to the ports of Denmark and Schleswig-Holstein which were still in German hands. The German Navy, still operational, attempted to defend the convoys against Russian submarines now known to be active in the Baltic.

But it was not only civilians that the Germans were attempting to move by sea. Within sight of British troops occupying the port of Lübeck, three German steamers lay at anchor, packed with 10,000 civilians, all of them locked below deck and watched over by SS guards. For these were concentration camp inmates, evacuated from Neuengamme Concentration Camp near Hamburg. The SS did not want them to fall into Allied hands. They had even removed all the ships' life-belts to discourage prisoners from sneaking over the side. In effect, those prisoners in their striped pyjama-like uniforms were condemned men and women; their only chance of survival now depended on the speedy arrival of the British.

On May 3rd, 1945, the British arrived. By air. From their new fields in Occupied Germany, squadron after squadron of rocket-firing Typhoon fighter-bombers rose into the air to carry out some of the last raids of the war. The targets were German shipping and coastal ports.

By midday they were ranging along the Bay of Lübeck. The first of the three prison transport ships was spotted, the *Athen*. The Typhoons zoomed down low. Skimming in over the water, rockets hissing from beneath their wings like flights of angry red and white hornets, they attacked the *Athen*. But just at that

Peter Kohn, a German war criminal was executed by the authorities for the murder of an American pilot.

moment, the *Athen*'s flak opened up, filling the sky with grey puffballs of smoke.

The Typhoons veered away. Captain Nobmann of the *Athen* seized his opportunity. He ran the ship against the quay at Neustadt, immediately hoisting the white flags and ordering the hatches opened to free his prisoners. Nearly two thousand of them sprang ashore, free and safe at last. The British had liberated them.[6]

But there would be no liberation for the men and women imprisoned on the two other ships, the *Thielbek* and the *Cap Arcona*.

At two thirty that afternoon, Flight Lieutenant Martin Rumbold's section of Typhoons came into sight. They saw the flak streaming up from the *Athen* and swept down to attack the other two ships. Rumbold, a twenty-two-year-old holder of the DFC, a veteran of the African Desert campaign and Normandy, picked as his target the *Cap Arcona*.

Line abreast, the nine machines hurtled down to attack. Rumbold, an insurance man in peacetime, now unwittingly became the man who caused more deaths from air attack than probably any other pilot in the RAF. He hit his firing button. Eight rockets streaked towards the motionless ship. Seconds later the rest fired. It was a terrifying salvo, which even impressed Pilot Officer Don Saunders flying below the rest. Nearly forty years later he recalled: 'Sixty-four rockets raced towards the ship. One went into the sea. The remaining sixty-three struck it. It was like a giant fireball bursting!'

Heinrich Mehringer, a German survivor, recalled in 1980: 'The ship started to burn in several spots immediately. It trembled as if an earthquake had started . . . Panic. The prisoners fought to get out. Everyone was screaming and shouting. Some of the prisoners wanted to put out the fires with the hosepipes. But they had been cut. Probably by the SS guards, for reasons known only to themselves.'[7]

Now the flames started to lick up about the panic-stricken concentration camp inmates. Mehringer threw some blankets to a Frenchman whose clothing was already ablaze. 'Water . . . water,' the Frenchman croaked. '*Alles kaputt!*'

Everything was indeed '*kaputt*'. Those few who managed to reach the upper deck were faced with a new danger. Having used up all their rockets, the RAF pilots were circling the helpless, drifting, burning ships, machine-gunning their decks. Now it was either the bullets or the water and most of the survivors could not swim.

As the *Thielbek* started to list at a fifty-degree angle her captain yelled: 'Off you go! The ship's going to turn turtle at any moment!'

The crew waited no longer. They clambered over the side and dropped into the water. Still the prisoners hesitated, for unlike the crew there were no life-jackets for them; they reasoned that even if the ship sank and they were below decks, they might still be rescued from the land which was tantalisingly close. They returned below to find a cabin and barricade themselves in against the flames and smoke, relying on the oxygen that would be trapped down there.

Tadeusz Kwapinski, a Polish prisoner, was not taking that chance. He went over the side with a handful of other prisoners. A boat picked them up, more dead than alive, and took them to the shore. There they faced another peril. Further up the beach, teenage Hitler Youth fanatics were busy shooting those of the prisoners who had managed to get ashore. The Pole and his comrades fled, running for their lives. Finally they met a British tank, and the soldiers gave them chocolate and cigarettes.[8] The Pole and his handful of comrades were among the very few who survived.

The Russian Aleksander Machnev was another. He managed to escape from the burning *Cap Arcona* after the ship had already been flooded below decks. He saw 'hundreds of people floundering and paddling in the incoming water, the few who could really swim being dragged under by their panic-stricken comrades.'[9]

Now he was one of the survivors trying to fight his way to the beach where fifteen-year-old Gerhard Schnoor was a witness to what happened next:

The harbour was full of naval shipping, but not one boat went out to the rescue of the concentration camp inmates, fighting for their lives in the Bay . . . After a while a single Navy boat left Neustadt and approached the swimming people, who cheered and cried piteously when they saw what they thought were their rescuers. But the officer in charge bellowed at them through a megaphone, 'We're only taking Germans on board!' And then the Germans struck at the swimmers with their weapons and forcibly released the grips of the others hanging onto the sides of the craft.[10]

Then, as Gerhard Schnoor and the cluster of other Germans looked on in horror, the sailors opened fire with their machine guns. 'Mercilessly they fired at their own comrades also in the water. Without a sound they sank beneath the surface.'

Another survivor was German communist Rudi Goguel. He was almost at the end of his strength when he saw a rescue boat. After an hour in the water he could hardly raise a shout, but somehow he managed to attract the attention of the sailors. What happened next was not what he had expected.

'Shooting broke out. They swept the sea with their machine guns, whole long bursts of bullets.' All around him other survivors went under for good. 'You poor fool,' Goguel told himself, 'can't you see that they're only rescuing uniformed SS men? *Do you really believe*

Members of the US Army dance with Red Army girls in celebration.

that in this world there are any decent human beings left?[11]

That day it seemed that Goguel was correct in his cynical assessment of the human race. Bogdan Suchowiak, a Pole, powerfully built and still well nourished, had now reached the shore safely – only to fall into the hands of nervous but fanatical fifteen-year-old Hitler Youth boys armed with rifles. Together with fifteen other former concentration camp inmates, Suchowiak was forced into a barn. There he and the rest cowered, listening to the chatter of machine guns some way off, whispering to each other that the German kids were soon going to shoot them. It was obvious that the order had gone out to both the Navy and the Hitler Youth that all prisoners were to be shot.

Suddenly it happened. Bogdan Suchowiak thought that his last moment on this earth had come. The door was flung open and German soldiers were standing there. They were going to be executed! 'Then a car appeared and its door was opened. I could not believe my eyes. In the middle of this group of German soldiers there stands an English captain. The German major in charge sprang to attention and saluted this English captain. I knew it was all over. The English were there!'

Tears of gratitude streaming down his face, Bogdan staggered over to the English captain, 'and for the first time in my life I attempted to make a speech in English. I said, "You have given us freedom. We thank you." '

The soldier's answer was brief and brutal. He shouted at the weeping Pole, '*Oh, will you shut up!*'[12]

Now it was about over. Of the 2,800 concentration camp inmates on the *Thielbek*, only 50 were rescued. From the *Cap Arcona*, which had held 4,500 prisoners, some 350 managed to reach the shore safely. In all, including those shot by the sailors, the Hitler Youth and the surviving SS guards, some 7,500 men and women perished that May afternoon. More people died that day than in the most celebrated sinking in the whole history of seafaring, that of the *Titanic*. It was the last great tragedy of the war in Europe.*

The surrender on the Hamburg front came at dawn that same day, May 3rd. The cavalry of the British 7th Armoured Division did not hear the ceasefire sounded by trumpet as in the past. Instead they heard the news over the earphones of their headsets. The Germans on the Elbe Front had laid down their arms. They would

* For nearly three decades, the skeletons of those unfortunate victims kept being washed up on the beaches of the area. The last was discovered by a twelve-year-old holidaymaker in 1971. The police told the boy: 'It happens every year. They are our *Cap Arcona* corpses.' They carried the bones away in a plastic bucket.

enter Hamburg without a fight.

They prepared themselves in true British Army fashion for the triumphal entry. Chins were shaved, boots were polished, collars done up, berets and helmets set at the regulation angle, brasses polished. 'The Germans respect a smart soldier,' was the word now from NCOs and officers, bustling about everywhere, readying the convoys of infantry and armour that would soon be crossing the Harburg bridges into the great port.

They set off. In front rode the infantry in their carriers, rifles and machine guns at the ready just in case some fanatic started shooting. Behind rolled the tanks, piled high with jerricans, bedrolls, spare tracks, the accumulated junk and loot of nearly a year's fighting. They were led by the only two tanks of the whole Division which had survived the campaign since the 7th had landed in Normandy the previous June. They were 'Sharpshooter' and 'Jerboa', after the little creature that had given the Division its name so long before, 'the Desert Rats'.

Passing through the tree-lined suburbs with their nineteenth-century houses and villas, they entered the city itself. Now they saw the tremendous damage that had been wreaked on Hamburg by the RAF in these last years. Whole sections of the city had been laid waste, 'dead zones', where no one went or lived. In their six years of war, the men of the Division had seen devastation enough – in London, Foggia, Caen. But never anything like this. Most of the awed soldiers thought that the city would have been abandoned and rebuilt elsewhere once the war was really over. BBC correspondent Wynford Vaughan-Thomas, who was going in with the 7th, reported:

We thought Bremen was bad, but Hamburg is devastated. Whole quarters have disintegrated under air attacks . . . miles upon miles of blackened walls and utterly burnt out streets. The docks are even more devastated than the town, the great shipyards of Bloem and Voss are a wilderness of tangled girders and in the middle of this chaos, fourteen unfinished U-boats still stand rusting on the slipways. Work on them finally stopped two months ago. After that date Hamburg was a dead city.[13]

The damage was so bad that one of the columns lost its way in the wasteland of ruined streets and was forced to ask directions from a policeman. In the end they continued the journey with an elderly *Schupo* in his leather helmet riding in the first carrier.

Colonel Bill Wainman, CO of the 11th Hussars – nicknamed 'the Cherrypickers' on account of their scarlet dress trousers – was not lost. As the commander of the Division's reconnaissance unit he knew the way and today he was ahead of the rest of the 7th. Now his little armoured car rolled into the big square in front of the grey Rathaus to find an imposing collection of elegant, bemedalled German officers waiting there to surrender

The shattered centre of Hamburg.

the keys of the city.

They clicked to attention as Colonel Wainman emerged from his vehicle, dressed in GI combat jacket, civilian trousers and desert boots. As befitted an old Desert Rat, Wainman dressed very casually.

He tugged at his cherry-coloured beret in acknowledgement, but otherwise ignored the Germans. Instead he fumbled in the interior of his armoured car for some compo biscuits, crushed them in his hand and started scattering the crumbs on the ground. Within seconds he was surrounded by hundreds of pigeons fluttering down from the ledges of the Rathaus.

Captain von Laun, the official interpreter, marched up to Wainman and said in his excellent English (learned at Oxford) that his senior officer, a General Wolz, 'would like to surrender, please'.

Wainman waved him aside; he'd have 'to leave that job to the Brigadier' he remarked, and went on feeding the pigeons.[14]

A few minutes later the Brigadier duly arrived, accompanied by two officers, and accepted the formal surrender of the city.

It was a fitting end to the Division's fighting career. It was almost five years since the first armoured cars of the Division had crossed the Egyptian frontier to begin offensive action against the Italians in Africa. Few were left of the men who had fought that month. Their graves mark the long road that leads from Alexandria to Tunis in the desert, and scatter the countryside in Southern Italy, Normandy, Belgium, Holland and Germany. Even now a burial party was preparing to bury the last two men of the Division to be killed in action right in the heart of the newly captured city. Their simple white crosses would be placed beneath the pompous stone memorial to the dead of Hamburg's own 69th Infantry Regiment, which in its turn was overshadowed by a tremendous statue of Bismarck. At last, however, the killing was over for the Desert Rats.

The war was finally petering out. The beaten German soldier was putting down his weapon at last, and, if he had the energy, attempting to escape Allied captivity while he still had a chance.

Actor David Niven, then a colonel in the British Army, bumped into one such escaper on a country road near Brunswick, newly captured by the Americans. He was a German general dressed as a farmer, trying to escape westwards in a horse and cart. Unfortunately his highly polished boots were a dead give-away and Niven stopped him.

For a while they just stared at each other. Niven thought he had 'never seen such utter weariness, such black despair on a human face before'. Niven knew it was his duty to arrest the general, but he just couldn't bring himself to do so. Instead he said in his usual jaunty fashion, 'Go ahead, sir.' Then he added, 'And please

Utilising their own vehicles, members of the Wehrmacht drive into British lines to surrender.

cover up your bloody boots!'[15]

But most German soldiers were simply too weak and weary to try to escape. Watching the mass surrender of General von Tippelskirch's 21st Army, one American eyewitness noted: 'Many walked until they could walk no further, then flung themselves down alongside the road until they recovered strength to push on.'

As von Tippelskirch's men desperately tried to reach the lines of the 82nd Airborne before the Russians caught them, one of the Airborne soldiers thought it was like a scene from the American Civil War: 'how you could have imagined the broken Confederate Army of the South must have looked at the end'.

Some, such as A. E. Evans, who had every reason to hate the Germans – he had spent several years in a German POW camp – could only feel pity for them now. Evans later recalled how he watched them stream into captivity:

They came in two's and three's at the double and many clearly were in the last stages of exhaustion. They were not permitted to cease running and if they showed any sign of doing so, an ugly snarl from the nearest Tommy and a raised rifle sent them off again . . . For a few minutes we stood in the shelter of a lorry watching this strange sight, for up till then I had not seen many Germans in the early stages of surrendering – it was a satisfying but not a pleasant sight, for these men were desperately in fear of death.[16]

Private Lester Atwell, the medic who had seen more than enough horror and misery caused by the Germans throughout the long campaign, also felt a twinge of sympathy for them now. Weary, footsore and anxious, the prisoners were shepherded through the town by armed guards. Atwell later remembered one scene in particular. Guarded by two GIs, 'a long double file of old men in civilian clothes, their hands up over their heads in surrender' passed him through the 'dull mustardly twilight'. He noticed that many of them were from the Volkssturm. They 'trudged past, their eyes straight ahead. Mixed in with them were a few gawky, stunned boys in their early teens. Our old codgers choked with laughter and jeered as their townsmen went by. The prisoners had evidently volunteered to hold the town, had run into the woods and there [had been] ingloriously captured. Our old men might rock with laughter, but the other old boys held themselves upright: at least they had tried.'[17]

In towns and cities all over Germany formal surrenders were being arranged, with German officers handing over their flags and their ceremonial swords as if this were the eighteenth century and not the century of total war. There was talk of 'honour among soldiers', a few words of polite disarming chit-chat between officers, a final heel-clicking and saluting. But when the bemedalled,

Surrender of the German Forces on the British Front at Luneburg May 4th 1945.

smartly uniformed officers marched into captivity, lustily singing 'O du schoener Westerwald' or the like, behind them came the shuffling mass of their men, down-at-heel, ill-kept and *beaten*.

Now it was up to Montgomery to put an end to the whole business. Deprived of the kudos of capturing Berlin, which had been his objective ever since Normandy, he took the surrender of what was left of the German Armed Forces, ranging from Norway down to the Channel Islands. It was against official Allied Policy to do so without the agreement of the Russians, but Montgomery did not bother even to consult them. And

so, with his usual nose for personal publicity, the little Field Marshal made headlines throughout the world.

As he exclaimed in triumph to a group of correspondents after the signing ceremony at Luneburg Heath: '*Good egg!*' Then he summoned the Army cameraman who had filmed the affair. 'Did you get that picture – under the Union Jack?' he asked, pointing to the flag flapping in the breeze above his head.

The photographer said he had.

'Good, good. A historic picture!' Montgomery rasped, very pleased with himself. This day he had upstaged even Eisenhower. Off he went to the correspondents again, telling them in a high good mood: 'I was persuaded to drink some champagne at dinner tonight . . . It looks as if the British Empire's part in the German war in Western Europe is over.'[18]

For the British and Canadian Armies, the news of the German Army's surrender came in the dry unemotional officialese of General Belchem's signal.* It read:

From: Exfor Main.
To: For action: First Cdn Army: Second Brit. Army L of C: GHQ AATPS. 79 Armd Div. Exfor Rear.
For Info: Second TAF: Exfor TAC: 22 Liaison HQ.
All offensive ops will cease from receipt this signal. Orders will be given all tps to cease 0800 hrs tomorrow Saturday 5 May. Full terms of local German surrender arranged today for 21 Army Gp front follow, emphasise these provisions apply solely 21 Army Gp.

Horrocks, commander of XXX Corps and victor of the Reichswald, heard the news in a very strange place. He wrote later: 'I had often wondered how the war would end. When it came it could hardly have been more of an anti-climax. I happened to be sitting in the military equivalent of the smallest room [i.e. a latrine] when I heard a voice on the wireless saying: "All hostilities will cease at 0800 hours . . ."'[19]

One of his divisional commanders, General Thomas of the 43rd Division, heard the news in the middle of a briefing for a further attack by the Division, which had already lost over 12,000 men in battle.

His staff officers were shocked to hear a thunderous knock on the door of the caravan where Thomas was planning the operation. Nothing was ever supposed to disturb a briefing. As Brigadier Essame later recalled: 'Even if the news had just come in that God had decided to come down from heaven and join in the war on our side, it still wouldn't have been grounds enough to disturb the General.'

The Brigade Major entered, a man named Chalmers, his face glowing with excitement.

'What is it?' snorted Thomas.

'Sir, the BBC have just announced the unconditional surrender of the German forces opposing Field Marshal Montgomery!' Chalmers answered breathlessly.

Thomas was not impressed. 'I take my orders from the Corps Commander and *not* the BBC,' he announced, and went on with his briefing.

Ten minutes Chalmers knocked on the door once more. This time he bore an official signal from Horrocks and he gave it wordlessly to Thomas.

The latter read it out aloud and the staff officers stared back at their divisional commander. He didn't appear to understand the message's import. His brow was fur-

'It's all over.'

* Belchem was Montgomery's Chief-of-Administration.

rowed as if he were still thinking hard. Then slowly he put the old frayed canvas cover over his map talc for the very last time and walked to the door in silence. It was over.

Essame followed him out and accompanied him to his waiting armoured car. Just before he clambered in, Thomas broke the heavy brooding silence. He looked at Essame and said: '*The troops have done us damn well!*'[20]

Standing bolt upright in his car, he acknowledged Essame's salute against a background of exploding flares. Next moment he vanished into the darkness. The 43rd (Wessex) Division would never fight another battle.

Some of the soldiers got drunk. In Bremen the Jocks of the 52nd Lowland Division went on a terrific bender, drinking from huge 50-litre crates of looted German gin. In their drunken enthusiasm, they fired their 'victory' mortar bombs right into their own lines. That night officer-led patrols of heavily armed men toured the shattered streets of Bremen in an urgent attempt to restore order.

Some did not trust the sudden calm. Captain R. W. Thompson was touring the front trying to find troops still in contact with the enemy; he discovered the battle-weary Dorsets, who had suffered severe losses in the last eleven months, 'still manning their weapon pits with their Brens, waiting dourly'. Their division, the 43rd, had fought a long hard battle since Normandy and they were taking no chances; for the enemy, as Thompson put it, had 'fought a slow retreat and taken severe toll'.[21]

Others reverted to 'real soldiering' almost at once. The men of the King's Shropshire Light Infantry, for example, were roused at dawn, given a breakfast of spam and biscuits, and transported into the surrounding countryside. There, as one veteran recalled, 'Sparks began to fly, not in the form of 88 mm shells, or "moaning minnies", but in the form of blanco, drill, PT, and last but certainly not least, DPIs [drill parades] turning . . . mud-begrimed battle veterans into a company of smart, clean-shaven and well-behaved men.'[22] In some parts of the British Army, bull reigned again.

Some were just numb. The men of the 8th US Infantry Division told a correspondent from the *New York Times*: 'We've left too many of our guys behind to feel like raising hell.'

The historian of the 3rd US Division recorded that the men had 'lived in constant apprehension of physical injury for the better part of two and a half years'. Thus:

. . . we were almost sceptical at first that the war was indeed over. The ultimate goal of every soldier who had fought to the end had seemed like the pot of gold at the end of the rainbow. It had been wonderful to dwell upon it. But it would never materialise. Then suddenly it was all upon them . . . and the impact failed to register . . . The full

Troops celebrate VE Day.

German ex POWs and civilians read the first edition of the Hamburg newspaper printed under the control of the Allied Military.

implications of it needed much time and serious consideration to sink in.[23]

A few were elated. The supply sergeant of the US 243rd Field Artillery had been the odd man out back in the heady, optimistic days of September 1944 when everyone had thought the war was almost over. He had placed a bet with his buddies that it would go on till May 1945. Now he was overjoyed to find he would 'enter civilian life richer by a cool eleven hundred and forty dollars!'[24]

Sometimes, however, the elation was mixed with weariness. Sergeant Giles wrote home to his wife Janice on May 7th:

The war is over! All we can think about is thank God, thank God . . . I'm sure everybody thought exactly what I did. I made it, I made it all the way. Nobody is going to shoot at me any more. I can't be killed. *I have made it!* Yet there is a queer kind of let-down. We have waited for this day so long. We don't yet believe it . . . My reaction has been a feeling of terrible weariness and then weakness and sleepiness. But I *am* happy! So *damned* happy! It's over![25]

Captain Charles MacDonald of the 2nd Division, now in Czechoslovakia, felt a mixture of pride, sadness and weariness as he watched the happy Czechs, who would be soon subjected to another tyranny, cheering his company. He watched his men's reactions:

Brilliant smiles wreathed their faces and they waved cheerfully at the shouting crowds, as if they had just won an election campaign and this was a personal triumph. Hardened, stubble-faced veterans had unashamed tears in their eyes. The unleashed joy of these oppressed people knew no bounds and it was too much for them.
Suddenly I began to realise what no one thus far had been able in the war to put into words – what we were fighting for. And I found a lump in my throat which I could not swallow.[26]

Private Atwell experienced a similar lump in his throat, but not from pride. He heard the news casually from a comrade while he was munching a sandwich. 'Really *over*?' he queried, putting down his sandwich.
'Yeah, there'll be no more fighting,' his comrade said.
The two men lapsed into silence. Atwell later recalled: 'I searched for some feeling, waited for it to develop. There was hardly any sensation at all. A moment later I was aware of an inward caving in, followed by a sore-throat feeling when I thought of all those who had been forced to give up their lives for this moment.'[27]
A few men carried out little private ceremonies, wandering off to be alone, away from the mass of khaki-clad men with whom they had lived for so long. A GI of the 76th Infantry Division, on hearing the news that the war had ended, told his buddy to stay in the

foxhole they were sharing. 'I have some business to attend to,' he said and moved off into some bushes. There, as his friend reported later, 'he raised his MI and fired it into the air, shooting off a whole clip at nothing – nothing at all.'[28]

Corporal Alexander McKee had made a little private pilgrimage along the route followed the previous month by the Canadians and the British of the 'Nymegen Home Guard'. But now it was getting dark and he abandoned that trail of dead bodies to return to Arnhem.

'Some freak of morbid curiosity impels me,' he wrote much later, 'to look through the window into that twilight room of the long dead' – he meant those who had been killed the previous September:

He's wearing a sniper's coat, I can see that now – the tough fabric has stood the decay better than the uniform, of which there is no sign; and his head is covered by rubble . . . if he has a head. The thing seems to have been mashed about, perhaps by a grenade. I creep cautiously round the corner. The shock wasn't so bad this time, though I nearly stepped on him. He's hideous, all huddled up outside a window of the room where the corpse of a German is lying.

It's small and like a mummy. All huddled up. The boots and gaiters are of British pattern, shiny and mildewed, and the only recognisable thing about it. The rest is just a mess. It has no head – the bones of the spine protrude from its mildewed collar; the thigh bones are visible and bare of flesh; but his legs where his trousers have been torn away or ripped by the rats have a cold mummy-like sickly covering that was once human flesh. The odour of putrescence is an atmosphere about him. This is flesh along the putrid limbs . . . that is bone along the thigh . . . that must be battledress, and yes! I can make out an army-issue jersey . . . But there is no beginning or end to these things, no demarcation line where one can say: that is flesh and this is bone and that is but cloth . . . it all merges into a decaying mess, smelling of evil. The rats jump about the corpse of the German three feet away.

Six feet away from this huddled, decayed ruin of a man, sprawled faced downwards on a heap of rubble, is a great bloated thing, so unhuman that it's hard to distinguish him from the earth and the wreckage on which he lies. It's green and shiny and the boots alone proclaim for what he died; that he, too, was once a Canadian infantryman. Dust to dust, they say . . . if they had seen this . . . It is not dust; it is disease, the antithesis of dust. Dust is clean. This is foul.

These decaying putrid things merge into the dusk in their surroundings. The Wehrmacht boy fits into the grey foul twilight of that deserted room so that he seems almost another bit of debris, only more foul; the two Canadians outside his window merge with the soil and the rubble so that we failed to see them as we passed the first time, though they lay but a few feet away. These are the glorious dead, the politicians' speeches . . .[29]

Three days later they had overcome their surprise, their sadness, their numbness, and they had grown accustomed to the strange silence that followed the end of the permanent barrage. Now that they no longer lived in fear of being killed suddenly and violently, they could count the cost.

By the end of the eleven-month campaign in North-West Europe, nearly five million Allied servicemen had come to Europe. While the fighting troops, the tankers and infantry, had amounted to only twenty percent of that huge force, they had absorbed seventy percent of the casualties. The final butcher's bill for the British, Canadian and American Armies came to 782,374 men killed, wounded and reported missing, plus another 10,308 for the US and British Navies and 61,624 for the combined air forces.* In essence, the equivalent of the population of a large-size British or American city had perished to achieve final victory.

Not that they were particularly proud of their victory. The sort of victory that the cheering, drunken throngs in London and New York thought they had achieved meant little to the average combat soldier. As Captain Critchell of the US 101st Airborne Division put it: 'We who had fought this war could feel no pride. Victors and vanquished, all were one. We were one with the crowds moving silently along the boulevards of Paris; the old women hunting through the still ruins of Cologne; the bodies piled like yellow cordwood at Dachau; the dreadful vacant eyes of the beaten German soldiers; the white graves and the black crosses and the haunting melancholy of our hearts. All, all were one, all were the ghastly horror of what we had known, of what we had helped to do.'[30]

And, now that the shooting was over, these young men were at last able to assess the changes that had taken place in themselves since they embarked on what their Supreme Commander and future President of the United States would soon call grandly 'the crusade in Europe'.

Physically and mentally they were much tougher, able to live under conditions that they would have thought impossible the year before. For months they had lived outdoors in holes in the ground, surviving the worst winter in Europe in living memory, on a diet of cheap pork and cheap beef. They had been afraid many times, of course, and some of them had been unable to bear the strain. They had broken down or run away. But the great mass hadn't. They had borne the strain and triumphed over themselves.

Alan Moorehead, the Australian war correspondent who had been there from the start, thought he had seen an immense change take place in the average British soldier in that year:

---

* These figures do not include non-battle casualties or men killed or injured in battlefield accidents.

(Above) Prisoners stand behind the wire at Dachau as one of their former guards is dragged from the moat.

(Below) These boys were captured by the 9th US Army as they rode into Rosslau with bazookas on their handlebars.

The clerk from Manchester and the shopkeeper from Balham seemed to me to grow in stature. You could almost watch him grow from month to month in the early days. He was suddenly projected out of a shallow and materialist world into a world where there were really possibilities of touching the heights, and here and there a man found greatness in himself. The anti-aircraft gunner in a raid and the boy in the landing barge really did feel at moments that the thing they were doing was a clear and definite good, the best they could do. And at those moments there was a surpassing satisfaction, a sense of exactly and entirely fulfilling one's life, a sense even of purity, the confused adolescent dreams of greatness come true . . . Not all the cynicism, not all the ugliness and fatigue in the world will take that moment away from the people who experienced it.[31]

These young men who had gone to fight in Europe had possessed less starry-eyed enchantment than those who had gone to France in 1914. Nor had they been gulled, particularly, by the patriotic slogans of the time. Hitler had been a very real menace and, in the case of the British, they had suffered at the hands of his followers in their own homeland even before they had set out on that long eleven-month march to Lübeck and final victory. That had been their real motivating force – 'Beat Adolf!' That was their only slogan.

Now for a little while they could also assess themselves as members of the nation to which they belonged. The British and the Americans had come a long way together since that summer's day in 1942 when their chief, the then unknown General Eisenhower, had arrived in London and first encountered that unlovely smell of boiled cabbage and brussel sprouts, which seemed to hang permanently over his headquarters at Number 20 Grosvenor Square.

These 'cousins from over the sea', as Churchill liked to call them, had been the new boys then, anxious to learn, deferential, ready to pay homage to the three-year struggle that the British had already undergone. But as more and more GIs poured into the island – which was only prevented from sinking by the barrage balloons, as the GIs wisecracked – American attitudes began to change.

In an area little larger than Colorado, two million GIs lived in relative luxury among a people who were underfed and overworked, stressed by the raids and the thousand scares and alarms of three years of war. Now these members of the AEF* – 'After England Failed', they jeered – started to look down upon their 'cousins'.

The Americans went into Europe feeling pretty sure of themselves. They had won the Old War; they would win this one, too. 'Hello, Lafayette – here we are for the second time!' Soon they were fielding three divisions for every one that the British could send to France. They were the big boys now. They were 'bailing England out of the mess she had gotten herself into'.

The hard battles of the German frontier and the Ardennes robbed them of some of that confidence. In the battles of the Hurtgenwald and the Bulge, where whole divisions cracked and battalions ran away, they learned that combat was not the glamorous thing that the Hollywood patriotic movies of the time made it out to be. It was dirty and very dangerous.

Never again would America respect the British or their Army as they had done back in 1942, and the USA would enter the second half of the twentieth century as *the* superpower in the West, while Britain slipped to the rank of a third-class nation. And yet they did begin to exhibit a grudging respect for British military professionalism.

The Germans, too, lost some of their overweening confidence in themselves as the best soldiers in Europe as the campaign progressed. At the beginning in Normandy, with their vast experience in Russia behind them, the Germans were the real professionals and, with a few exceptions, the British, Canadians and Americans rank amateurs.

But as the Allied soldiers learned, the Germans lost in ability. At Aachen, Colonel Engel's 12th Infantry Division, for example, was thrown into battle piece-meal and was decimated by the 'Big Red One'. On the Rhine, the German defenders bungled every defensive operation and the Allies crossed successfully. One month later, at Bremen, Horrocks' XXX Corps even found the enemy gunners of the German Marine Division *facing the wrong way!* It was not only Allied matériel superiority that beat the Germans, but their own lack of morale and poor leadership. Never again could there be another *dolchstoss* legend for the Germans. They lost World War Two in North-Western Europe because they wouldn't fight to the bitter end. In the final analysis, the Allied soldiers were quite simply better than they were.

But now it was the last time they would be all together. 'Demob' and 'separation' from the service would soon take them home. Many would be posted to the Far East for service against the Japanese. 'BLA,'* the Tommies would joke, 'means *Bloody Burma Looms Ahead!*'

So on this Tuesday May 8th, 1945, they celebrated one last time. On this 'V-E Day'** they prepared to go on a 'wing-ding', a 'bender', a 'right old piss-up', as the expressions of the time had it. But first there were the parades, the speeches, the radio recordings of London and New York going crazy yet again.

In London, the King told his soldiers to 'remember those who will not come back; their constancy and

* American Expeditionary Force.

* The official title of Montgomery's Army: 'The British Liberation Army'.
** Victory in Europe Day.

A concentration camp victim is buried in a mass grave.

courage in battle; their sacrifice and endurance in the face of a merciless enemy: let us remember the men in all the Services and the women* in all the Services who have laid down their lives. We have come to the end of our tribulations and they are not with us at the moment of our rejoicing.'[32]

His soldiers really did not need reminding. The cost was still there before their mind's eye. The gaps in their ranks could no longer be filled; even their vehicles bore

the scars of the long campaign. Preparing for a ceremonial parade that day, Captain Foley watched his tankers cleaning up their tanks: '*Avenger* still bore the line of bullet marks across the turret from the first day of the Reichswald battle and the little splash of molten metal on the cupola flap was still shining evidence of the sniper at Le Havre. *Angler*'s tracks needed adjusting and I thought of how we had battled to do this task in the Ardennes blizzard.'

Suddenly Foley realised that they would never need these metal monsters ever again. He stared at 'the sunshine winking on the polished muzzle-brake of *Avenger* where McGinty was slowly, but quite pointlessly, cleaning it . . .'[33]

* The first British servicewoman Corporal Lydia Alford flew into Normandy on D − 3 to evacuate wounded. Later, British women were employed in mixed flak batteries in Belgium and Germany. Some 1,000 women were killed in action, winning five Military Medals, but there are no exact figures for North-West Europe.

A German woman walks through devastated Schweinfurt.

Then the parties started. Corporal Arthur Hare, the killer-sniper who wanted to be a gardener, couldn't believe their colonel had really ordered rum punch for the whole battalion. But he had, and the battalion erupted in an orgy of shooting. They fired a barrage that would have done them credit in a real war. In the end the CO had to summon his company commanders and order them to tell their drunken soldiers to stop firing because 'bullets were dropping like confetti' all around.

Perhaps that last night they saw themselves once again as they had been back in the line – in the free air of good comradeship, away from the jealousies and petty rivalries of the 'rear echelon wallahs'; moving up once again with the guns rumbling uneasily in the distance, the sky flickering its silent ugly pink, laden down with the impedimenta of war, ammo, weapons, picks, shovels, bazookas, each man carrying some treasured personal possession, their faces red and weatherbeaten, their clothes an odd assortment of British, American and German pickings, which defied the description 'uniform'; going up once more, moving into that first high-pitched hysterical burr of the Spandaus . . .

Or perhaps they simply got drunk.

Para-medic James Byrom was on duty at the great Luftwaffe hospital at Wismar that night. While his comrades of the 6th Airborne got drunk – 'according to a long-cherished plan' – he remained 'as sober as a judge'. Long afterwards he remembered:

. . . standing at a dormer window in the . . . hospital at Wismar, looking at the magnificent sunset and thinking I had now come almost the full circle back to the sea that washed the shores of Sweden. On a ward balcony below me the wounded Germans talked quietly. Presently, as the glow of their cigarettes confirmed that it was dark, the victory celebrations began. Up from the British lines came brilliant flares, singly and in clusters, but without pattern or prodigality, as if one soldier in each platoon had been given an official coloured hat and told to fling it into the air. But further away, in the Russian lines, the glow of bonfires steadily lit up the sky. Distance subdued the flickering, making static cones that were slightly blurred by smoke, or mist; and I could fancy that they were ghost fires, the fires of other historic triumphs, so strongly did I feel them as a symbol of the unreality of victory in relation to the recurring failure to keep peace.[34]

Fifty miles away at Plauen, another medic Lester Atwell was approached that day by 'a small, humorous-looking German' who grinned at the American and stretched out his hand. 'Ofer,' he announced, 'war ofer. Gut friends.'

Atwell stopped, looking around to see that no MPs were watching, then allowed his hand to be heartily shaken.

'Now,' said the German with his codger's grin, 'togedder we fight the Russians . . .'[35]

ENVOI

So ends their tale. The tale of those once young men of forty years ago who are now old – or long dead. Today, you could follow the course of that battle which took eleven long bloody months in 1944/45 in eleven short hours. The *autoroute* and the *autobahn* make that easily possible.

But, for the boots that hit the wet sand of Normandy that June, it was a long, long way. Plodding down those long white Norman roads to the first menacing rumble of the barrage and into the waist-high corn with the machine guns chattering frighteningly. Crouched, sweating with fear, in the *bocage* while the 'moaning minnies' ripped the morning calm apart. Boots slogging over the glistening wet *pavé* of Belgium and Luxembourg, with the cheers, the kisses, the wine and beer, and the Flemish carillon playing the songs of the Old War. Boots squelching through the slush and mud of the Ardennes towards the enemy frontier. Boots pelting in panic through the snow-heavy firs. Boots stilled for good . . .

Today there is little to see of their long march from the Channel to the Baltic. The official cemeteries are there, of course, Patton, lying in the midst of the six thousand dead of his old Third Army at the US Military Cemetery at Hamm, Luxembourg. Or the tiny British Military Cemetery just outside Münster, Germany, buried in the heart of a wood. Here the last of Montgomery's dead are interned, the handful of graves bearing dates such as '30 March '45' or '4th April 1945'. Here lie the remains of his eighteen- and nineteen-year-olds, the reinforcements killed at the very moment of victory, dead before they had ever begun to live.

Now, forty years on, there is little else to be seen of that tremendous effort, those scenes of desperate action, where young men – British, Canadian, American *and* German – fought, suffered and died. Time and the green earth itself have drawn a cloak over them. The fields once littered with the debris of war – rusting tanks, abandoned equipment, ragged brown shell-holes, still figures in khaki and field grey – have long since reverted to their former state. Now, when old men return to visit the places of their youth, there are only the gentle

A US 7th Reconnaissance Army jeep roars down a deserted street in Wurzburg, Germany.

sounds and scents of a soft summer's day.

Here and there you can still catch a glimpse of that terrible time. The grey chipped bunkers that were once the *Atlantikwall*, slowly slipping into the green sea. The old Sherman or Panther, freshly painted for every new tourist season, in odd corners of the Low Countries and Northern France. The foxholes and dugouts in the heart of the Ardennes Forest, with their rotting roof-timbers, half buried in moss and piles of rusty shell-cases and empty C-ration cans. The bullet-pocked walls of the village houses in the Eifel and Moselle. Each grim height still dotted with the heap of concrete rubble that was once the Siegfried Line. The rows of 'dragon's teeth', the concrete tank traps, still running across the hills like the bared spine of some long dead primeval monster.

On to the Rhine. The shell-scarred red-brick pillars of that bridge at Remagen which was, for a short while, the most famous bridge in the world. The weathered stone pillar at Speyer commemorating Sergeant Bertout's 'assault crossing' of the last natural barrier. The faint depressions in the fields below Paderborn, caused by mortar bombs at the place where General Rose was trapped and shot dead by the Waffen SS. The lonely wood where Field Marshal Model declared, 'A German field marshal does not surrender' – and then shot himself. The Heath at Luneburg, where it all ended and where all trace of that 'historic' ceremony which brought the long struggle to a close has long since vanished.

Up to the Elbe at Lauenburg and Bleckede where those young men, British and American, made their last assault crossing; and there it is – *die Mauer*. 'The Wall', that mocking monstrosity, which made – *and makes* – all their sacrifice and effort in vain.

That high, triple-wired fence, with all its watchful guards, machine-gun towers, minefields, lethal booby traps, running through the heart of a divided Germany for five hundred long miles. Today it separates two worlds, East and West – as effectively as did once, in another age, the English Channel and the Atlantic Wall, lying in wait for that great and desperate assault which began it all . . .

NOTES

Chapter 1
1   Pieker, H., *Hitler* (Stalling Verlag)
2   Johnson, J., *Wing-Leader* (Corgi)
3   Toland, John, *Battle: The Story of the Bulge* (Random House)
4   Clostermann, Pierre, *The Big Show* (Corgi)
5   Personal interview
6   MacDonald, Charles, *Company Commander* (Ballantine)
7   Toland, op. cit.
8   Marshal, H. A. L., *Men in Combat* (Bantam)
9   Toland, op. cit.
10 MacDonald, op. cit.
11 Giles, Janice, (ed.) *The GI Journal of Sergeant Giles* (Houghton Mifflin)
12 McKee, Alexander, *The Race for the Rhine Bridges* (Souvenir Press)
13 Essame, Hubert, *The Battle for Germany* (Batsford)
14 Atwell, Lester, *Private* (Popular Library)
15 Personal interview
16 Patton, George, *War As I Knew It* (Bantam)
17 Saunders, Hilary St George, *The Red Beret* (Four Square)
18 Foley, John, *Mailed Fist* (Panther)
19 *BBC War Report* (Oxford)
20 Personal interview
21 Thompson, R. W., *Men Under Fire* (Macdonald)
22 Ibid.
23 Toland, op. cit.
24 Personal interview
25 Anderson, Dudley, *Three Cheers for the Next Man to Die* (Robert Hale)
26 Codman, Charles, *Drive!* (Atlantic Monthly Press)
27 Personal interview
28 Huie, E., *The Execution of Private Slovik* (Bantam)
29 Ibid.
30 Quoted in Huie, op. cit.
31 Ibid.
32 Ibid.
33 Ibid.
34 Ibid.

Chapter 2
1   Anderson, Dudley, *Three Cheers for the Next Man to Die* (Robert Hale)
2   Personal interview
3   Quoted in Shulman, M., *The Other Side of the Hill* (Corgi)
4   Ibid.
5   Essame, Hubert, *The Battle for Germany* (Batsford)
6   Horrocks, Brian, *A Full Life* (Leo Cooper)
7   Foley, John, *Mailed Fist* (Panther)
8   Woollcombe, Robert, *Lion Rampant* (Leo Cooper)
9   Fergusson, Bernard, *The Black Watch* (Collins)
10 Quoted in Wingfield, Robert, *The Only Way Out* (Hutchinson)
11 Horrocks, op. cit.
12 Quoted in Essame, op. cit.
13 Foley, op. cit.
14 Woollcombe, op. cit.
15 Thompson, R. W., *Men Under Fire* (Macdonald)
16 Foley, op. cit.
17 Personal interview
18 Personal interview/correspondence
19 Wingfield, op. cit.
20 Horrocks, op. cit.
21 Thompson, op. cit.
22 Personal interview
23 Quoted in Flower, D., *The Taste of Courage* (Harper & Bros)
24 Personal interview
25 Wynne, B., *The Sniper* (New English Library)
26 Quoted in Essame, op. cit.
27 Thompson, op. cit.
28 *Maple Leaf*, 1945
29 *Daily Express*, April 1945
30 Ibid.
31 Horrocks, op. cit.
32 Woollcombe, op. cit.
33 Personal interview
34 Thompson, op. cit.
35 Wingfield, op. cit.
36 Foley, op. cit.
37 Essame, op. cit.
38 Prebble, John, *The Edge of Darkness* (Corgi)
39 Foley, op. cit.
40 Thompson, op. cit.
41 Wilson, Andrew, *Flame Thrower* (Panther)
42 McKee, Alexander, *The Destruction of Dresden* (Souvenir Press)
43 Personal interview
44 Quoted in McKee, op. cit.
45 Interview, *Sunday Times*, 1983
46 Quoted in McKee, op. cit.
47 Ibid.
48 Flower, op. cit.
49 Quoted in McKee, op. cit.
50 Toland, John, *The Lasty 100 Days* (Random House)
51 *Westdeutsche Allgemeinzeitung*, March 1945
52 *Sunday Times*, 1983

(Right) German woman flees burning area in Siegburg.

Chapter 3

1   Ayres, Frederick, *Patton* (Little Brown)
2   Eisenhower, Dwight D., *Crusade in Europe* (Heinemann)
3   Irving, David, *The War Between the Generals* (Allen Lane)
4   Nobuesch, Johannes, *Zum Bitteren Ende* (Bitburg)
5   Personal interview
6   Personal interview
7   Personal interview
8   Atwell, Lester, *Private* (Popular Libary)
9   Giles, Janice, (ed.) *The GI Journal of Sergeant Giles* (Houghton Mifflin)
10 Irving, op. cit.
11 Personal interview
12 *Stars and Stripes*, March 1945
13 Atwell, op. cit.
14 Ibid.
15 Personal interview
16 Personal interview
17 Personal interview
18 Nobuesch, op. cit.
19 Personal interview
20 Moorehead, Alan, *Eclipse* (Hamish Hamilton)
21 Quoted in Hechler, K., *The Bridge at Remagen* (Ballantine)
22 Toland, John, *The Last 100 Days* (Random House)
23 Ibid.
24 Hechler, op. cit.
25 Ibid.
26 Ibid.
27 Quoted in Essame, Hubert, *The Battle for Germany* (Batsford)
28 Personal interview
29 Wilson, Andrew, *Flame Thrower* (Panther)
30 Ibid.
31 Eisenhower, op. cit.
32 Quoted in Saunders, Hilary St George, *The Green Beret: The Story of the Commandos, 1940–45* (Four Square)
33 *BBC War Report* (Oxford)
34 Quoted in McKee, Alexander, *The Race for the Rhine Bridges* (Souvenir Press)
35 *Maple Leaf*, 1945
36 Ibid.
37 Fergusson, Bernard, *The Black Watch* (Collins)
38 Ibid.
39 *Maple Leaf*, 1945
40 Ibid.
41 Ibid.
42 Ibid.
43 Ibid.
44 Ibid.
45 Ibid.
46 Ibid.
47 Toland, op. cit.
48 Ibid.
49 *Rhine* (Time-Life)
50 Flower, D., *The Taste of Courage* (Harper & Bros)
51 Toland, op. cit.
52 Thompson, R. W., *Men Under Fire* (Macdonald)
53 Toland, op. cit.
54 Ridgway, Matthew, *Soldier: Memoirs* (Harper & Bros)
55 Flower, op. cit.
56 McKee, op. cit.
57 *BBC War Report*
58 Flower, op. cit.
59 Anderson, Dudley, *Three Cheers for the Next Man to Die* (Robert Hale)
60 McKee, op. cit.
61 *BBC War Report*
62 Quoted in McKee, op. cit.
63 *BBC War Report*
64 Toland, op. cit.

Chapter 4

1   *BBC War Report* (Oxford)
2   Ibid.
3   Bradley, Owen, *Soldier's Story* (Dell Paperbacks)
4   Toland, John, *The Last 100 Days* (Random House)
5   Flower, D., *The Taste of Courage* (Harper & Bros)
6   Anderson, Dudley, *Three Cheers for the Next Man to Die* (Robert Hale)
7   Whiting, Charles, *Battle for the Ruhr Pocket* (Ballantine)
8   Personal interview
9   Codman, Charles, *Drive!* (Atlantic Monthly Press)
10 Foley, John, *Mailed Fist* (Panther)
11 Atwell, Lester, *Private* (Popular Library)
12 *Rhine* (Time-Life)
13 Atwell, op. cit.
14 MacDonald, Charles, *Company Commander* (Ballantine)
15 *BBC War Report*
16 Whiting, Charles, *Bounce the Rhine* (Secker & Warburg)
17 *After the Battle*, Summer 1977
18 *Rhine* (Time-Life)
19 Whiting, Charles, *Battle for the Ruhr Pocket* (Ballantine)
20 *A History of the 17th SS Panzer Division* (Munin Verlag)
21 Personal interview
22 Personal interview
23 Personal interview
24 Giles, Janice, (ed.) *The GI Journal of Sergeant Giles* (Houghton Mifflin)
25 Quoted in McKee, Alexander, *The Race for the Rhine Bridges* (Souvenir Press)
26 *BBC War Report*
27 McKee, op. cit.
28 Ibid.
29 Ibid.

Chapter 5

1   Personal interview
2   Personal interview
3   Personal interview
4   Toland, John, *The Last 100 Days* (Random House)
5   Personal interview
6   Stern, *Cap Arcona* (Gruner & Jahr Verlag)
7   Ibid.
8   Ibid.
9   Ibid.
10 Ibid.
11 Ibid.
12 Ibid.
13 *BBC War Report* (Oxford)
14 *A Short History of the 7th Armored Division* (privately printed)
15 Niven, David, *The Moon's A Balloon* (Fontana)
16 Personal interview
17 Atwell, Lester, *Private* (Popular Library)
18 Moorehead, Alan, *Eclipse* (Hamish Hamilton)
19 Hörrocks, Brian, *A Full Life* (Leo Cooper)
20 Essame, Hubert, *The 43rd (Wessex) Division At War* (William Clowes)
21 Thompson, R. W., *Men Under Fire* (Macdonald)
22 Personal interview
23 *A History of the 3rd Infantry Division* (privately printed)
24 *Stars and Stripes*
25 Giles, Janice, (ed.) *The GI Journal of Sergeant Giles* (Houghton Mifflin)
26 MacDonald, Charles, *Company Commander* (Ballantine)
27 Atwell, op. cit.
28 *Stars and Stripes*
29 McKee, Alexander, *The Race for the Rhine Bridges* (Souvenir Press)
30 *Combat: A Selection of Writings from 'Yank' Magazine* (Dell)
31 Moorehead, Alan, *Eclipse* (Hamish Hamilton)
32 *Daily Express*, May 1945
33 Foley, John, *Mailed Fist* (Panther)
34 Flower, D., *The Taste of Courage* (Harper & Bros)
35 Atwell, op. cit.

(Right) German snipers searched by 3rd US Army.

INDEX

Aachen, 22, 77
Airborne Landings, *112, 114*, 115–8
Aircraft
   Allied, *15, 16*, 18, 20, 112, 114–5, 118
      C47 Transport, 20
      Dakota, 8
      Flying Fortress, 18, 20, 114
      Halifax, 76
      Lancaster, 76, 84, 104
      Mosquito, 84
      Mustang, 84
      Spitfires, 16, 18, 20
      Thunderbolt, 35, 38
      Typhoon, *18*, 20, *36*, 67, 110, 160–2
   German, 20
      Focke Wulf 190, 14, 16–8, 20
      Junkers 52, 'Auntie Jus', 14–6
      Junkers 88, 8, 14
      Messerschmidt 109, 14, 16–8
Airfields Allied, attacked by Luftwaffe, 14–20
   Aachen Field, 18
   Brussels-Evre Field, 18
Alsace, 22, 32
American troops, bitterness of, 23; attitude to Germans, 22, 90, 92–6; attitude to USAAF, 76–7; lack of equipment, 24; desertion by, 11, 23, 28, 47–9, 58; drunkeness of, 92–4, 96, 100, 130; killing civilians, 94; looting by, 90, 94, 96, 133–4; morale of, 30; raping by, 92, 133; also see Russian–American contacts
Anderson, Corporal Dudley, 40, 44, 54, 118, 130
Antwerp, 40
Ardennes Offensive, 'Battle of the Bulge', 11, *12*, 22–4, 28, 30–2, 34, 40, 58, 148, 178, 183; desertion during, 47–9; weather

during, 23–4, 26, 30, 32
Armies
   American
      First, 40, 88, 136, *155*; joins up with Third 32–4
      Third, 22, 28, 30, 88, 92, 126, 140; joins up with First, 32–4
      Seventh, 96, 123
      Ninth, 102, *134*
   British
      Eighth, 62
   French
      First, 140
   German
      First Parachute, 56
      Twenty First, 160, 168
Arnhem, first battle of, 56, 112; second battle of, 118, 152, *152*, 153, 176
Artillery, 59–60, 70–1, 92–4, 102–4
Aschanfenburg, 128
Athen, 100, 162
Atwell, Private Lester, 28, 92, 94, 132–4, 136, 168, 175, 181

Bad Kreuznach, 147
Baer, Lt-Colonel, 16
Barr, Robert, 31–2
Barrance, Private, 62, 70
Bartholomew, Major, 104
Bastogne-Marche Highway, 24
Bauman, Bodo, 84
Bausendorf, 92
BBC, (British Broadcasting Corporation), 31, 104, 118, 124, 138, 164, 170
Belgian civilians, attitude to Allies, 40, 44; revenge on, 40; starvation of, 40
Belgium, 11, 16, 20, 22, 24, 38, 40, 124
Bellinger, Major, 131
Berchtesgaden, 140, *144*, 146
Berlin, 78
Betts, General, 92
Bielfield, 128
Bienen, 104, 108
Billets, 9, 11, 54, 133
Bitburg, 77, *82*, 92, 96

Bittrich, 56
Blackmarket, 11
Blijenbeek Castle, 72, 74
Bombing,
   American, 14–16, 77, 78, 128
   British, 76, 78, 104, 164
   German, 8, 16–20
Bombing Strategy, 77; doubts over, 78
Borken, 67
Bradley, General Omar, 6, 144; crosses the Rhine, 98; in Aschaffenburg, 128
Bremen, 164, 172
British troops, attitude to RAF, 76–7; desertion by, 11, 27, 58; looting by, 70, 76, 133, 134; morale of, 56; house clearing, 111; also see Russian–British contacts
Brodie, Major Alex, 62–4
Brooke, General Sir Alan (CIGS), 120, *121*
Brothels, 11, 44
Brussels-Evre, 20
Brussels, 44
Buchanon, Private Malcolm, 104–5, 110–1
Buehlingen, Oberst, 16
Bure, 30
Byrom, Private James, 117–8, 181

Caen, 76, 77
Calcar, 52, 67, 72
Canadian troops, 16, 18, 52, 56, 59, 65, 104–5, 108, 111, 118, 156
Cap Arcona, 162–3
Capa, Robert, 112, 114–5
Carrier, Sergeant, 30
Casualties,
   American, 6, 20, 22, 26, 32, 34, 104–5, 176
   British, 6, 8, 20, 22, 30, 32, 34, 67, 70, 76, 117, 119, 176
   Canadians, 52, 65, 67, 108, 111, 114–5
   German, 23; in Dresden, 85
CBS Radio, 151

Cleves, 52, *75*, 76, *80*
Closterman, Flt. Lieutenant Pierre, 20
Chemnitz, 78
Chenogne, 22
Cherbourg, 77
Churchill, Winston S., 11, 40, 74–6, 178; Dresden Raid, 78; goes to the Rhine, 112; on the Rhine, 119; at Wesels, *86*, 120; on the Siegfried Line, *121*
Codman, Colonel Charles, 44, 132
Collins, Private, 118
'Colmar Pocket', 44, 47–8
Combat Fatigue, 26–8, 49
Concentration Camps, 84, 147, 160, 163, 176, *177, 179*
Cota, General 'Dutch', 48
Court Martial, 48, 131
Cousins, Sergeant Aubrey, 68
Cramer, Staff Sergeant, 119
C rations, 23, 183
Critchell, Captain, 176
Crutchfield, Captain Wilfred, 38
Cummings, Father, 48
Cunningham, Captain, 58

Davis, Major Franklin, 133
Deaden, Corporal Sam, 108, 111
Deeves, Major, 100
Desertion, attitude of US Army to, 47–9
Drabik, Alex, 100
Dresden, Allied soldiers in, 78, 82; bombing of, 84; casualties in, 85; consequences of bombing, 85
Dudeldorf, 92
Dueron, 77
Duffy, Major, 76
Duisburg, 146
Dysentery, 32

(Right) Peace at last.

Eifel, 88–90, 92, 94, 96, 183
Eindhoven, 20
Eisenhower, General
    Dwight D., 6, 35, 49,
    102, 131, 136, 146, 169,
    178; armies stalled, 22;
    attitude to fraternisation,
    88–9; visits Rhine
    crossing area, 104, 112;
    threatens French, 140;
    attitude to Concentration
    Camps, 147
Elbe, 84, 153, 163
Elson, Colonel Edward, 48
Equipment,
    American
        BAR Automatic rifle, 8
    British
        Besa gun, 64
        Bren gun, 60, 71, 105,
        108
        Bofors gun, 59
        PIAT, 130
    German
        Bazookas, 126
        75 mm Cannon, 111
        85 mm Flak Cannon,
        14, 26
        Mortars, 110
Essame, Brigadier H., 27,
    58, 74, 170–2
Eupen, 38
Execution, of American
    soldiers, 47–9, 92

Ferguson, Private, 65
Fergusson, Major Bernard,
    58
Firestorm, in Dresden, 84
Fodor, Captain, 115
Foley, Captain John, 30–1,
    58–61, 72, 74, 132, 179
Formations
    American
        Corps
        XXI, 48
        Engineer, 26
        Divisions
        Airborne
        17th, in the Ardennes,
        24, 34; cross the
        Rhine, 116–7, 119
        82nd, in the Ardennes,
        24; 21st Army
        surrenders to, 160, 168
        101st, 176; at
        Berchtesgaden, 140, 146
        Armored
        2nd, links up with
        Third Army, 34; in the
        Ruhr Pocket, 130–1,
        3rd, in the Ruhr

Pocket, 130–1
6th, rout of, 28; enter
German towns, 90
7th, contact with
Russians, 159
9th, 98, 155;
Infantry
2nd, in the Ardennes,
22; in Leipzig, 136
3rd, 150, 172;
5th, 128; transferred
from Italy, 76
8th, 172
28th, execution of
Eddie Slovik, 47–9
30th, cross the Rhine,
104
45th, 150
69th, in Leipzig, 138
71st, 128
76th, capture Wittlich,
90–2
79th, cross the Rhine,
104
106th, surrender in
Ardennes, at
Rheinbach, 148
Regiments
15th Infantry, 150
109th Infantry, 48
291st Combat
Engineers, 35
243rd Field Artillery,
175
513th Parachute, 134
British
    Corps
    XXX, in the
    Reichswald, 52, 62;
    casualties, 67
    Royal Armoured, 58,
    67
    Royal Army Medical
    Corps, 117; in the
    Reichswald, 71
    Division
    Airborne
    1st, at Arnhem, 56
    6th, 40, in the
    Ardennes, 30; cross
    the Rhine, 112, 117–8,
    120; at Wismar, 156,
    158–60
    Armoured
    7th, in Hamburg, 163
    Infantry
    3rd, 20
    15th Scottish, in the
    Reichswald, 52, 58,
    64; reach the Rhine, 74
    49th, Battalion of is
    routed, 58; at

Nymegen, 152
51st Highland, in the
Reichswald, 52, 62;
cross the Rhine, 104
52nd Lowland, in the
Reichswald, 72; victory
celebrations, 172
53rd Welsh, in the
Reichswald, 52, 62
Guards Armoured, in
the Reichswald, 52
Regiments
Argyll and Sutherland
Highlanders, 7 Bn,
104
Black Watch, 58, 60–1,
108, 110–1; 5 Bn 104; 7
Bn 105
Dorsets, 172
Dragoon Guards,
4/7th, 59
Gordon Highlanders, 1
Bn, 65; 2 Bn, 70
Hussars, 4th, 112; 7th,
164
Kings Own Scottish
Borders, 70
Kings Shropshire Light
Infantry, 172
Lincoln, 104
Manchester, 70
Middlesex, 62
Northumberland
Fusiliers, 20
Parachute, 13 Bn, 30
Queens Royal, 59, 64,
71
Royal Artillery, 103rd,
104
Royal Tank, 104
Ulster Rifles, 1st, 118
3rd Parachute
Engineers, 158
Canadian
    Corps
    2nd, in the Reichswald,
    67
    Division
    2nd, in the Reichswald,
    52, 62, 67
    3rd, in the Reichswald,
    52, 62, 67
    Brigades
    1st Parachute, crosses
    the Rhine, 118
    Regiments
    Cameronians, 65
    Essex Scottish, 68
    Highland Light
    Infantry, 104–5, 108,
    110–2
    North Nova Scotia

Highlanders, 54, 108
Regina Rifles, 67
Royal Winnipeg Rifles,
67
French
    Division
    2nd Armored; at
    Berchtesgaden, 140,
    144
    Regiment
    De Tirailleurs
    Algerien, cross the
    Rhine, 139
German
    Division
    Parachute
    7th, on the Rhine, 119
    8th, on the Rhine, 119
    Panzer
    15th, on the Rhine, 108
    Infantry
    84th, on the Rhine, 119
    Regiment
    69th Infantry,
    memorial, 166
Folkestone, 20
Foy, Colonel, 34
France, 16, 22, 124
Fraternisation, 88, 89, 90,
    91, 92, 132–3, 138; attitude
    of Eisenhower to, 88–9;
    attitude of Patton to,
    88–90
Free French, 20
French, attitude to
    collaborators, 47
Freudenstadt, 139
Freyburg, Alfred, 138, 139
Freyer, Margaret, 84

Gabel, Private Kurt, 24, 26,
    34–5
Gare du Nord, 44
Gaulle, General Charles de,
    22
German troops, assessment
    of Allies, 56; in retreat,
    32, 94, 126; reaction to
    defeat, 92, 134; fear of
    Russians, 146, 156, 158,
    160, 168
German civilians, reaction
    to Americans, 92, 94, 96;
    looting, 133, 134; reaction
    to defeat, 150
Gestapo, 40
Giles, Staff Sergeant, 26,
    92, 150–1, 175
Gliders, 112, 114, 114,
    118–9
    Hamilcars, 118
    Horsa, 118

190

Waco, 118
Goch, 52, 65, *69*, 70, *73*, 74, 76, 77
Goering, Hermann, 59, 146
Graves Registration Unit, 34–5, 49
Gregg, Lieutenant, 26
Grolman, Police General von, 136

Halton, Matthew, 151–2
Hare, Corporal Arthur, 67, 181
Hamburg, firestorm in, 84; surrender in, 163–4, 168
Haminkeln, 118
Harling, Squadron Leader Davis, 16, 18
Harris, Sir Arthur 'Bomber', 76–8, 82, 104
Hauptmann, Gerhart, 85
Hermes, Alois, 94
Hines, Colonel, 28, 30, 128, 130
Hitler, Adolf, 14, 88, 90, 140, *142*, 160
Hitler Youth, 158, 162–3
Hitler Youth Division, 32
Hoarding, 6
Hobart, General, 60
Hochwald, 67
Hodges, General Courtenay, 88; rivalry with Patton, 136
Hoge, General, 99
Holland, 16, 18, 20, 58, 114
Home Front, 6, 8
Hood HMS, 8
Horrocks, Lieutenant-General Brian G., 104; in the Reichswald, 52, 58–9; pushes reserves up, 64; worries about troops, 70; congratulates troops, 72; news of victory, 170
Houffalize, 32
Howard, Conan, 114
Huertgen Forest, 58
Hummel Captain, 49

Isner, Lieutenant, 110
Inspector General, 35

Jensen, Marvin, 100
Johnson, Wing Commander 'Johnnie', 16, 18
Jolly, Captain, 104
Jones, Colonel, 115
Jones, Corporal Alf, 65
Jungenfeld, General von, 160

Karlsruhe, 139
Kervenhiem, 71
King, Major, 105
Knowlton, William, 159–60
K rations, 34, 136
Kyll, 94

Lambert, Major von, 128
Latrines, 11
Le Clerc, 140, 144, 146
Leipzig, 78, 136, 138
Leitz, Hilda, 92
Liege, 26
Lindsay, Colonel, 65
Lissendorf, 92
Looting, 70, 74, 76, 90, 94, 96, 100, 132–4, *133*, *134*
London, 11
'Lord Haw Haw', 76
Louvain, 20
Luftwaffe, 156; attacks Allied Airfield, 14–20
Lubeck, 160
Luneburg, *168*, 169–70, 183
Luxembourg, 22

MacDonald, Captain Charles, 22, 26, 136, 138, 175
Malmedy 'Massacre', 22, 35, 38
Maquis, 47
Marshal, Brigadier-General H.A.L., 24
Martindale, Lieutenant Stuart, 94
Maxeiner, Sergeant Walter, 146
Maxted, Stance, 118
McKee, Corporal Alex, 26–7, 77
McKendrick, Sergeant, 49
McMillan, Richard, 104
Medics, 23, 26, 28, 65, 96, 118, 132
Mehs, Eric, 94
Merril, Joseph, 150
Meyer, Lieutenant-Colonel, 18, 20
Milburn, General Frank, 48
Military Police, 11, 48
Miller, Colonel Allen C., 112, 114–6
Mines, 28, 30, 64–5, 126
Mine detector, 30
Minton, Flight Lieutenant, 18
Model, Field Marshal, 146–7, 183
Montgomery, Field Marshal Bernard, 20, 52,

78, *86*, 90, 98, 133, 152–3, 169, 170; reinforcements for, 6; personal plane destroyed, 18; against death penalty, 27; attitude to troops, 56; plans for Rhine crossing, 76; attitude to Harris, 77; Rhine crossings, 102, 104; meets Churchill, *120*, 121; German surrender to, *168*, 169
Moorehead, Alan, 96, 98, 176
Mortara, Joe, 132–3
Moselle, 90, 92, 94, 183
Moyland, 67

NAAFI, 11
Nicklin, Colonel Jeff, 118
New York Times, 172
Normandy, 6, 20, 27–8, 30, 58, 62, 67, 70–2, 102–4, 114, 117, 152, 164

Oberaden, 90
O'Farrel, Colonel, 34
Olsen, Fred, 150
Operation Thunderclap, 77
Ostend, 20
Ouerthe, 34

Paris, 90
Patton, General George, 132, 182; did not take prisoners, 22; losing the war, 30; views on troops, 88; attitude to fraternising, 88–90; attitude to liberation, 92; rivalry with Hodge, 136; reaction to Concentration Camps, 147
Patton, 'War Memorial', 92
Pedley, Colonel George, 92
Penicillin, 26
Plasma, 23, 26
Piesport, 94
Prebble, John, 74
Press, effect of, 20, 34, 74, 136
Prisoners
Allied, 6, 130; condition of, 82; in Dresden, 82; SS treatment of, 126–8; liberated, 136
German, *24*, 74, 105, 117, *119*, *147–8*, *166*, 168; conditions of, 147–150; ill treated, 90; shooting of, 22, 24, 26, 94, 128
Prum, 38

Purvis, General, 94

Radar, 16, 20
RAF, 8, 72, 77, 84, 164; casualties, 76
Railway Transport Officer, 9
Red Cross, 23
Red Army, 78, 156, *159*, *163*
Rees, 104
Reich, 14, 22, 32, 67, 78
Reichswald, 52–78, 104; supplies for, 58; barrage during, 60; effect of mud in, 62; sown with mines, 65; casualties during, 67
Reidel, Sergeant, 104
Remagen Bridge, (Luddendorf Railway Bridge), capture of, 98–100; effect on strategy, 102, 183
Rennie, General, 104, 108
RFC, 77
Rheinbach Camp, 148–50
Rhine, 14, 30, 47, 58, 62, 74, 78; banks opened, 64; capture of Remagen Bridge, 98–100, crossing of, 99–105, *102*, *105*; bombardment of, *103*, 104; crossed by Canadians, 104–5, 108; Churchill goes to, 112; bridgeheads established, 119; airborne crossings of, 112, 114–117; crossings exploited, 124
Richardson Lieutenant-Colonel, 170
Ridgeway, General Matthew, 116, 159
Roosevelt, Franklin Delano, 11, 40; near death, 92
Rose, General Maurice, 130, 183
Rougelot, Doctor, 49
Rudder, Colonel James E., 48
Ruhr Pocket, later Rose Pocket, 130–132, 146
Russian–American contacts, 132, 158–60, *158*
Russian-British contacts, 132, 153, 159, 163

Sabia, Sergeant, 99–100
Saint Lo, 27
Saint Vith, 38
Saundby, Sir Robert, 78
Saunders R., 104

Siegfried Line, also known as the West Wall, 32, 52, 54, 58–59, *121*, 183
Simmonds, General, 67
Simpson, General, *86*, 112, 120, *121*
Slovik, Private Eddie, 48–50
Smith, Wing Commander, 84
Sniping, 67, 92, 94, *99*, *100*, 111, 118, 132
Sondag, 90
Spa, 40
Speldorp, 104–5, 108, 110–11
SS, troops, 20, 64, 126, 128, 130; Dutch, Landstrum Nederland, 34th Division, 151–2; Free American Corps, 82; French, 144; Guards, 160–3, *177*; 6th Mountain Division, 126–8
Stacey Lieutenant-Colonel, 67
Stars and Stripes, 23, 90, 144
Ste Marie-Aux-Mines, 47–9
Strasbourg, 22
Stuttgart, 139–40
Suicide
    Allied troops, 11
    Germans, 138, 147
Sunday Times, 64
Surrender, German forces,

24; at Luneburg, 168–70; German towns, 88, 90, 92, 94, 136, 138, 140; of Hamburg, 163–6, 168
Supply problems, 62

Tanks
    American,
        Pershing, 131
        Sherman, 62, 68, 94, *100*, 124, 126, 151, 183
    British
        Churchill, 30, 31, *31*, *53*, 60–1, 124
        Crocodile, 60
        Flail, *124*
    German,
        Panther, 183
        Tiger, 62, *129*, 130–1
Tank Warfare, 124–6
Thompson, Captain R. W., 34, 60, 64, 67, 70–1, 76, 115, 172
Tilburg, 26
Tiltson, Major, 68
Time, 102
Time Life, 150
Timmermann, Lieutenant Karl, captures Remagen Bridge, 98–102
Thielbek, 162–3
Tippelskirch, General von, commander 21st Army, 160–8

Topham, Corporal, 118
Trenchfoot, 118

Uden, 76
USAF, United States Air Force, 38, 76–7
US 9th TAC Air Force, 'American Luftwaffe', 77
122nd Wing, 20
487th Fighter Squadron, 18

Vaughan-Thomas, Wynford, BBC correspondent, 104, 118–9, 124, 126, 164
V-Bombs, *9*, 117
V.C., 68, 118
VD, 9, 26, 44, 90, 92
Vehicles
    Allied,
        Alligator, 116
        Buffaloes, 62, 104
        Lloyd carrier, 65
        Kangaroos, 60
        Wasp carrier, 152
        effect of weather upon, 30
    German
        Self propelled gun, 110
        destroyed by Allied aircraft, 38
Verviers, 26
Victory, celebration of, 172; reaction to, 175–6

Volkssturm, (German Home Guard), 119, 168
Vonnegut, Kurt, 82, 85
Vosges, 47–8
Voss, Private O.B., 20, 22

War Correspondents, 31, 34, 60, 67, 70, 76, 96–8, 104, 112, 114–5, 118, 124, 176
Ward, Edward, 138–9
Wainman, Colonel Bill, 164–6
'Water Rats, 62
Watts, Lieutenant-Colonel, 118
Werner, Bruno E, 84
Wesel, 104, *109*, 120
Wheldon, Major Huw, 118–9
Whores, 11
Wilson, Captain Andrew, 76, 104
Wingfield, Lance-Corporal R. M., 59, 64, 71–2
Wismar, 156–60, 181
Wittlich, 90
Wood, Sergeant Douglas, 32–4
Woollcombe, Lieutenant, 58, 60, 70

Xanten, 74

Yalta Conference, 78

ACKNOWLEDGEMENTS

We are most grateful to the Robert Hunt Picture Library (many of whose photographs come courtesy of the US Army) for permission to use the photographs which appear on the jacket and for many of the photographs which appear in the book.

We also thank The Imperial War Museum for permission to use the photographs which appear on the following pages: 2, 7, 12, 14, 16, 18, 19, 23, 25, 27, 31, 32, 35, 36/37, 38, 40/41, 42/43, 44, 45, 50/51, 52/53, 54, 73, 82, 87, 95, 98, 99, 102/103, 105, 109, 117, 119, 120, 124, 152, 164, 179, 189.